Using the *Sams' Teach Yourself in 24 Hours* Series

Welcome to the *Sams' Teach Yourself in 24 Hours* series! You're probably thinking, "What, they want me to stay up all night and learn this stuff?" Well, no, not exactly. This series introduces a new way to teach you about exciting new products: 24 one-hour lessons, designed to keep your interest and keep you learning. Because the learning process is broken into small units, you will not be overwhelmed by the complexity of some of the new technologies that are emerging in today's market. Each hourly lesson has a number of special items, some old, some new, to help you along.

Minutes

The first 10 minutes of each hour lists the topics and skills that you will learn about by the time you finish the hour. You will know exactly what the hour will bring with no surprises.

Minutes

Twenty minutes into the lesson, you will have been introduced to many of the newest features of the software application. In the constantly evolving computer arena, knowing everything a program can do will aid you enormously now and in the future.

Minutes

Before 30 minutes have passed, you will have learned at least one useful task. Many of these tasks take advantage of the newest features of the application. These tasks use a hands-on approach, telling you exactly which menus and commands you need to use to accomplish the goal. This approach is found in each lesson of the *24 Hours* series.

Minutes

You will see after 40 minutes that many of the tools you have come to expect from the *Sams' Teach Yourself* series are found in the *24 Hours* series as well. Notes and Tips offer special tricks of the trade to make your work faster and more productive. Warnings help you avoid those nasty time-consuming errors.

Minutes

By the time you're 50 minutes in, you'll probably run across terms you haven't seen before. Never before has technology thrown so many new words and acronyms into the language, and the New Terms elements found in this series will carefully explain each and every one of them.

Minutes

At the end of the hour, you may still have questions that need answered. You know the kind—questions on skills or tasks that come up every day for you, but that weren't directly addressed during the lesson. That's where the Q&A section can help. By answering the most frequently asked questions about the topics discussed in the hour, Q&A not only answers your specific question, it provides a succinct review of all that you have learned in the hour.

Ned Snell

SAMS
Teach Yourself
Microsoft®
Publisher 98
in 24 Hours

SAMS

A Division of Macmillan Computer Publishing
201 West 103rd St., Indianapolis, Indiana, 46290 USA

Sams' Teach Yourself Microsoft® Publisher 98 in 24 Hours

Copyright © 1998 by Sams Publishing

International Standard Book Number: 0-672-31304-9

Library of Congress Catalog Card Number: 98-84446

Printed in the United States of America

First Printing: May 1998

00 99 98   4   3   2   1

Trademarks

PUBLISHER
Jordan Gold

EXECUTIVE EDITOR
Mark Taber

MANAGING EDITOR
Jodi Jensen

ACQUISITIONS EDITOR
Mark Taber

PROJECT EDITOR
Tonya R. Simpson

COPY EDITOR
Kate Givens

TECHNICAL EDITOR
Nan Chastry

COVER DESIGNER
Erin Howell

BOOK DESIGNER
Gary Adair

INDEXER
Kelly Talbot

PRODUCTION
Michael Henry
Linda Knose
Tim Osborn
Staci Somers
Mark Walchle

Contents at a Glance

Contents

Dedication

For my family.

About the Author

Ned Snell is the former editor of the graphic arts magazine *Art & Design News* and an award-winning computer journalist. He is the author of *Sams' Teach Yourself the Internet in 24 Hours, Second Edition, Laura Lemay's Web Workshop: Netscape Navigator Gold*, and several other Internet, Windows 95, and Microsoft Office 97 books.

Introduction

I'm sure you didn't pick up this book to learn how to use Microsoft Publisher 98—not really, anyway. You're here because there's something you need to communicate—on paper or on a Web site—and you've decided that Publisher can help you say it.

Well, I'm on your side. A PC program is just a means to an end. This book is built to give you the skills to produce the end you want, quickly and easily. Even before you spend a full 24 hours with it, you'll know exactly how to bring your message to life. Sure, along the way you will become a fully functioning Publisher 98 pro—but that's the tail, not the dog. Don't worry, I know which one wags the other.

Actually, I wanted to call this book *Sams' Teach Yourself How to Create Really Wonderful Print Publications and Web Pages (and Learn Microsoft Publisher 98 Along the Way) in 24 Hours or Less*. But my editors reminded me that: A) All long titles sound like *Everything You Always Wanted to Know About Sex (but Were Afraid to Ask)*, and B) Economy is the key to effective communication.

Comment B) is a good example of the sort of straightforward publishing advice I'll pass along to you over the next 1,440 minutes (or less) in the course of this fast, fun tutorial. Welcome aboard!

Meet Me at the Pub

You can create many different kinds of publications in Publisher, from flyers to posters, from books to brochures to business cards.

But to keep things simple, when referring generally to Publisher projects, I'll call them "publications," or just "pubs." Publishing pros often use the short term "pub" to describe their work, so you and I will do likewise.

What's "Desktop Publishing," Anyway?

You already know what *desktop publishing* (DTP) is, but you might be unfamiliar with the term itself and a few useful details about it.

Until very recently, all print publications were created by individually producing strips of text, photos, and artwork (each on a different system), then carefully pasting them onto boards to create an attractive layout. The finished boards were then photographed onto plates for the printing press. This traditional "paste-up" approach is slow and skill intensive and makes last-minute changes costly and sticky.

With desktop publishing (or *DTP*), you can create text and artwork and arrange those elements into a finished layout, all on your PC screen. Before you print a thing, your PC has shown you exactly (well, almost exactly) how your finished pub will look on paper, enabling you to easily experiment with the text and layout and make the pub perfect before it goes to press. Then, in many cases, modern electronic presses can print your pub directly from your DTP files.

FIGURE IN.1.

Publisher displays your pub much as it will look when printed, so you can create and edit it almost entirely on your PC.

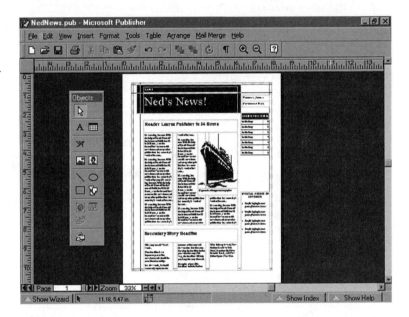

Matching the onscreen display of a document to its printed appearance is known as *WYSIWYG* (*What You See Is What You Get*), pronounced "wizzy-wig." Most word processors for Windows and the Mac are also WYSIWYG programs you can use to create publications. But compared to a word processor, a true DTP program like Microsoft Publisher or Adobe PageMaker provides far greater control of the layout, text style, color, and other aspects of the publication.

Control makes the difference between a pub that looks like your high school newsletter and one that looks like *Vanity Fair* magazine, or a Fortune 500 company's annual report and an award-winning ad. A word processor lets you say it, but DTP lets you say it with *style*.

Why Publisher?

Among popular DTP programs, Publisher stands out for its simplicity: It's the ideal DTP program for folks who lack a background in graphic arts or publishing. Publisher enables anybody who can use Windows to create professional-looking print publications and Web pages.

Publisher also makes a great training ground for a beginner who aspires to become a professional layout artist, one who'll probably move up one day from Publisher to a more advanced (and more difficult) DTP program like PageMaker.

Who I Wrote This Thing For

This book's publisher and I have designed the book expressly for the benefit of folks who

- Are new to DTP in general and new to Publisher in particular.
- Want a quick, easy, common-sense way to learn how to create and print publications—and maybe create Web pages, too.
- Don't appreciate having your intelligence insulted.

Because I know you want an easy way to learn Publisher, I give you all the help and hints you need. But I also give you credit for not being an "idiot" or a "dummy" in other respects. I understand that you've devoted your life thus far to more important tasks than learning a software program. Good for you.

What You Need to Know Already

To get started with this book, you do not need to know a single thing about Publisher, publishing—desktop or otherwise—or biochemistry. (Not that you'll learn anything about biochemistry here, but isn't it nice to know you don't have to? One less thing to do.)

Before diving into this tutorial, however, you do need to know the basics of getting around in Windows 95 (or Windows NT, if that's what you have). You needn't be a Windows expert, by any means. But you do need to know how to

- Open and close folders and programs
- Use the Start menu

- Use your mouse to point to stuff, such as a button or menu item, and single- or double-click on it
- Click the arrow at the end of a drop-down list box to open the list

If you know just that much, I'll take you the rest of the way.

But if you're completely new to Windows 95 or NT, I recommend learning the basics first. You can take Windows's own built-in tour, or consult any of the better beginner's books, such as *Sams' Teach Yourself Windows 95 in 24 Hours*.

Do I Need the Internet to Use Publisher?

Just because I mention the Internet now and again, don't assume that the Internet is at all necessary to using Publisher or this book.

Yes, you *can* enhance your Publisher practice with an Internet account and *Web browser* such as Internet Explorer, which is included on the Publisher 98 CD-ROM, or Netscape Navigator. On the Internet's World Wide Web you can find hints, help, and other Publisher resources, many of which I'll point out during the tutorial and also in Appendix A, "Internet Resources for Publisher Users." You might even be able to get a free trial version of the Publisher program right from the Web, as you learn in Hour 1, "Setting Up Publisher 98."

Nevertheless, you don't need an Internet account to learn Publisher or to use it productively; with Publisher, everything you need to create great pubs is right on your PC.

How This Book Is Organized

This book is divided into six parts, each containing four chapters—or rather, four "hours":

- **Part I, "Start Publisher, Start a Publication,"** starts you up and starts you off. It begins by showing how to install Publisher, moves quickly through an orientation to getting around in Publisher, and finishes up in Hour 4, "Starting a New Publication," with creating your first publication layouts.
- **Part II, "Page Design,"** picks up where Part I leaves off, showing how to edit, arrange, and fine-tune a layout, create multipage pubs, and print drafts and final output on your own printer.
- **Part III, "Text and Type"** could be retitled "Everything You Always Wanted to Know About Text." (There I go again.) You'll create new text, copy text from other documents, fix spelling and punctuation (or make Publisher fix it), create tables,

and most important, make text look fantastic. You'll also learn how to set up Publisher to fill in names, addresses, and other text automatically.

- **Part IV, "Pictures, Backgrounds, and Color,"** does for pictures what Part III did for text, showing you how to capture, create, or borrow all the visual stimuli your pub needs and to manipulate pictures in exciting, surprising ways. You also learn in Part IV how to work with colors and color schemes.

- **Part V, "Publishing on Paper,"** wraps up your print projects, exploring your printing options, showing you how to choose and use a printing service, and offering tips for checking the proofs you get from a printing service, making corrections and fine-tuning your page design for the press. You'll also discover how to easily produce a mass mailing and about other, advanced DTP tools you might want to learn next.

- **Part VI, "Publishing Online,"** shows you how to create and publish documents *online*—on the Web or on your company network. Building on skills from Parts I through IV, Part VI shows how to create new online publications (or transform print pubs for use online); how to add animation, sound, and other kinds of multimedia sizzle; and how to publish your document on the Web for all the world to see.

Bonuses at the Back of the Book

After Hour 24, you'll discover reference resources, all containing stuff that's potentially useful and absolutely optional:

- **Appendix A, "Internet Resources for Publisher Users,"** provides a directory of DTP- and Publisher-related Internet resources. You learn where online you can find hints, reference materials, software updates, fonts, and pictures for your pubs, and much more.

- The **Glossary** provides easy reference to DTP and Publisher terms. (Note that I keep the use of technical terms to a bare minimum and that all new terms are defined as the book goes along. If you follow the hours in order, you'll probably never need the Glossary. But it's there, just in case.)

Things You'd Probably Figure Out By Yourself

Again, you're no dummy, so all by yourself you'd probably figure out everything I'm about to tell you. But just to make sure you're clear on what you're about to see, here's a quick guide to some special elements on this book's pages.

Tips, Terms, and "To Do"

Here and there, I show a quick list of step-by-step instructions, called a "To Do," to show you exactly how to do something. The text ahead of each To Do provides a pretty good overview of the task at hand, so feel free to skip a To Do when the overview is enough for you.

Any time you feel like you don't completely understand something, work through the To Do, and you'll quickly get the picture. Sometimes you teach yourself best by doing.

NEW TERM I call attention to important new terms by tagging them with the New Term icon. It won't happen a lot because I won't bury you in terminology you don't really need. But wherever knowing a term is important, let this icon lead your attention to the definition.

You'll also see three different kinds of tips set off in boxes:

A Tip box points out a faster, easier way to do something, a way to get something done quickly, or a way to save time by *not* doing something.

A Note box pops out an important consideration, tip, or interesting tidbit related to the topic at hand. Just something to keep your eye on.

A Caution box alerts you to situations where something bad could happen, like accidentally deleting an important file or violating someone else's copyright. Because there's very little you can do in Publisher that's in any way dangerous, you'll see very few Cautions—so when you see 'em, take 'em seriously.

Workshops

At the end of each hour, there's an easy, fun workshop designed to reinforce the most important skills and concepts covered in the hour. Each workshop contains

- **Q&A Session:** One or more quick questions and answers explaining interesting stuff that wasn't included in the hour because it doesn't directly contribute to teaching yourself Publisher (even though it's interesting).

- **Quiz:** Three or four multiple-choice questions that help you recall important points, and also provide me with a good place for jokes I couldn't work into the book elsewhere.
- **Activity:** Something you can do to practice what you learned in the hour or to prepare for the hour that follows.

Ready?

Time to get on your way to your first pubs. Start the clock, and hit Hour 1. Twenty-four working hours from now you'll have the skills to commit your ideas to print (and to the Web) clearly, simply, and beautifully.

Thanks for setting aside a few hours to spend with me!

Tell Us What You Think!

As a reader, you are the most important critic and commentator of our books. We value your opinion and want to know what we're doing right, what we could do better, what areas you'd like to see us publish in, and any other words of wisdom you're willing to pass our way. You can help us make strong books that meet your needs and give you the computer guidance you require.

As the team leader of the group that created this book, I welcome your comments. You can fax, email, or write me directly to let me know what you did or didn't like about this book—as well as what we can do to make our books stronger. Here's the information:

E-mail: newtech_mgr@mcp.com
Fax: 317-817-7070
Mail: Mark Taber
Macmillan Computer Publishing
201 W. 103rd Street
Indianapolis, IN 46290

PART I

Start Publisher, Start a Publication

Hour

HOUR 1

Setting Up Publisher 98

Somebody told me there are two ways to train eager, first-time skydivers:
a) Suppress their eagerness long enough to cover the basics on the ground,
and then jump; or b) Take 'em up, jump with them, and explain the basics
on the way down.

I want to turn you loose in Publisher as quickly as possible, but I would
rather not push you out of the plane without first covering a few basics such
as "Your Friend the Parachute" and "Gravity: Pros and Cons." So I will split
the difference: After a minimal ground session, I will jump with you. Before
the end of Hour 4, "Starting a New Publication," you will dive into your first
Publisher projects.

In this first hour, you pick up valuable background on Publisher 98 and
desktop publishing. And in case you haven't already done so, you will spend
part of this hour installing Publisher on your PC. At the end of the hour, you
will be able to answer the following questions:

- Where do you get Publisher 98?
- What handy tools and other resources are included with Publisher in
  addition to the Publisher program?

- How must my PC be equipped to run Publisher?
- How do you install Publisher on your PC?

Where Do You Get Publisher?

I guess you probably already have your copy of Publisher 98, ready to go. But just in case you don't, note that you can get Publisher 98 in three different ways:

- *Packaged alone*—Publisher 98 is available on CD-ROM from any software retailer. (Note that Publisher is not available on disks; you must have a CD-ROM drive to install Publisher.)

- *On the Internet*—Microsoft periodically makes Publisher available in a "free trial" version. If you have an Internet account and Web browser, you can download the trial version (if it is currently offered) from Microsoft's Publisher Web site (www.microsoft.com/publisher; see Figure 1.1), or order the trial version on CD for a small shipping fee. The free trial version includes the basic Publisher program, but none of the other valuable tools and resources that make up the full Publisher 98 CD.

- *Packaged with the Windows version of Office*—Microsoft's Office 97 program suite is available in several different versions for Windows, each with a different family of programs included. The Office 97 Small Business Edition version 2.0 includes Publisher 98, along with Word (a word processor), Excel (a spreadsheet), and several other business programs.

The Office 97 Small Business Edition is bundled as free software with new PCs from many manufacturers. If you are in the market for a new PC and haven't already purchased Publisher 98, you may want to look for a PC pre-equipped with the Office 97 Small Business Edition version 2.0.

Note that only version 2.0 includes Publisher 98. Some PCs may still come equipped with version 1.0 of the Office 97 Small Business Edition, which includes Publisher *97*, not 98.

FIGURE 1.1.

If you have Internet access, you can download a free trial version of Publisher from the Web.

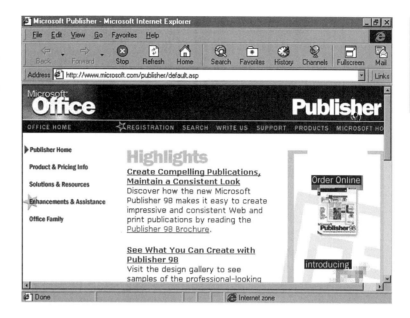

As a member of the Office family (although not included with all Office versions), Publisher 98 shares many features in common with the core products in Microsoft's Office program suite.

If you use Word, for example, you will find that you perform many document editing and formatting activities in Publisher exactly as you do in Word. Publisher also integrates with the other Office programs for some activities; for example, you can jump directly from Publisher to Word to edit the text of a Publisher file. (You will learn how to do this in Hour 9, "Getting the Words Into Your Publication.")

Of course, you need not have Office to use Publisher; you need not know a thing about Office to learn Publisher; and experience with Office doesn't begin to teach you the whole of Publisher. But the better you know Office (or Word, especially), the more naturally you will pick up new Publisher skills.

What Is Included?

Publisher 98 includes the Publisher program itself, of course. Now is a good time, however, to learn that Publisher also includes an elaborate supporting cast of programs and files that you can call on for certain kinds of projects. You will learn more about Publisher's supporting cast as you work through this tutorial.

The cast includes, but is not limited to the following:

- *Fonts.* A huge gallery of *fonts* (type styles) is included on the CD and installed automatically when you install Publisher. You can use these fonts to make great-looking text not only in Publisher, but in most other Windows programs on your PC.
- *Clip Gallery* (see Figure 1.2). An enormous collection of artwork for your pubs (10,000 graphic images, 500 photos and 300 animations), all cataloged and accessible through Publisher's Clip Gallery facility. You learn how to use the Clip Gallery in Hours 13, "Getting Graphics," and 23, "Adding Links, Motion, and Other Web Goodies."
- *Microsoft Photo Editor.* A full-featured image editor you can use to customize and manipulate photos and other image files for your pubs.
- *Microsoft Draw and WordArt.* Two great tools for creating logos and other drawings to dress up your pubs.
- *Internet Explorer 4, the Web Publishing Wizard, and Web page materials.* As support for Publisher's Web-page creation capabilities, the CD includes the Internet Explorer Web browser and other valuable tools and files. You learn how to use these tools in Part VI, "Publishing Online."

If you choose to install the Internet Explorer 4 Web browser included with Publisher (as described in Hour 21, "Understanding Online Publishing"), you will be presented the option to install Web Integration. Also called the Active Desktop, Web Integration overhauls Windows in many surprising ways. After installing Web Integration, for example, you no longer double-click icons in Windows to open them—one click is all it takes.

Web Integration doesn't really affect anything you do within Publisher. Because it changes the way you use Windows overall, however, consider reading an Internet Explorer 4 book that explains Web Integration, such as *Sams' Teach Yourself Internet Explorer 4 in 24 Hours.*

In Hour 21, when you learn how to install IE4, you will learn how to choose whether to use the Active Desktop.

FIGURE 1.2.

Publisher includes a huge gallery of clip art, photos, and animations to liven up your publications.

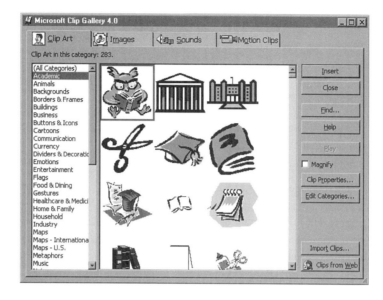

1

To Do: Explore Your Publisher CD

You never know what Microsoft will throw on a CD—the company frequently piggybacks unadvertised, bonus programs and files on the CDs of unsuspecting applications. To learn exactly what you got on your Publisher 98 CD, and to learn where certain files and folders are located for later reference, it is a good idea to take a peek at your CD's contents.

1. Insert your Publisher CD in your CD-ROM drive, and wait a moment. (If a dialog box opens, starting the Publisher installation, click Cancel in that dialog box; you will install later.)

2. Open the My Computer icon on the Windows desktop.

3. In My Computer, find the icon for your CD-ROM drive (it looks like a CD), and click on it to select it.

4. Choose File | Open. A folder opens, showing the contents of the Publisher CD.

Take special note of the following folders and file:

- *Actors folder.* Contains characters you can choose for Publisher's "Assistant" animated Help facility (see Hour 2, "First Steps: Open, Close, and Save").

- *MSIE folder.* Contains the Internet Explorer Web browser and related files (see Hour 21).

- *ClipArt folder.* Contains thousands of images and other files for the Clip Gallery (see Hour 13).

- *Readme.txt file.* Contains any important notes, tips, and instructions not included in your Publisher manuals or this book.

What Hardware Do You Need?

Unlike some Microsoft programs and many other desktop publishing programs, Publisher 98 is monogamous: It is available only for the Windows family (Windows 95 and Windows NT)—not for the Macintosh, Windows 3.1, or any other system.

Because the minimum requirements for running Publisher exceed those for running Windows, not all PCs running Windows 95 or Windows NT are up to handling Publisher (although most can). Table 1.1 shows the minimum system requirements for Publisher under each member of the Windows family.

When considering hardware, keep in mind that the *minimum* requirements for running a program are rarely *practical* requirements. A PC equipped with just the official minimums will run Publisher, but it will tend to do so slowly and unreliably, and may prevent you from *multitasking*—running other programs such as Word at the same time as Publisher—which can be handy.

Therefore, in addition to the official Microsoft minimums, Table 1.1 shows what I think are the practical minimum requirements for running Publisher with acceptable performance and reliability.

TABLE 1.1. SYSTEM REQUIREMENTS FOR PUBLISHER 98.

Windows Version	Minimum Requirements	Practical Requirements
95	486 DX2 or Pentium, 12MB of RAM, 110MB of free space on hard disk, CD-ROM drive	Pentium 133 or faster, 24–32MB of RAM, 300MB of free space on hard disk, CD-ROM drive
NT (4 or higher)	486 DX2 or Pentium, 16MB of RAM, 110MB of free space on hard disk, CD-ROM drive	Pentium 133 or faster, 32MB of RAM, 300MB of free space on hard disk, CD-ROM drive
NT (below 4)	Not supported by Publisher 98	

When it comes to hard disk size on a PC that will be used for desktop publishing (DTP), too much is never enough. Publications often take up a surprising amount of disk space. Therefore unless you have a fat hard disk, you may soon run short of space.

Note that Windows requires a certain amount of empty hard disk space to run smoothly; if you let your disk get anywhere near full, your system may periodically lock up or crash, even when some space remains on the disk.

What About Windows 98?

As this book goes to press, Windows 98 has not yet been released. When it does appear, however, Windows 98 will support all Windows 95 application programs; therefore, Publisher 98 will run on Windows 98 just fine.

Using Publisher on Windows 98 will be no different than using it on Windows 95. If you intend to do that, note that all the information and instructions in this book concerning anything you do within Publisher will also work fine if you are using Publisher under Windows 98.

Windows 98 will demand somewhat more memory and disk space for itself than Windows 95 does. Therefore the Windows 95 minimums shown earlier in Table 1.1 may be insufficient for running Publisher on Windows 98. Use the Practical Requirements listed for Windows NT 4 as a good rule of thumb for running Publisher 98 smoothly under Windows 98.

After the release of Windows 98, you will find the Windows 98 system requirements for using Publisher on the Publisher Web site at www.microsoft.com/publisher.

To Do: Find Out What's in Your PC

If you are not sure about the specifications of your PC and whether it is up to handling Publisher, use the System Information accessory to display a profile of your PC's contents.

1. From the Start menu, choose Programs | Accessories to open the Accessories menu.

2. On the Accessories menu, choose System Tools | System Information. The System Information accessory opens, as shown in Figure 1.3.

On a few systems, the System Information item may not show up on the Accessories menu. If that happens to you, point to My Computer on your Windows desktop, click your right mouse button, and choose Properties from the menu that appears. A dialog box appears on which you may find your system's processor and RAM listed.

▼   3. In the left column, beneath the heading System Information, click on the word
          System. The right column reports the details of your system configuration.

    In the report, pay particular attention to the following:

    • *Processor.* Indicates the type of processor (486, Pentium, and so on) in your PC.

    • *Total physical memory.* This number shows the total memory, or RAM, in your PC,
      expressed in kilobytes (KB). There are 1024KB in a megabyte, so divide by 1,000
      to get a rough idea of the megabytes of RAM In your PC. The computer profiled in
      Figure 1.3 has about 22000KB of physical memory—around 22MB.

    • *Available space on drive.* This number tells the amount of free space (space not
      already occupied by files or programs) on your hard disk, in KB. Divide by 1,000
      to learn the rough number of MB.

FIGURE 1.3.

*The System
Information accessory
can tell you exactly
what is in your PC.*

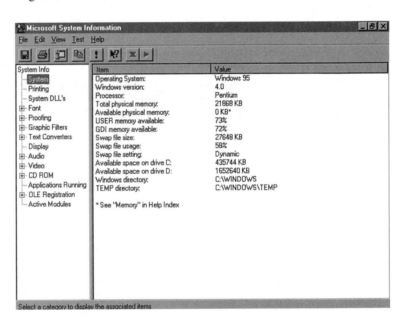

▲

What *Else* Do You Need?

In addition to the PC hardware shown in Table 1.1, the following optional devices can be
very useful in producing professional-looking Publisher projects.

They really are optional—don't feel you need any of them to start learning Publisher. If
you are still hardware shopping or if you're expecting to use Publisher for heavy-duty
publications, however, you should consider the value of these optional devices.

You will learn more about most of these devices in the hours where they come into play.

Large-Screen Monitor

The Holy Grail of desktop publishing is true WYSIWYG editing, which enables you to completely create and edit the document onscreen and to know that it will look the same when printed.

But a computer monitor, no matter what its size, cannot precisely match the appearance of a printed document. That is partly because even the highest monitor resolutions are far lower than the resolutions possible in print, and also because it is very difficult to match colors made of light (like those onscreen) with colors of ink and paper.

NEW TERM *Resolution* describes the number of lines or dots that make up the grid from which an image is produced, onscreen or on paper. *Color depth* describes the number of colors that can be displayed or printed simultaneously by a device.

> You will learn more about resolution and color depth as you move ahead in this tutorial. For now, however, just keep in mind that you will see resolution and color depth listed as specifications for all types of DTP devices, including monitors, scanners, and printers.
>
> In general, the higher the resolution and color depth supported by a device, the better its results and the more it costs. Choosing DTP hardware is often a matter of finding the highest resolution and color depth you can afford.

A large monitor—one with a diagonal screen measurement of 17, 21, or even 27 inches—will enable you to work in Publisher at the highest display resolution supported by your PC's internal graphics card. Very high resolutions are often impractical on smaller monitors because icons, small text, and other objects may become too small to work with effectively.

On a large screen, high resolutions of 1024×768 or higher make what you see a much better match for what you get. Most large color monitors also support the maximum color depth of your PC's graphics card, improving the match between display color and printed color.

Scanner

A scanner is a device that captures images from paper or photographs, converting them into computer graphics files that you can use in your pubs. Scanners can also capture text from printed pages.

Flatbed-type scanners are the best choice for desktop publishing because they enable you to scan just about anything—even images bound in books—and because they typically offer the highest specifications for image resolution and color depth.

Digital Camera

One way to get original photos into your pubs is to shoot them with a regular camera, get them developed, and then scan the printed photos with a scanner. By using a digital camera, however, you can bypass the film, developing, and scanning.

A digital camera captures the images you snap as graphics files. All you need to do is transfer the file from the camera to your PC, using the cable and software (or built-in disk drive) included with most digital cameras. As you will learn in Hour 13, if your digital camera is equipped with TWAIN software, you can use Publisher to pull your snapshots directly from the camera's memory into a pub.

Color Printer

A color inkjet or color thermal printer enables you to print and evaluate your color projects as you work on them, and even to produce final printouts of projects where professional-quality printing is not required. Color laser printers are also available, and are dropping in price. However, these are still extremely expensive and not always any more useful than the cheaper alternatives.

Many folks use inexpensive inkjet printers to test their pubs while working on them, and then use a *printing service* to produce the final prints.

NEW TERM　No affordable home or office printer produces the perfect, professional-looking text and color possible from the devices at printing services (sometimes also called *service bureaus*)—companies that take your desktop publishing files and print them with magazine-quality results. You learn about using printing services in Part V, "Publishing on Paper."

Tape Drive or Writable CD-ROM Drive

Again, publications take up a lot of disk space, especially when they include pictures and color. A high-capacity storage device such as a tape drive, high-capacity removable disk drive (sometimes called a "ZIP" drive), or writable CD-ROM drive enables you to archive your old projects off your hard disk but still have access to them when needed.

For large projects that will be printed by a printing service, a writable CD-ROM drive enables you to hand the bureau a single CD holding the entire project, rather than a pile of disks.

High-Speed Modem

A fast PC modem (33.6kbps or 56kbps) comes in handy for the following three Publisher-related tasks:

- *Sending pubs to printing services*. Many printing services can accept DTP files via modem. By sending your projects via modem, you can transmit them to the printing service the moment they are ready, and you can even use a printing service that is nowhere nearby. Because DTP files are large, a fast modem is needed to transmit them quickly.

- *Web publishing*. To tap Publisher's Web page creation and publishing features (see Part VI), you will need a modem and Internet account to put your pages online and to evaluate them there.

- *Getting extra help and resources*. Through a modem and Internet account, you can get free help and resources (such as fonts or clip art) from Microsoft and many other companies online (see Appendix A, "Internet Resources for Publisher Users").

Installing Publisher 98

If Publisher is included with your copy of Office, you will install it while installing Office. During Office installation, watch for dialog boxes that list the available programs and make sure Publisher has been selected.

If you have purchased Publisher by itself, install it by running its setup wizard, as described in the following To Do.

To Do: Run Publisher's Setup Wizard

1. Close all programs and files (except Windows, of course).

2. Insert your Publisher 98 CD in your CD-ROM drive, and wait a moment. If nothing happens, continue to step 3. If you see a prompt asking whether you want to install Publisher 98, skip to step 5.

3. From the Windows Start menu, choose Run. The Run dialog box opens.

4. In the Run dialog box, type the letter of your CD-ROM drive, followed by \setup. If your CD-ROM drive is the E: drive, for example, type

   `E:\setup`

5. Click OK. A Welcome dialog box opens. Click on Continue. The Name and Organization Information dialog box opens (see Figure 1.4).

▼ 6. Check that your correct name and organization are shown. (If not, make corrections.) Then click OK.

The Name and Organization Information dialog box shown in Figure 1.4 is more than just a formality. Publisher automatically uses the information on this dialog box to put your name and organization into appropriate spots in your pubs, saving you the trouble of typing it.

Publisher does this through a feature called *personal information sets*, which you will first encounter in Hour 4 and explore in detail in Hour 9.

FIGURE 1.4.

Publisher collects your name and organization information during setup, in part so that it can insert this information automatically in pubs you create.

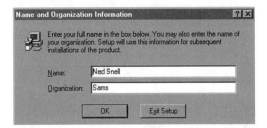

7. A dialog box asks you to confirm the name and organization info you typed in step 6. If it is correct, click on OK to move on; if not, click on Change to return to step 6.

8. A dialog box reports a Product ID number that can be useful if you need to call Microsoft for help. Jot the number someplace, and then click on OK.

9. The next dialog box tells you where on your hard disk Publisher will be installed. If the folder shown is OK with you (and why wouldn't it be?), click on OK; otherwise, click on Change Folder to choose a different folder.

10. After a few moments, a dialog box shows two buttons: Typical Installation and Custom Installation. Click on Typical to conveniently install Publisher with its most popular options, or click on Custom to open a dialog box on which you can pick and choose which parts of Publisher to install.

Publisher's Typical installation includes practically everything in Publisher and is the best choice for nearly all users. The Custom option is really useful only if you want to optionally leave out a component of Publisher, such as Microsoft Photo Editor.

Regardless of which installation option you select, you can use the Publisher Installation Maintenance program at any time to add or remove components, or to re-install Publisher from scratch. See the section titled "Changing Your Publisher 98 Setup," next.

▼

▼   11. After you choose an installation option, Publisher begins copying files to your hard disk. After several minutes, a dialog box appears to report that installation is complete. Click on OK to clear the dialog box.

12. No dialog box tells you to do so, but it is always a good idea to restart your PC after installing a major Windows program. Do that, and Publisher and your PC are ready to go.

> After you install Publisher, you may remove the CD and store it in a safe place. You will not need it for most day-to-day Publisher activities.
>
> However, some activities—such as using Publisher's Clip Gallery—may require that the Publisher CD be in your CD-ROM drive. Whenever you begin such an activity, Publisher reminds you to insert your CD.

▲

Changing Your Publisher 98 Setup

If you decide later to add or remove Publisher components, to re-install Publisher or even to remove Publisher, you can do so by running the Publisher 98 Installation Maintenance program.

To run the program, repeat steps 1 through 5 of the To Do shown earlier for installing Publisher.

In step 5, the Installation Maintenance program opens, offering the following three buttons:

- *Add/Remove*. Opens a dialog box listing components of Publisher. Next to each component, check the check box to add that component or clear the check box to remove it.

- *Reinstall*. Starts the installation program over again, from step 6 of the To Do. This option is useful if you are experiencing general problems that might be fixed by just clearing the decks and starting over with a fresh installation.

- *Remove All*. Removes Publisher from your hard disk to make room for something else (such as more recipes).

Summary

See how much you can pick up in an hour? In the same 60 minutes as a single, blood-curdling episode of *Melrose Place*, you have developed an appreciation of the range of tools and resources bundled as "Publisher," learned how and where to get it, discovered optional hardware you may want for advanced Publisher tasks, and installed Publisher on your PC.

That is a strong foundation on which to build. Now take a break—have some Triscuits or Yoo-Hoo—and then move ahead to Hour 2, and *into* Publisher proper.

Workshop

The following workshop helps solidify the skills you learned in this lesson.

Q&A

Q Can you use Publisher on a notebook PC?

A Many folks use notebook PCs as all-purpose computers, whether in the office or on the go. If you are one, note that a notebook can certainly run Publisher as long as it meets the specifications shown earlier in Table 1.1.

Except for the simplest projects, however, I recommend using the external monitor and mouse ports (included on most notebook PCs) to connect a full-size monitor and mouse to your notebook. Even the largest notebook screens are still too small for the precise work of desktop publishing, and the touchpads or tiny trackballs built into notebooks in lieu of a mouse are similarly too clumsy for Publisher mousework.

Quiz

Take the following quiz to see how much you've learned.

Questions

1. Where and how can you get Publisher 98?

    a. Packaged by itself, at any software store

    b. As part of the Office 97 Small Business Edition version 2.0

    c. From Microsoft's Publisher Web site (depending on availability), in a free-trial version

    d. All the above

2. If your PC can handle Windows and other Windows programs, it can handle Publisher 98. (True/False)

3. To change my Publisher installation choices after installation, you can

    a. Erase your hard disk

    b. Click on the button on your Windows desktop labeled "Oops"

    c. Repeat the first steps of the installation procedure to open the Installation Maintenance program

    d. Have some Yoo-Hoo and hope everything's OK in the morning

Answers

1. (d) All choices are ways you can get started with Publisher 98.

2. False. Some PCs running Windows 95 have as little as 8MB of RAM in them; Publisher requires a minimum of 12MB, and really wants even more.

3. (c) is the only right answer, though I often wish (b) and (d) were reasonable options.

Activities

Begin developing your eye for page design. When an ad in a magazine or a billboard catches your attention, study it, and consider what you like about it. Did the color draw you in, or a particular picture? Is the composition of the various elements—pictures and text—balanced and pleasing to the eye? Are boxes, borders, or lines used to frame or divide the page in an attractive or exciting way?

The more carefully you study publications that impress you, the better you will be able to create publications that impress others.

HOUR 2

First Steps: Open, Close, and Save

Here's an easy hour, but an important one. Before doing anything else in Microsoft Publisher, you need to know how to get into and out of it, round-trip. Along the way, you will learn how to save your work and discover some of Publisher's handy features, such as the Publications Catalog.

Even if you're an old hand at opening and closing other Windows programs and saving your work there, you will notice that Publisher 98—although faithful to many techniques you already know—has its own quirks and twists on common tasks. To know Publisher, you must approach it with an open mind, ready to adapt to the way it wants to do things—which often is not what you'd expect, based on experience with other programs.

At the end of the hour, you will be able to answer the following questions:

- How do I open and close Publisher 98?
- What's that Catalog thing I see when I open Publisher, and what do I do with it?

- How do I save my publications, and save changes I make to them?
- Does Publisher help me remember to save my work?
- After closing, how do I find and open the pubs I've saved so that I can work on them again?

Opening Publisher and Closing the Catalog

To open Publisher from the Windows Start menu, choose Programs | Microsoft Publisher 98 (see Figure 2.1). Note that this is the way to open Publisher whether you installed it alone *or* as part of Office.

FIGURE 2.1.

Opening Publisher from the Windows Start menu.

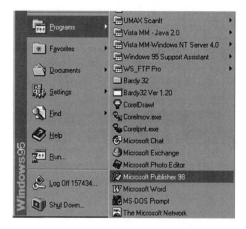

After you have created some pubs, you can open Publisher another way—by opening a file icon right from a Windows folder, the Desktop, or the Documents menu. See the Q&A at the end of this hour.

When Publisher opens, it immediately displays the Publications Catalog (see Figure 2.2), the usual starting point for your Publisher sessions.

NEW TERM   The *Publications Catalog* is a handy dialog box on which you start a new publication or open an existing one. It is divided into four parts, or *tabs*. You use the first three tabs to create new publications, and the fourth tab (Existing Publications) to locate and open pubs you've already created.

FIGURE 2.2.

The Catalog provides a helpful starting point for starting new pubs or opening old ones.

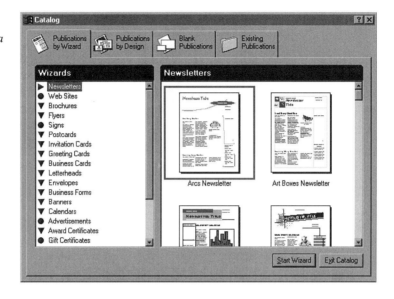

You will learn later in this hour how to open an existing pub from the Catalog, and in Hour 4, "Starting a New Publication," you will learn several ways you can use the Catalog to get a head start on a great layout. For right now, however, you need to know how to get the Catalog out of your way.

To close the Catalog, click on the Exit Catalog button in its lower-right corner. When the Catalog closes it reveals the new, blank pub that is created automatically whenever you open Publisher (see Figure 2.3). That new pub is always called Unsaved Publication, and it looks like a blank sheet of paper in the middle of Publisher's workspace.

Saving Your Work

I know, I know…. You haven't created anything yet, so what's to save? But look at it this way: Do you really want to spend an hour creating your first masterpiece, and then lose it because you haven't learned to save yet?

Starting a publication isn't difficult, but Publisher rewards you for making some smart choices when doing so. Therefore, starting pubs can wait until Hour 4, where I can show you not merely how to start a pub, but to do it in the way that gets you the quickest, best-looking results.

In the meantime, you might as well get saving out of the way here and now, especially considering that Publisher has created an Unsaved Publication you can use for practice.

FIGURE 2.3.

Beneath the Catalog at startup, Publisher creates a new, blank Unsaved Publication in case you want to use it to start a new pub.

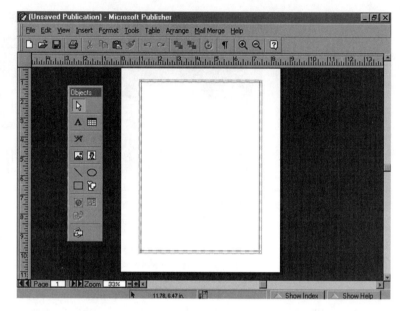

Saving a Pub the First Time

To save a new publication for the very first time, you can do any of the following (all three have the same effect):

- Press Ctrl+S
- Click on the Save button (the disk) on Publisher's toolbar
- From the menu bar, choose File | Save

Any way you go, the Save As dialog box shown in Figure 2.4 opens. You are probably familiar with this dialog box from other Windows programs. All you really need to do on it is click in the box next to File Name, and type a short, descriptive name for the file. Don't bother typing a *filename extension*—the period and three-letter suffix that come at the end of a filename (.txt, .exe, and so on). Publisher automatically adds the correct filename extension for Publisher files: .pub.

After typing a filename, click on the Save As dialog box's Save button to save the file.

Publisher supports Windows 95's file-naming conventions, which means you can type just about anything you want for a filename, of any length (up to 255 characters!).

However, it is best to avoid using any punctuation in a filename, and to keep filenames fairly short (10 characters or so).

Descriptive filenames help you easily locate a particular project later. But the dialogs from which you will open your saved Publisher projects display a preview of each file. Therefore unless you create a long list of pubs to sort through, filenames need not be excessively descriptive; the previews make it easy to find out what each file contains.

2

FIGURE 2.4.

Use the Save As dialog to choose a name, location, and options for your pub file.

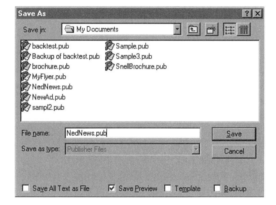

Choosing Options When Saving

Before clicking the Save As dialog's Save button, you can take advantage of the dialog's optional items: the Save In list and the check boxes.

Unless instructed otherwise, Publisher saves your publications in the folder C:\My Documents. On the Save As dialog, you may optionally drop down the Save In list shown at the top of the dialog to select a folder in which to save your publication. (You can also choose Desktop from the top of the list to save the pub on your Windows desktop.) The large box beneath Save In shows the names of any pub files in the selected folder. (Note that the selected folder may contain other files of other types, but only the pub files appear in the box.)

In Figure 2.4, observe the row of check boxes at the bottom of the Save As dialog. The Save Preview box is always checked automatically, but you may click any of the check boxes to add or remove check marks according to your needs:

- *Save All Text as File*. When checked, this option saves just the text (no pictures or layout) into a separate Publisher, word processing, or ordinary text file. You will learn more about this option in Hour 9, "Getting the Words Into Your Publication."

- *Save Preview*. When this box is checked, a *preview* is saved along with the pub, to make it easy later to locate the pub and remember what it contains.

- *Template*. Check this box to create a *template*, a special version of a pub file that you can use as a head start on creating new, similar pubs. You will learn more about templates in Hour 4.

- *Backup*. Check this box to save—in addition to the pub file—a *backup*: a separate, identical copy of the publication. A backup uses the same filename as the pub file it matches, but has the filename extension .bak rather than .pub. A backup makes a handy failsafe in case something happens to the original pub file.

NEW TERM A *preview* is a small, rough image of a publication or of the first page of a multi-page pub. When a preview has been saved, it is displayed when you select the pub's name from any dialog on which you would open a pub. That helps you locate and open the pub you want. See the section titled "Opening a Pub You've Saved," later in this hour.

Saving a Pub After the First Time

After the first time you save a pub, using any of the regular save steps—Ctrl+S, the Save button on the toolbar, or File | Save—no longer displays the Save As dialog box.

Instead, whenever you apply any of these save steps, the file is just saved (with all its latest changes) using the filename, location, and options you selected the first time you saved. No dialog box appears, and there's nothing else to do.

If you want to change anything on the Save As dialog box—such as the file's name or location—you can make the dialog reappear by choosing File | Save As.

To Do: Open Publisher and Save a Pub

1. From the Start menu, open Publisher by choosing Programs | Microsoft Publisher 98. Publisher opens and displays the Catalog.

2. In the Catalog's lower-right corner, click on the Exit Catalog button to close it. Unsaved Publication—the new pub created automatically when you opened Publisher—appears in the workspace.

3. In the toolbar, click on the Save button (the disk), or choose File | Save from the menu bar. The Save As dialog box opens.

4. Click in the box next to File Name, and type Sample.

5. Click on the dialog's Save button. You have saved the file Sample.pub in your My Documents folder.

Dealing with AutoSave

After long experience, my fingers now instinctively press Ctrl+S—with no help from my brain—every time I stop to breathe. My body has developed its own useful rut, a personal autosave. But just in case your body hasn't, Publisher's AutoSave reminds you to save.

Any time your pub contains changes you've made since you last saved it, if 15 minutes pass during which you do not save the file, a dialog appears to remind you (see Figure 2.5). To save, just click on Yes in the dialog. (If you've never saved the current file before, the Save As dialog box then opens so that you can choose the pub's filename.)

If you don't want to save—as you might if you're not sure you want to keep the current changes—click on No. AutoSave will leave you alone, until you go another 15 minutes without saving.

FIGURE 2.5.

When you go 15 minutes without saving your work, AutoSave displays this prompt to remind you.

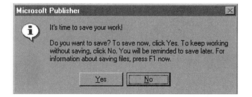

In Hour 3, "Tools, Views, Menus, and Measures," you will learn how to customize many aspects of Publisher's behavior, including changing the number of minutes AutoSave waits before reminding you to save, or disabling AutoSave altogether.

Opening a Pub You've Saved

From inside Publisher, you've got three (count 'em!) ways to open a pub you've previously saved; each of which you discover next.

Regardless of how you open a new pub, keep in mind that Publisher can have only one pub open at a time. Therefore you need not bother closing the current pub (even Unsaved Publication) before opening a different one. The current pub closes automatically when you create or open a different one. See the section titled "Closing a Pub," later in this hour.

In addition to the three ways shown here for opening a pub from within Publisher, you can open an existing pub from the *outside*, in Windows, without first opening Publisher. See the Q&A at the end of this hour.

Choosing from the Catalog

Usually, the Catalog's Existing Publications tab (see Figure 2.6) is the most convenient way to find and open existing pubs. To display the Existing Publications tab, follow these steps:

- When the Catalog is closed, choose File | Open. Doing so opens the Catalog and goes straight to Existing Publications.
- When the Catalog is already open (as at startup), click on the tab labeled Existing Publications, along the top of the Catalog.

FIGURE 2.6.

The Catalog's Existing Publications tab offers a convenient way to preview and open publications.

Recently used files ——

Directory ——

Preview ——

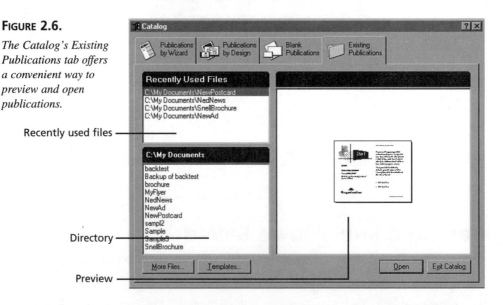

The Existing Publications tab is made up of the following three parts, or *panes*:

- *Preview*. The large pane on the right displays a preview of any file you select in the lists shown by the other two panes.
- *Recently Used Files*. This pane lists the pubs you've created or edited recently, showing the filename preceded by the disk letter and folder in which the file is stored.

- *Directory*. This pane lists the pub files in the My Documents folder, the default folder for publications.

To see a preview of any pub listed on the Existing Publications tab, single-click the pub's name. To open a pub, double-click its name, or display the pub's preview and then click on the Open button on the Existing Publications tab.

To find and open a file not listed on the Existing Publications tab, click on the tab's More Files button to display the Open Publication dialog box. See the section titled "Calling Up the Open Publication Dialog," later in this hour.

Many Windows applications enable you to edit multiple documents simultaneously, switching from one to another from a "Window" menu or even displaying them all at once in multiple, tiled windows. But not Publisher. Publisher handles one pub at a time, period.

That doesn't mean you can't enjoy the benefits of working in multiple documents, however, such as copying text or pictures from one pub to another. You will learn how to perform such multipub operations—Publisher-style—in upcoming hours.

Picking from the File Menu

Files you have edited recently—the same files listed in the Existing Publications tab's Recently Used Files pane—also appear in a list at the bottom of Publisher's File menu (see Figure 2.7). When the Catalog is closed and you want to open a recently used file, you will find doing so quicker if you choose File, and then click on the file's name in the list.

Calling Up the Open Publication Dialog

Publisher's Open Publication dialog (see Figure 2.8) is your basic everyday Windows file-opening dialog, like those you've probably seen in other programs. You can open it in the following two ways:

- If the Catalog is closed, click on the Open button (the folder icon) in Publisher's toolbar.
- If the Catalog is open, click on the More Files button on the Existing Publications tab.

FIGURE 2.7.

You can conveniently open any file you've used recently by choosing it from the bottom of the File menu.

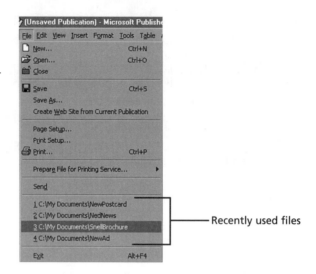

Recently used files

FIGURE 2.8.

The Open Publication dialog enables you to preview and display pubs stored anywhere on your PC.

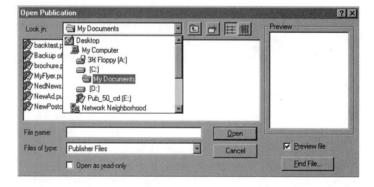

You call on the Open Publication dialog to preview or open pubs that don't appear on the Existing Publications tab. Drop down the Look In list at the top of the dialog to select the folder containing the pub. The box beneath Look In lists all pub files in the selected folder. (The folder may contain files of other types, but only the pub files appear in the box.)

Single-click any pub listed in the box to display its preview in the Preview pane on the right side of the dialog. (Make sure the check box for Preview File, underneath the Preview pane, is checked.) To open a pub, double-click its name or display the pub's preview and then click on the dialog's Open button.

If you're experienced with Windows applications, you may expect the New and Open buttons on Publisher's toolbar (the little page icon and folder icon) to do the same thing as File I New and File I Open, respectively. But as you've seen already, that's not the case (another Publisher quirk).

Those toolbar buttons do open dialogs for creating or opening publications, but they don't open the Catalog, as do File I New and File I Open.

You will learn more about toolbar activities as you go along. For now, just remember that the File I Open and File I New lead to the Catalog; whereas the Open and New buttons on the toolbar lead to alternative, Catalog-free ways to open or create files.

2

Closing Publisher

When finished working on a pub, close Publisher by choosing File I Exit. The current pub and Publisher close.

If you attempt to close a pub, or Publisher, when the current pub contains changes you haven't saved, a slightly modified AutoSave dialog opens to ask whether you want to save the pub before closing. On that dialog, you may do the following:

- Click on Yes to save the pub and close Publisher.
- Click on No to close without saving, discarding all changes made to the file since it was last saved.
- Click on Cancel to change your mind about closing. Publisher stays open, and you can continue work on the current pub.

Think of the closing AutoSave prompt as an auto airbag: It is a useful safety device, but it's not a license to be careless. Make a habit of saving your pubs before closing, rather than relying on the dialog. If you rely on the dialog, and you're working too fast, it's pretty easy to accidentally click on No and blow your last chance to save.

Closing a Pub

To close a pub without closing Publisher, choose File I Close. Note, however, that compared to most other Windows applications, Publisher has two file-closing idiosyncrasies:

- Publisher must always have an open pub; so when you close a pub, Unsaved Publication reappears. You cannot close Unsaved Publication; you can only replace it in the workspace with another pub, or edit and save it to make it a new pub.

- The current pub closes automatically any time you start a new pub, open an existing pub, or close Publisher—therefore it is unlikely you will ever need to deliberately close a pub. Closing a pub might be useful only if you suddenly decide you don't like a bunch of changes you made; you can discard them by closing the pub and clicking on No when prompted to save.

To Do: Open an Existing Pub and Close Publisher

Practice closing Publisher and opening files using the practice file (`Sample.pub`) you created in this hour's earlier To Do.

1. Close Publisher if it is open.

2. Open Publisher and don't close the Catalog. (If you've already closed the Catalog, open it by choosing File | Open.)

3. On the Catalog, choose the Existing Publications tab.

4. In the tab's Recently Used Files pane, find `Sample.pub`.

5. Single-click `Sample.pub`. Its preview appears in the Preview pane. (Note that because you didn't actually put anything in `Sample.pub` when you created it earlier, its Preview appears blank.)

6. Click on the Existing Publications tab's Open button. The Catalog closes, and `Sample.pub` opens in the Publisher workspace.

Summary

Got the hang of opening Publisher, saving publications, and opening existing pubs? It sounds like pretty basic stuff, but as I'm sure you noticed, in the course of exploring those basics you were introduced to some of Publisher's features and its quirky approaches to some activities. Knowing those quirks will keep you out of trouble in the hours to come.

Workshop

The following workshop helps solidify the skills you learned in this lesson.

Q&A

Q If I want to work on a particular pub-in-progress, it seems like a lot of steps to open Publisher from the Start menu, open the Catalog's Existing Publications tab, and then choose the pub. Tell me there's a faster way.

A Okay, there is a faster way: Don't open Publisher; just open the pub. Publisher automatically configures Windows to make itself the *default program* for any file with a `.pub` filename extension. So when you open a pub file anywhere in Windows, Publisher opens too.

2

Just navigate through Windows's folders (or in Windows Explorer) to the folder where the pub file is stored, and then double-click on the file's icon. Publisher opens and immediately shows the file—bypassing the Catalog and Unsaved Publication—so you can get straight to work.

And if the pub you want is among the files you've used most recently in Windows (including files you have opened in other programs), you will probably find it listed in the Windows Documents menu. From the Start menu, choose Documents, and then choose the pub file from the list that appears. Try it now. Is `Sample.pub` listed?

Quiz

Take the following quiz to see how much you have learned.

Questions

1. The filename extension for a Publisher file is always

   a. `.bar`

   b. `.pub`

   c. `.cafe`

   d. `.saloon`

2. Which of the following saves a pub?

   a. Ctrl+S

   b. File | Save

   c. The Save button (the disk) on the toolbar

   d. Any of the above

3. You need not close the current pub before starting a new pub, opening a different pub, or closing Publisher. (True/False)

4. Which two things happen automatically any time you open Publisher from the Start menu (Programs | Microsoft Publisher 98)?

    a. The Catalog opens, and a happy jingle plays on your speakers.

    b. Your modem dials Microsoft, so Microsoft can see what you're up to.

    c. The Catalog opens, and a new, blank Unsaved Publication is created.

    d. All the above.

Answers

1. (b) A Publisher publication always uses the .pub extension.

2. (d) Choices (a), (b), and (c) all save the current pub.

3. True. The current pub closes automatically when you start or open another pub or close Publisher. If the current pub needs saving, however, you will be prompted to save it before it closes.

4. (c) At startup, the Catalog opens and Unsaved Publication is created. You can use or close the Catalog and ignore Unsaved Publication—it will go away as soon as you open or create another pub.

Activities

Click on the Catalog's Publications by Wizard tab, and study the right-hand pane to examine just a few of the dozens of publication layouts Publisher can create for you. Do any resemble the kinds of publications you want to create? You will begin working with these layouts in Hour 4, after you learn your way around Publisher's interface in Hour 3.

HOUR 3

Tools, Views, Menus, and Measures

At first glance, Microsoft Publisher appears to have a lot in common with any Windows word processor. You may already recognize the familiar toolbars, scrollbars, and other common interface elements. However, Publisher adds to that mix some unique interface objects you may not recognize, and also turns a few twists on the common objects.

In this hour, you tour the Publisher interface, discovering what's what and—more important—learning how to tap features that can *tell* you what's what, any time you need a refresher. At the end of the hour, you will be able to answer the following questions:

- What are the parts of the Publisher window?
- How does Publisher help me automatically when I point?
- How can I use toolbars and identify their buttons?
- How do I modify Publisher's display so that I see all of my pub at once, or zero in on just a small part of my pub?

- How do I get help?
- How do I customize Publisher's appearance and behavior?

Getting the Lay of the Land

Figure 3.1 shows Publisher, with a sample publication opened as the current pub. Following the figure are descriptions of the important parts of the Publisher window.

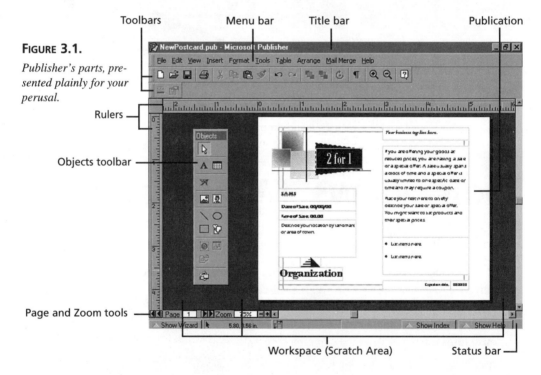

Toolbars   Menu bar   Title bar   Publication

FIGURE 3.1.

Publisher's parts, pre-sented plainly for your perusal.

Rulers

Objects toolbar

Page and Zoom tools

Workspace (Scratch Area)   Status bar

- *Title bar.* The bar at the top of the screen always tells you the filename of the current pub.
- *Menu bar.* Right beneath the title bar, the familiar menu bar offers a row of menu names—File, Edit, View, and so on. Click on a name to drop down a menu of related items.
- *Toolbars.* In the area between the menu bar and the workspace, Publisher displays its toolbars (sometimes). See the section titled "Using Toolbars," later in this hour.

- *Objects toolbar*. The Objects toolbar is always available in Publisher for working with the objects that make up your pub. Like any toolbar, objects can appear "floating" in the workspace (as in Figure 3.1), in the toolbar area below the menu bar, or along either side of the screen. (See "Using Toolbars," later in this hour.)
- *Object*. Almost everything you put in your pub—a block of text, a picture, and so on—is an *object*. You add new elements to a pub by creating new objects; and you design a page by arranging, sizing, and shaping the objects on it, as you learn to do in Hour 6, "Arranging Frames and Columns."

> To perform many Publisher activities, you need a skill called *drag and drop*. Using your mouse, you point to an object, click and hold the button, and then move the mouse (without letting go of the button) to "drag" the object to a new location. Release the button, and the object "drops" in the spot where you dragged it.
>
> If you're new to drag and drop, moving toolbars is a great way to practice. See "Moving Toolbars," later in this hour.

3

- *Rulers*. The rulers serve two purposes: Because your pub is rarely displayed at its actual, printed size (see the section titled "Zooming In, Zooming Out," later in this hour), the rulers provide a scale by which you can visually judge the actual printed size of objects and the space between them. As you learn in upcoming hours, you also use the rulers to position objects precisely.
- *Workspace (Scratch Area)*. The workspace is the whole area between the toolbars and the status bar (described a little later), with the current pub in the middle of it. Any empty parts of the workspace not covered by the pub are known as the *scratch area*, where you can temporarily put objects aside while working on the layout.
- *Page and Zoom tools*. This small set of buttons and indicators provides you with a convenient way to move among the pages of a multipage document and control the Zoom factor. See the section titled "Zooming In, Zooming Out," later in this hour.
- *Status bar*. The status bar provides buttons for getting help (see the section titled "Getting Help," later in this hour) and indicators near the center that tell you precisely where in the workspace the mouse pointer is located. The indicators can be valuable for a few advanced activities you will discover in upcoming hours.

Publisher works best when it is *maximized*, with its window covering your
entire display. A maximized Publisher window enables you to see the most
of your pub while you work. The only time you will want to display
Publisher in a window smaller than the whole screen is when dragging text
or pictures between documents, as you learn to do in upcoming hours.

If Publisher isn't maximized when you open it, double-click on its title bar to
maximize it.

How Publisher Shows You What's What

Publisher is an unusually helpful program, offering you support and guidance even when
you haven't asked for any. As you explore Publisher, you will notice the following types
of mostly unsolicited assistance at work, all of which come into play when you move
your mouse to point to something.

ToolTips ("ScreenTips")

You can learn the name of any toolbar button by pointing to it and waiting a second.
After a moment, a tiny label—a *ToolTip*—appears to tell you the button's name (see
Figure 3.2). ToolTips make finding any particular toolbar button easy while you're learning your way around. (After a little practice, you will know the buttons by their icons,
and won't really need the ToolTips.)

Many Windows programs have ToolTips, but in Publisher ToolTips have a new name—
ScreenTips—because they work for more than just toolbar buttons. You can point to all
sorts of objects in Publisher—including objects within your pub—and a ScreenTip pops
up to tell you what you're pointing to.

FIGURE 3.2.

*This ToolTip, or
ScreenTip, tells you
that you're pointing to
the Print button.*

To conveniently learn the names of a whole row of toolbar buttons, point to
a button at one end of the toolbar and wait a second for the button's
ToolTip to appear (don't click). Then slowly slide your mouse left or right
across the row. As you pass each button, its name pops into view.

TipPages

Publisher automatically displays little hints in yellow balloons, called *TipPages*, when it thinks you need a hint. The difference between ScreenTips and TipPages is that ScreenTips tell you what something *is*; TipPages tell you how to *do* something.

To display the TipPages, Publisher must guess what you're trying to do; it doesn't always guess right. If a TipPage tells you how to do something you don't want to do, just ignore it and continue working; TipPages vanish as soon as you do anything in Publisher, regardless of whether you follow their advice.

"Helpful" Mouse Pointers

As you work on a pub, you will notice that your mouse pointer changes depending on what you're doing. When you point to an object that you can drag to change the size of something, for example, the pointer changes to the Resize pointer (see Figure 3.3).

Sometimes you must point very precisely to a particular part of an object to perform a particular type of action, such as changing the size or shape of a picture. These "helpful mouse pointers," as they're called, tell you when you're pointing to the perfect spot to perform a particular action. You will learn more about helpful pointers in Parts II, "Page Design," and III, "Text and Type."

FIGURE 3.3.

Helpful mouse pointers tell you what you can do with your mouse at the spot where you're pointing.

Publisher makes good use of Windows's pop-up menus, sometimes called *context menus*. You display a pop-up menu by pointing to something and then *right-clicking*—clicking your right mouse button rather than the usual left button. (If you're a lefty who's configured Windows so that you do most mouse operations with your right button, you click your left button to "right-click.")

Each onscreen object—including toolbars, the workspace, and objects in your pub—has its own pop-up menu that contains only choices related to working with that object. Try right-clicking on the middle of Unsaved Publication, and see what's on its menu. Then right-click a toolbar, and observe how different the choices on its menu are.

To Do: Explore the Interface

1. Open Publisher and close the Catalog, to reveal Unsaved Publication.

2. Move the pointer up to the toolbar area, point to any button, and pause a moment. A ScreenTip appears to identify the button.

3. Point to a button in the Object toolbar, and pause. A ScreenTip appears.

4. Point to a ruler, and pause. The pointer changes to a two-pointed arrow, and the tip, Move Ruler, appears to tell you that you can move the ruler when pointing to it.

▲

Using Toolbars

Publisher has three toolbars, whose buttons you will learn about and use as you move through this tutorial:

- *Standard.* The Standard toolbar includes all the basic housekeeping buttons such as Open, Save, and Print.

- *Formatting.* The *Zelig* of toolbars, Formatting transforms itself to please you. This toolbar always contains buttons for formatting pages or objects, but its buttons change depending on what you're doing. Click on text in a pub, and the Formatting toolbar shows tools for formatting text. Click on a picture, and the Formatting toolbar shows a different set of buttons for formatting pictures.

- *Objects.* The Objects toolbar shows tools for creating and manipulating objects in your pub.

When you first use Publisher, the Objects toolbar floats in the workspace and the other two toolbars reside in the toolbar area (with the Standard toolbar on top). That's a good setup in which to learn, so you've no reason to change it now.

But one day, you might work on a project that's so large or complicated that you want to free up more screen area for the workspace. Or you may want to move a toolbar to a location you find more convenient. As you learn next, you can move any toolbar, and you can hide toolbars (except for the Objects toolbar, which moves but can't hide) to free up more workspace within the Publisher window. You can even hide the status bar.

You will notice that some toolbar buttons appear faded and colorless, as if covered in fog. Such buttons are temporarily "grayed out" because you're engaged in an activity for which they're irrelevant. Publisher grays out irrelevant buttons to help you focus on those that really are useful to the task at hand.

When the current publication is blank, many buttons are grayed out because the pub contains no objects for which they would be useful. As soon as you begin adding objects, you will see the color come back to these buttons, indicating their availability if you need them.

Moving Toolbars

Using drag and drop, you can position any or all of the toolbars—including Objects—in the toolbar area (and choose their order, top to bottom). You can also float any toolbar, and you can move any toolbar to a side of the window, or the bottom (see Figure 3.4).

At the left end of each toolbar in the toolbar area, a pair of vertical lines appears (see Figure 3.4). To move the toolbar, you click on the lines, hold down the mouse button, and then drag:

- Drag a short way up or down, and then drop to change a toolbar's place in the top-to-bottom order of toolbars in the toolbar area.

- Drag into the workspace, and then drop to float the toolbar.

- Drag all the way to a side or the bottom, and then drop to position the toolbar there. (Be careful when dragging to the bottom not to release on top of the Windows taskbar.)

FIGURE 3.4.

Any toolbar can reside in the toolbar area, float, or rest on a side or bottom of the window.

Vertical lines

Formatting toolbar, floating

Standard toolbar

Objects toolbar, moved to side

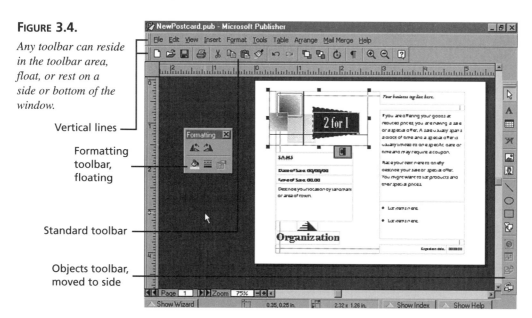

When a toolbar is floating, you can move it by clicking its title bar, holding the mouse button, and dragging to a new position and dropping:

- Restore a floater to the toolbar area by dropping it there.
- Drag all the way to a side or the bottom, and then drop to position the toolbar as a single row there.

Hiding a Toolbar or the Status Bar

To hide a toolbar (except for Objects) or the status bar, choose View | Toolbars to display the Toolbars menu. In the menu, the currently displayed toolbars have check marks next to them. To hide a toolbar, click on its name in the menu. To redisplay it later, return to the Toolbars menu and click on it again, restoring the check mark.

Do you suffer from too-tiny toolbar buttons?

If you work on a small monitor or run Windows at high resolution (or both), you may find that Publisher's toolbar buttons look awfully small. Too-tiny buttons are not only hard to identify, but also tricky to point to and click.

To get bigger buttons, choose View | Toolbars | Options to display the Toolbar Options dialog box, and then click on the check box for Large Icons. Note that the Toolbar Options dialog box also contains options for choosing when and whether ScreenTips appear.

Zooming In, Zooming Out

With most pubs, it is not practical to always display the pub at its actual, full printed size while working on it.

For one thing, the printed size of many publications is much larger than the actual measurements of the Publisher workspace on your monitor—so at full size, you can't see the whole pub at once to evaluate its overall appearance. For another, even if you can display a particular pub full size, you will often need to magnify a portion of it to do close, careful work, such as dealing with small text.

You enlarge or reduce the onscreen appearance of your pub by changing the *zoom factor*. Note that changing the zoom factor affects only the size at which your pub is represented onscreen; zooming has no effect on the actual, printed size.

NEW TERM *Zoom factor*, often shortened to just *zoom*, describes the extent to which your pub's appearance is magnified or reduced onscreen. A zoom of 100% means that the pub appears onscreen at roughly its printed size.

Zoom factors higher than 100% indicate that the pub is shown larger than its actual size; zoom factors below 100% indicate that the pub is shown smaller than actual size.

Increasing the zoom is often called *zooming in*, because it makes the pub appear larger, as if you had moved your eyes closer to it. *Zooming out*—decreasing the zoom factor—makes a pub appear farther away.

Because of the variability among computer monitors, Publisher can't determine how to display your pub at *exactly* its actual size. A zoom of 100% is a "best guess," ballpark stab at representing actual, printed size.

Changing the Zoom Factor from a Menu

The current zoom factor is displayed as a percentage in the Page and Zoom tools area near the bottom of the window. You can also visually judge the effects of the current zoom by looking at the rulers. When the zoom factor is 50% (half size), one inch on the rulers looks like a half inch. At 200%, an inch on the rulers looks like two inches.

You can change the current zoom factor from the Zoom menu, which you display in either of two ways:

- Choose View | Zoom.

- In the group of Page and Zoom tools, click on the Select Zoom Mode button (the word *Zoom*), as shown in Figure 3.5.

FIGURE 3.5.

The Zoom menu, displayed from the Select Zoom Mode button.

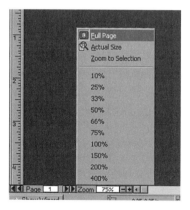

The top two choices in the Zoom menu automatically adjust the zoom factor based on the size of your pub:

- *Full Page* adjusts the zoom so that the full page can be seen all at once, without scrolling. At Full Page, the pub may or may not appear actual size.
- *Actual Size* adjusts the zoom to 100% so that your page is displayed at its rough actual size, the size it will be when printed. At Actual Size, the pub may or may not fit within the window; you may have to scroll to bring unseen parts of the pub into view.

Rather than choosing one of the top choices from the Zoom menu, you may instead select an exact zoom factor from the menu, from 10% (one-tenth actual size) to 400% (four times actual size).

Any time you open a publication or create a new one, it always starts out at the Full Page zoom setting, calculated to make the whole pub visible in the workspace at once.

In the Page and Zoom tools, you will see a tiny plus button (+) and a minus button (–). These buttons move you up and down through the same zooms (10% to 400%) listed on the Zoom menu. Each time you click on +, the zoom increases to the next-highest zoom on the menu. The – button does the opposite.

Don't confuse these buttons with the Zoom In and Zoom Out buttons on the Standard toolbar, which are described next.

Choosing What to Zoom

Often when zooming in, and sometimes when zooming out, the part of the document you see after zooming isn't the part you wanted to work on. You are then forced to scroll around to bring the desired area into view.

The Zoom In and Zoom Out buttons on the Standard toolbar solve this problem by making the spot you click the center of the zoomed image.

To use Zoom In or Zoom Out, click the button, and then point to the general spot within your pub that you want to be at the center of what you will see after you zoom. Click, and the zoom factor increases (if you're using Zoom In) or decreases (Zoom Out) by one level of the choices in the Zoom menu (peek back at Figure 3.5). The spot you clicked appears at the center of your screen.

> Suppose you want to zoom so that one particular area of the pub fills the window. Click on Zoom In, and then point to a corner of the area you want displayed. Click and hold the button, and drag diagonally across the area to the opposite corner. (As you drag, a box appears to mark the area you're selecting.)
>
> When you release the button, the zoom is automatically adjusted so that the area you selected roughly fills the window.

To Do: Play with Zoom

1. Open Publisher and close the Catalog to reveal Unsaved Publication. Note that Unsaved Publication starts out at the Full Page zoom setting.

2. In the Page and Zoom tools near the bottom of the window, click on the word *Zoom*. The Zoom menu opens.

3. Choose Actual Size. Unsaved Publication expands to its rough actual size. Scroll around to bring other parts into view.

4. Open the Zoom menu again, and choose 10%. Unsaved Publication shrinks to postage-stamp size.

5. Return to Full Page zoom.

6. On the Standard toolbar, click on the Zoom In button.

7. Point to a spot anywhere within Unsaved Publication, click and hold the mouse button, drag to form a box, and release. The zoom is adjusted so that the area in the box you formed fills the window.

▲   8. Return to Full Page zoom.

Getting Help

The aforementioned ScreenTips and TipPages are a form of help, but they offer no more than object identification and the occasional hint. For more detailed answers to your questions, you need *real* help text, the kind you can get in Publisher from three sources: the Assistant, the Help index, and Microsoft's Internet-based, online help.

Asking the Assistant for Help

If you've used Microsoft Office 97, you've probably already met the "Assistant," who also pops up in Publisher.

The Assistant is a little animated cartoon character that appears in a small window (see Figure 3.6), supplies quick access to help text, and sometimes supplies unsolicited advice. Some folks love the Assistant, others shut him off to shut him up. It's your call.

- To open the Assistant, press your F1 key or click on the Microsoft Publisher Help button at the right end of the Standard toolbar, or choose Help | Microsoft Publisher Help.

- To move the Assistant, drag him as you would a floating toolbar, and drop him in a spot where he's out of your way.

- To close the Assistant, click on the X button in the Assistant's upper-right corner.

FIGURE 3.6.

Click on the Assistant to display its What would you like to do? *balloon.*

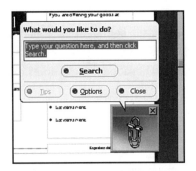

While the Assistant is open, it offers *context-sensitive* help—another way of saying it monitors your activities and tailors its suggestions to what it thinks you're doing. From time to time, it may automatically display a hint related to what you're doing, even if you don't ask. You can follow the Assistant's advice or click on the Close button that appears with the hint to ignore it and get back to work.

You can also ask the Assistant to help you. You begin by clicking on the Assistant to display its What would you like to do? balloon. (To close the balloon later, click anywhere in your pub.) Then ask for help in any of the following ways:

- At the top of the balloon, the Assistant may show a short list of help topics it guesses relate to what you're currently doing. Choose an item to display the help text.

- Type a simple question in the box provided, such as How do I print? Then click on the Search button. The Assistant displays a short list of options relating to your question.

- Click on the Tips button to display a tip related to what you're doing.

Not that it matters, but you can change the Assistant's cartoon character from the playful paperclip to any of several animated alternatives, including a grumpy Albert Einstein and a doggy with a superhero cape. (I am not making this up.)

Click on the Assistant to open its balloon, and then click on the Options button. The Office Assistant dialog box opens. (Observe that this dialog box offers a variety of options for customizing the Assistant's behavior.)

Choose the Gallery tab, and then click the Next button to flip through the available characters. When you see one you like, click on OK.

Consulting the Contents and Index

The Publisher Help Contents and Index (see Figure 3.7) provide access to old-fashioned, detailed help text for almost any Publisher activity.

3

- Display the Contents menu by clicking on the Show Help button on the status bar, or by choosing Help|Contents. The Contents menu starts off with a list of broad topics. Click on a topic, and you get another list of more specific choices. Keep clicking, and eventually you will reach help text (see Figure 3.7).

The little backward-pointing arrow in the set of controls at the bottom on the Contents takes you "back" one level from where you are in the Contents. While investigating a menu of options, you may click this back button to move backward to the preceding menu.

- Display the Index by clicking on the Show Index button on the status bar, or by choosing Help|Index. The Index lists all help topics alphabetically. Scroll through the list to find the topic for which you need help, or type a *keyword*—a word relating to the topic—in the box at the top of the Index; the Index narrows the list to topics that match your keyword.

After using Contents or Index, you can close both simultaneously by clicking on the Hide Help button on the status bar. To close just the Index but leave Contents open, click on the Hide Index button.

FIGURE 3.7.

*Use the Contents and
Index to find and dis-
play help text for any
topic.*

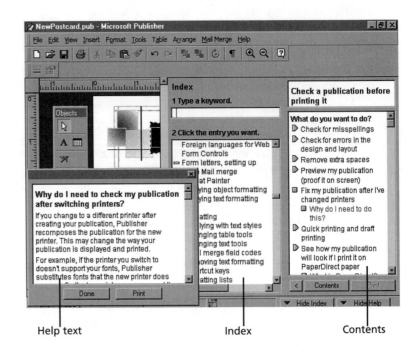

Help text   Index   Contents

What's This? is a very handy, little-used help feature of many Windows programs, Publisher included. While working in any dialog, you can use What's
This? to display a description of any box, button, or other item on the dialog, to learn how to use that item.

To use What's This?, click on the tiny question mark button (?) that appears
in the upper-right corner of nearly all dialogs. (The pointer turns into a
question mark.) Then point to the item you want to know more about, and
click.

To Do: Play a Demo

Publisher's Help system includes a collection of "demos" to help you learn Publisher
(see Figure 3.8). They don't replace this book, but they're kind of fun, and every little bit
helps.

1. Open the Contents by clicking on Show Help on the status bar or choosing Help |
   Contents from the menu bar. The What Do You Want to Do? page of the contents
   appears.

2. From the menu, choose Learn about using Publisher.

▼   3. From the next menu, choose A Publisher demo. A list of demos appears.

4. To start any demo that looks interesting to you, just click on it.

5. Use the arrow buttons in the upper-right corner of the demo to click your way through the demo's pages.

6. Click on the Done button on the demo to close the demo.

Figure 3.8.

From the Help Contents menu, you can navigate to a list of demos, such as this one, that demonstrate basic Publisher activities.

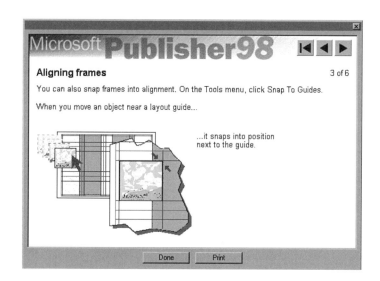

▲

3

Getting Extra Help from the Internet

If you have an Internet account and a Windows Web browser (such as Internet Explorer or Netscape Navigator) set up on your PC, you can get help, tips, updates, and more from Microsoft's Publisher Web site. To reach the site, choose Help | Microsoft Publisher Web Site. Your browser should open automatically and go to the site. If your PC is not configured so that your browser opens automatically, you can reach the Publisher site by pointing your browser to its address:

`www.microsoft.com/publisher`

Customizing Publisher

Right now is a good time to discover that you can customize many aspects of Publisher's behavior to fit the way you work. However, it's not yet a good time to actually customize Publisher.

Publisher comes preconfigured to meet the needs of beginners, so it is best to leave the customization settings alone until you gain enough experience to make smart choices about what to change. As you move through this tutorial, I will return to the Options dialog from time to time, pointing out customization options that affect the task at hand.

That said, you will find Publisher's customization settings on the Options dialog (see Figure 3.9), which appears when you choose Tools I Options.

FIGURE 3.9.

Choose Tools I Options to open Publisher's customization settings.

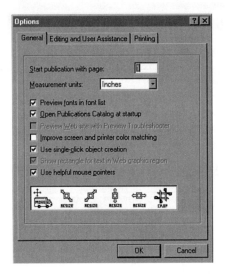

The Options dialog is made up of the following three tabs:

- *General*. Contains options for customizing the general behavior of Publisher.
- *Editing and User Assistance*. Contains options for customizing editing and help features, such as choosing whether TipPages appear.
- *Printing*. Contains options for printing on your local printer (see Hour 8, "Printing Proofs").

To customize, you choose from among settings on the tabs, most often adding or clearing check marks. On the Editing and User Assistance tab, for example, change the number for minutes between reminders to choose the number of minutes AutoSave waits before reminding you to save. To disable AutoSave so that no reminders appear, clear the check box next to Remind to save publication.

Summary

If you have a background with any Windows word processor (especially Word), Publisher probably feels pretty familiar to you. But even if you're new to such programs, you have discovered in this hour how simple—and helpful!—Publisher's interface is. You're ready at last to apply that understanding to starting a pub, as you do in the next hour.

Workshop

The following workshop helps solidify the skills you learned in this lesson.

Q&A

Q In Windows, my taskbar is configured to the auto-hide setting, so that it pops up whenever I move my mouse to the bottom of the screen. So when I go to the bottom of Publisher to click a button on the status bar, the silly Windows taskbar jumps up and gets in my way. How can I fix this?

A You can beat this by moving your mouse carefully. The taskbar doesn't pop up until the pointer reaches the absolute bottom of the screen. But you needn't go that far to click a button on the status bar. When moving to the status bar, just be careful to stay above the very bottom of the screen, and the taskbar won't intrude.

To disable auto-hide, right-click on an empty area of the taskbar, and choose Properties from the pop-up menu. On the Taskbar Properties dialog box that appears, clear the check mark next to Auto Hide. To make the Publisher window sit above the taskbar (so the taskbar is always available), check the Always On Top check box. To enable Publisher to fill your screen entirely (covering the taskbar), clear the Always On Top check box.

Quiz

Take the following quiz to see how much you have learned.

Questions

1. Which of the following lists types of help that Publisher provides?

    a. TipPages, ToolTips, screenblurbs, and the Helper Man

    b. Friendly help, surly help, co-dependent help, unreliable help

    c. Web help, free help, pay-per-use help

    d. TipPages, ScreenTips, Helpful Pointers, and the Assistant

2. When you lower the zoom factor, your pub appears to be

    a. Dimmer

    b. Farther away

    c. Smarter

    d. Closer

3. To put a floating Objects toolbar into the toolbar area with the other toolbars, you do what?

    a. Choose View | Toolbars | Objects | Unfloat.

    b. Float another toolbar.

    c. Click and hold on the Objects toolbar's title bar, drag to the toolbar area, and release.

    d. Trick question! The Objects toolbar always floats.

Answers

1. (d) Some parts of the other choices are correct, but only (d) contains legit Publisher help types.

2. (d) Lowering the zoom, or "zooming out," makes a pub look farther away; raising the zoom, or "zooming in," makes it look closer.

3. (c) To put a floater back in the toolbar area, just drag it and drop it there.

Activities

Don't change anything yet, but explore the customization options on the Options dialog (Tools | Options). Use the What's This? technique you discovered in this hour to learn more about each option. By studying the options now, you will develop an awareness of how the current settings affect your Publisher experience, and you can begin considering how you may want to change the settings later.

Hour 4

Starting a New Publication

By now you may have expected to hear a word or two about layout concepts, something along the lines of "Don't put pictures too close together," or "Stay inside the margins." The reason I haven't mentioned that stuff yet is that, depending on your personal Publisher ambitions, you may not need to know any of it.

Publisher includes a huge collection of pre-fab publications, called *templates*, that you can modify to create a great-looking pub in a heartbeat. If all you do is plug your own text and/or pictures into a template, you needn't know a thing about how to create an attractive layout—Publisher has already taken care of that. (Of course, in the hours following this one, you will learn how to build a beautiful layout from scratch, as well.)

In this hour, you discover the ways Publisher helps you start a pub, including some that give you a big headstart on *finishing* the pub. At the end of the hour, you will be able to answer the following questions:

- What's a wizard, and what can it do for me?
- How can I start a matched set of interrelated pubs?
- Can I just start a blank pub and build its layout from scratch?
- How can I convert other kinds of documents, such as word processing files, into pubs?
- How can I use an old pub to create a new one?

Wizarding Up a Layout—*Fast!*

You've met wizards before—you used one to install Publisher, just as you use a wizard to install most Windows programs. A wizard is just a program that leads you through a series of simple questions to help you do something easily.

In Publisher, wizards help you start new publications based on *templates*.

NEW TERM   A *template* is a publication that's already been completely designed, save for personal touches such as your own words. By using a wizard to build new pubs from templates, you can save most or all of the time required to develop a design from scratch.

Publisher includes dozens of templates you can use through wizards. You can also create your own templates, as you learn near the end of this hour.

The Catalog shows previews of all Publisher's templates, organized into categories to help you locate templates that serve a certain purpose or have a certain style.

You explore the Catalog's categories to locate a preview whose appearance is a close match for the publication you want to create. Then you run the wizard to select from among a range of options for that template such as paper size, colors, or other options. When you finish, you will have what I call a *proto-pub* (see Figure 4.1).

NEW TERM   *Proto-pub*, an unofficial term (I made it up!), is how I describe what you get after running a wizard. A proto-pub has a finished layout, but usually does not contain your own, finished text or custom pictures. The text in a proto-pub is just a placeholder for text you will add later. Sometimes you can actually use the pictures in a proto-pub, but often you will want to replace them with your own pictures, as well.

How Publisher Knows Your Name

When you begin running wizards, you will soon discover that some of the text in your proto-pubs isn't just a placeholder.

A wizard produces a proto-pub, a finished design whose place-holder text (and some-times pictures) must be replaced with your own.

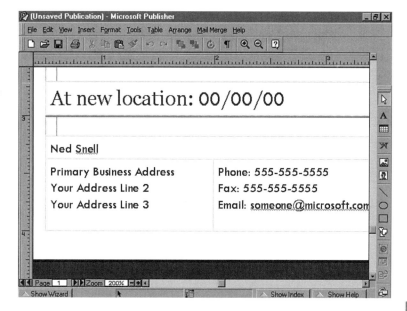

If you run a wizard that creates a business card or resume, for example, you will proba-bly see that your real name, and maybe your company name, appears automatically in the proto-pub. Publisher has filled in this information automatically, from one of your *personal information sets*.

NEW TERM A *personal information set* contains information about you or your company, such as your name, company name, and address. When you insert a personal information set in a pub, the text it contains appears in the pub automatically, saving you the time of typing it.

Publisher maintains four different personal information sets, so you can easily insert dif-ferent information for different kinds of pubs—personal pubs, business pubs, and so on.

Publisher collects your name and company name from dialogs you fill in during installa-tion and setup (see Hour 1, "Setting Up Publisher 98"). But the rest of the information in the personal information sets must be collected later, as you create pubs. In Hour 9, "Getting the Words Into Your Publication," you will learn much more about creating and using personal information sets.

Choosing a Wizard

In the Catalog, the template previews are grouped into two tabs. Each tab shows pretty much the same templates as the other; the difference is the way the templates are grouped on each tab:

- *Publications by Wizard* organizes the templates by type of pub: newsletters, brochures, and so on.
- *Publications by Design* (see Figure 4.2) groups together different types of publications that share a similar appearance, so you can easily choose templates for creating a matched set of related pubs—such as a flyer, banner, and Web site all announcing the same event.

On either tab, you select a category from the left column of the Catalog to display the previews for that category in the right column.

FIGURE 4.2.

The Publications by Design tab groups together different types of pubs with a common style, to help you create a matched set of pubs.

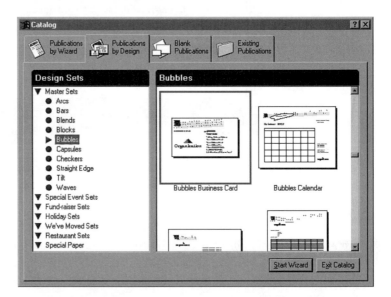

To Do: Check Out the Wizards and Templates

1. Open Publisher and don't close the Catalog. (If you've already closed the Catalog, choose File | New to open it.)

2. Click on the Catalog's Publications by Wizard tab to show the choice of available templates, grouped by type of pub (or more accurately, by the wizard that works on each type of pub).

   In the left Wizards column, the top choice (Newsletters) is selected. On the right, previews of newsletter templates appear.

3. Using the scrollbar on the right side of the Catalog, scroll through the newsletter previews to get a look at the range of newsletter templates available to you.

▼ 4. Point to any preview, and single-click. A gray box appears around the preview, indicating that you have selected it. (When you start a wizard, the wizard always uses the selected template.)

5. In the Wizards column, click on Postcards. The postcard template previews appear, but a list of subcategories also appears under the Postcards category in the Wizards column (see Figure 4.3). You can scroll through all the previews, or click a subcategory to jump directly to the previews for a particular type of postcard.

FIGURE 4.3.

Some categories in the Catalog group their templates into a list of subcategories to make finding a particular group of templates easy.

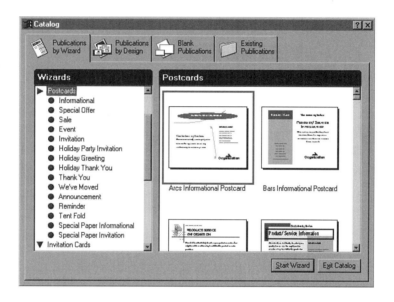

Just for kicks, scroll to the bottom of the Wizards column. There you will see categories for Airplanes and Origami.

If you run the wizard for one of these and print out the proto-pub, you will get a sheet of paper on which dotted lines show where to fold to complete your plane, boat, or parrot.

6. Click on Postcards again. The subcategory list closes.

7. Click on the Catalog's Publications by Design tab. On the tab, note that a list of subcategories already appears under Master Sets in the left column—which is now labeled Design Sets rather than Wizards.
▼

▼   As with the Postcards, you can scroll through all the Master Sets (which are general-purpose sets of matched pub templates), or click on a subcategory to jump straight to a particular set.

8. In the Design Sets column, click on Fund-Raiser Sets. The fund-raiser previews appear, and a list of subcategories appears under Fund-Raiser Sets.

When you explore the Catalog, you will notice plenty of previews whose names include the words *Web Site*. These templates help you start a new Web page rather than a regular pub.

Creating a Web page in Publisher draws on many of the same skills you will learn creating regular pubs—including running a wizard from the Catalog. But Web page publishing is different in many important ways. You will learn all about creating Web pages in Part VI, "Publishing Online."

▲

Running a Wizard

The easiest way to understand a wizard is to run one, so you will dive into a wizard in the next To Do. You will start up a wizard, answer its questions, and crank out a proto-pub that's ready for your final touches.

Before starting, it helps to know what a wizard's three buttons do (see Figure 4.4):

- Click on *Next* to advance from one part, or "page," of the wizard to the next. Note that you do not have to answer all the wizard's questions; you can click on Next on any page to skip a question.

- Click *Back* to move backward to a page you already saw, to change any choices you made there. You can go back and forth among the questions all you want.

- Click *Finish* when the preview appears as you want it to, to create the proto-pub.

Different wizards ask different questions, depending on the kind of pub that they create.

FIGURE 4.4.

Use a wizard's Next and Back buttons to move among the questions, and the Finish button to create the pub.

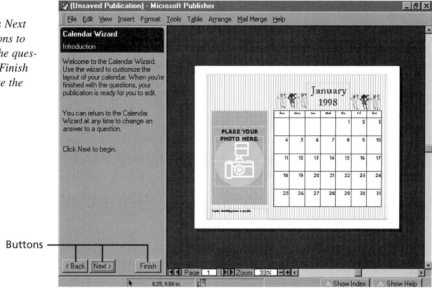

Buttons ──

To Do: Wizard Up a Basic Business Card

Begin at the Catalog's Publications by Wizard tab.

1. In the Wizards column, click on Business Cards.

2. Scroll the previews until you see a preview named Bubbles Business Card. Single-click Bubbles Business Card to select it.

3. Click on the Start Wizard button at the bottom of the Catalog.

   The wizard opens, showing its questions on the left and a larger preview on the right (look back at Figure 4.4). As you respond to each question, the preview changes to show you the results of your choice.

> While a wizard is open, Publisher won't let you do anything else, such as open a menu from the menu bar. You must click Finish to close the wizard before you can move ahead to other activities.

4. Click on Next. A column of *color schemes*—coordinated colors to be used together in a pub—appears. (You will learn more about color schemes in Hour 16, "Controlling Color.")

5. Click any color scheme in the list. The colors in the preview change to show the results. You can now try another scheme, or click on Next to move ahead.

4

▼   6. On the next page, choose an *orientation*: Portrait or Landscape.

Like most business cards, Bubbles begins in landscape orientation. Click on Portrait to see how it will appear if remodeled into portrait orientation. Then click Landscape again to return it to landscape orientation, and click Next to move ahead.

New Term   Because most pubs are printed on rectangular paper, you must choose an *orientation* for the layout—the way the paper is turned when the words are upright.

When the page is taller than it is wide (like Unsaved Publication or the pages of this book), it is in *portrait* orientation. When the page is wider than tall (like a dollar bill), it is in *landscape* orientation. You learn more about orientation in Hour 5, "Fitting Page to Paper."

7. The long, rectangular graphic at the top of the card is a placeholder for a logo, intended to create a spot in the layout that you can easily fill later with your company's real logo. If you choose No on this page, Publisher creates a fun picture in that spot—which includes your company name—to serve as a logo. (Try it!) Click on Next to move ahead.

8. In case you didn't know, business cards are printed as a grid of card images "tiled" across a page. After printing, that sheet is sliced into the separate cards. If you will print your cards yourself, or will send your file to a service bureau for printing, you will want to choose the Several tiled on the page option. Click on Next after making your choice.

9. On the final page, you can insert a personal information set. Because you're just starting out and haven't filled out your sets yet, most of the text inserted—other than your name and company name—will be placeholder text. (You will learn all about personal information sets in Hour 9.)

▲   10. Click Finish.

That's it! Your finished proto-business card appears as the current pub, ready to be edited and enhanced in any way you wish. (Be sure to save it soon, if you want to keep it.)

When you begin selecting templates for your own projects, keep in mind that the template you choose need not be an exact match for the design you intend.

As long as you choose a template that's in the right ballpark, you can use the wizard's options to make the pub a better match. After running the wizard, you can edit the proto-pub any way you want, changing the layout or any other aspect of the pub.

But the more closely the template you choose matches your goal, the less editing you will have to do later. That's why investing a little time carefully choosing the best template *saves* time, in the long run.

Using a Wizard to Edit a Layout

After you complete a wizard, a special version of the wizard remains in the left column (see Figure 4.5). This wizard version—which is available any time you open or edit a pub that was created with a wizard—enables you to change any of the choices you made when running the wizard the first time.

In the top half of the Wizard column, a list appears; each item in the list represents a particular page of the wizard. The bottom half of the column shows the wizard page that's selected in the top half.

FIGURE 4.5.

When you have used a wizard to create a pub, that wizard is available any time you edit that pub. Therefore you can change the pub by changing your answers.

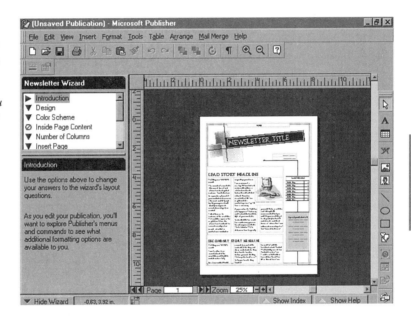

To use the wizard to make changes, click on the name of the page on which the item you want to change is dealt with, and then change your choices. The pub instantly shows the change.

- To hide the wizard while you work on a pub, click on the Hide Wizard button at the left end of the status bar.
- To redisplay the wizard, click on the Show Wizard button at the left end of the status bar.

Starting a Layout Solo

Even when no preview seems like a good match, it is almost always smart to start with a template and wizard. Doing so gives you raw material with which to play around, instead of staring down that most frightening of starting points: a blank, empty page.

Still, I ought to point out that you don't have to go through a wizard. You have a number of options for starting a pub more quickly (and with less help from Publisher), including the following:

- Using a template, but ignoring the wizard. Just start the wizard as always, and then immediately click on its Finish button. A prompt appears, asking whether you want to skip the questions. Click on Yes.

- Choose a layout from the Catalog's Blank Publications tab. The blank publications supply a headstart on layout, but no proto-content. To start a pub, click on the layout you want, and then click on the Create button. A blank pub with the selected layout appears, ready to accept your content.

- Edit Unsaved Publication.

You can also make a new, blank publication (identical to Unsaved Publication) *outside* of Publisher, in Windows.

Right-click in a folder or on the desktop to display a pop-up menu, and choose New | Microsoft Publisher Publication. An icon for the new pub appears; double-click the icon to open Publisher and edit the new pub.

Converting a Different Document into a Pub

If you have documents—files from word processor programs, presentation programs, other DTP programs, and so on—you can *import* them into Publisher, converting them into new pubs with the same content as the original document.

What's Importing?

Publisher comes with a family of *filters*, programs that convert the contents of other file types into Publisher .pub files. That enables you, for example, to transform a word processor file containing your resume into a pub so that you can apply to it all of Publisher's bells and whistles.

Importing a document makes sense only when you want to preserve the general appearance of the original. If all you want to do is copy the text or pictures in the document into a pub with a completely different design, it is smarter to create that design, and then copy the text and pictures from the document into the pub.

You will learn how to do that in Hour 9 (to copy text) and Hour 13, "Getting Graphics" (to copy pictures).

Before importing anything, note that the pub you will get will probably not be identical to the document from which it was created. The pub will likely contain all the text and images from the original, but the document's design elements—layout, fonts, color and such—may or may not be perfectly re-created in the pub.

How closely the pub's design matches the original varies with many factors, including the file type of the document and the complexity of its design. There's no way to predict the level of success—you just have to go ahead and import (which is easy), and see what you get. Usually, Publisher manages a pretty good match.

Importing a Document

To import a document into Publisher, click on the Open button on the Standard toolbar to display the Open Publication dialog (see Figure 4.6). Drop down the Files of Type list at the bottom of the dialog, and select the file type of the document; the box on the dialog now shows all files of that type in the current folder.

4

If the file type of your document does not appear on the Files of Type list, Publisher has no filter installed for that file type, and you can't import the document.

You can download new filters from the Publisher Web site (www.microsoft.com/publisher), however, and install them in Publisher, to expand the range of documents Publisher can import.

Use the Look In list at the top of the dialog to navigate to the folder where the document is stored. When the document's file icon appears in the box, double-click on it.

Publisher takes a few moments converting the document, and then displays it as the current pub. You may then save the pub, and work on it as you would any other.

FIGURE 4.6.

Use the Open Publication dialog to convert another type of file into a Publisher .pub *file.*

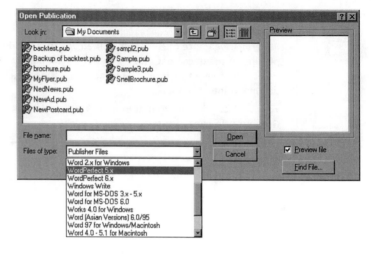

Importing a document makes a pub file that's a copy of the document file— it doesn't actually change or erase the original document file. After importing, you can still use the original document file in its original program.

Using Old Pubs to Make New Ones

After taking the time to create a design that you are proud of, you may want to use it again and again. To do that, you can create a new template based on your own design (or even your own modifications of existing Publisher templates).

To get a feel for creating and using templates, run the following exercises, in which you will create a new template from an existing pub, and then create a new pub based on that template.

To Do: Make a Template

1. Open or create a pub from which you want to make a template. (For practice, use the business card you created in this hour, or any other saved pub.)

2. Choose File | Save As to open the Save As dialog.

3. At the bottom of the dialog, check the check box next to Template, and then click the dialog's Save button. The pub is saved, and a new template—matching the pub—is created.

To Do: Use a Template You Made

1. Make at least one template.

2. Choose File | New to open the Catalog, and choose the Existing Publications tab.

3. On the tab, click on the Templates button. The Open Template dialog opens, showing all the custom templates you have created.

4. Click the name of the template, and then click on Open. A new pub opens, based on the contents and formatting of the template.

When you create a pub from a template, you can edit the pub all you want without affecting the template.

To actually change the template itself so that all further pubs created from it show the changes, create a new pub from the template, make the changes, and then create a new template from the changed pub.

Summary

The simple, sensible starting point for most Publisher projects is choosing a template from the Catalog, and then running a wizard. Doing so gives you a solid head start, often leaving you with only the remaining task of adding your own words (some of which may even be added for you, from a personal information set) or making minor tweaks to the design.

When no regular template/wizard pair meets your needs, however, Publisher provides a variety of other starting points: beginning with a blank publication; importing an existing document; or using your own, homemade templates.

Workshop

The following workshop helps solidify the skills you learned in this lesson.

Q&A

Q **So now I know how to import a document from another program, converting it to a pub file. Can I convert a pub file *into* another file type for use in another program?**

A Sure…. Filters work both ways. To *export* a pub (make a copy of it in a different file format for use by a different program), choose File | Save As, drop down the

Files of Type list on the Save As dialog, choose the file type you want, and then click on the Save button. Note that when you export, only the text winds up in the new doc; the pictures don't export.

As with importing, exporting is rarely perfect. Depending on the file type you export to, the appearance of the copy will vary somewhat from the original.

Quiz

Take the following quiz to see how much you have learned.

Questions

1. Your personal information sets are created
   a. By osmosis
   b. When you type information about yourself into pubs in which a personal information set has been inserted
   c. When you complete the Fill In Personal Information Set dialog
   d. By The Amazing Kreskin

2. After locating in the Catalog a template you want to use, you start its wizard by
   a. Single-clicking the preview to select the template, and then clicking on the Start Wizard button
   b. Dropping down the Select Wizard/Template list, and then clicking on the template's name
   c. Clicking your heels together and repeating "There's no pub like mine... There's no pub like mine..."
   d. All the above

3. After using a wizard to create a pub, you can change that pub in absolutely any way you want to, whether using the wizard or making manual edits to the pub's content and design. (True/False)

Answers

1. (b) As you use a personal information set in pubs and add information to those pubs, the information is automatically incorporated into the set (see Hour 9).

2. (a) Click a preview, click on Start Wizard, and you're on your way.

3. True. A wizard and template only help you get a pub started. You can then change that pub in absolutely any way your little heart desires—a wizard and template place no limits on the flexibility of their results.

Activities

Know your templates! Spend some time exploring the Catalog and discovering the range of templates available. When you come across one you think you may use one day, run its wizard, just to become familiar with the options available for that template. (You can always run a wizard just for practice—you're under no obligation to save the results.)

The better you know the templates, the faster—and smarter—your pub-starting choices will be.

4

PART II
Page Design

Hour

HOUR 5

Fitting Page to Paper

Most print projects evolve from the edges of the paper to the middle. In other words, before one can really begin dealing with the size, shape, and arrangement of the objects in a page, one has to know the size and shape of the paper, and other physical aspects on the pub such as whether the pub folds, and where.

In this hour, you will learn how to map out your pages. At the end of the hour, you will be able to answer the following questions:

- How do I choose the paper size and type for a project?
- How do I define the area of the paper within which my pub will be printed?
- What's "special paper," and how does Publisher help me use it?

As a practical matter, you can ignore everything in this hour if the layout aspects of a template you've selected meet your needs as-is, with no changes to anything other than content (words, mostly).

Still, until you know how to manipulate the layout, you're stuck with whatever a template gives you, regardless of whether it meets your needs. So take an hour to learn your way around the making of a page.

Choosing Basic Layout and Paper

The first choice in creating any pub (other than a Web page) is choosing the size and shape of the paper on which the pub will be printed. After you have made that choice, you need to tell Publisher about it so that Publisher can tailor the pub onscreen to the size, shape, and other aspects of the paper you've selected.

In many ways, this is the most important decision you make when creating a pub because it affects every other choice you will make—the number, size, and shape of the text and graphics elements on the page; the number of pages; and so on.

Setting Up the Page

You choose your paper size and basic layout on the aptly named Page Setup dialog (see Figure 5.1). To open the Page Setup dialog, choose File | Page Setup.

On the dialog, you choose three items that together define the size, shape, and configuration of your page and pub: Publication Layout, size, and orientation. You will learn about each of these over the next few pages.

On the Page Setup dialog box, it is important to work from top to bottom, choosing a Publication Layout before choosing a size or orientation. That's because when you change the Publication Layout, the options in the other two boxes change as well.

Choosing a Publication Layout

The Page Setup dialog offers five different Publication Layouts, each built to fit a particular kind of paper:

- *Normal.* This layout is designed to match the kind of paper in the printer selected for this pub (see Hour 8, "Printing Proofs"), printed flat out on one side. This is the choice to make when you will print your pub on a full sheet of paper, in your own printer, and the pub will not be trimmed, folded, or assembled in its final form.

FIGURE 5.1.

First things first: Set up your page on the Page Setup dialog.

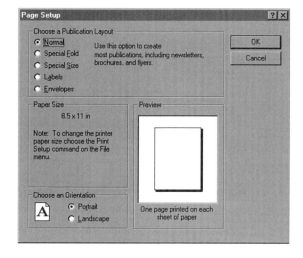

- *Special Fold.* This layout enables you to choose from among a variety of layouts in which the paper will be folded after printing, as with a brochure or greeting card.

- *Special Size.* This layout enables you to choose from among a variety of different publication sizes, from a tiny business card to a 15-foot banner.

Here's a good place to point out that paper size and pub size are not always one and the same.

As you saw in Hour 4, "Starting a New Publicaton," multiple business cards are often printed on one large page, and then cut apart—so the paper size is much larger than the pub size. Other kinds of pubs are printed smaller than the paper size, and after printing the excess paper is trimmed away.

And in some cases, pub size is larger than the paper size. You can use Publisher to print long banners across multiple sheets of paper, for example, that you will tape together after printing.

- *Labels.* This option sets up your pub to match any of the standard sheets of labels (those produced by label makers Avery or Formtec) for printing multiple labels on a sheet.

- *Envelopes.* This option sets up your pub for printing on any of the standard envelope sizes.

5

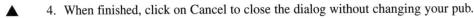

To Do: Explore Layout Options

1. Open or start any pub.

2. Choose File | Page Setup to open the Page Setup dialog.

3. One by one, choose each of the radio buttons in the top of the dialog: Normal, Special Fold, and so on. As you choose each, examine the Preview to see what that type of pub looks like.

4. When finished, click on Cancel to close the dialog without changing your pub.

Choosing Layout Options

After you choose a publication layout, the box beneath Publication Layout (whose name changes, depending on your layout) presents any options for the layout you have selected (covered next).

As you select among the options in the box, watch the Preview to see the shape and size of the pub you're setting up.

> When your pub layout choice is Normal, you get no further options on the Page Setup dialog box (besides orientation, covered next), because the pub size and the paper size are the same.
>
> To change the Normal pub size, you must change the paper size selected for your printer (see Hour 8).

Special Folds

If you have chosen Special Fold as your layout, the box shows a list of options for the configuration of folded pubs (see Figure 5.2).

In all special folds, the paper is printed on only one side. When you fold the paper, however, you not only make the pub smaller than the sheet of paper, but also make two or four printed pages out of one printed side.

Your special fold choices are as follows:

- *Book Fold.* The paper is folded in half, side-to-side, to form two half-sheet printed pages. This choice works well for a simple two-page folder flyer or program.

- *Tent Fold.* The paper is folded in half, top-to-bottom, to form two half-sheet printed pages. This choice works well for a tent card or sign.

- *Side-Fold Card.* The paper is folded twice to form a small booklet in which all four sides—front, back, inside-left, inside-right—are printed. The fold runs along the left side, as in a book. This choice works well for a greeting card or similar small pub that requires print on all sides.

- *Top-Fold Card*. The paper is folded twice to form a small booklet in which all four sides are printed. The fold runs along the top, as in a flip-chart or pad of paper.

By default, all the special fold options assume that they will be printed on a full sheet of the paper currently selected in your printer setup, as described in Hour 8.

You can change the dimensions and shape of a special fold pub by reducing the width and height measurement in the Page Setup dialog. If you do, you will see that Publisher displays in gray the parts of the paper that must be trimmed away after printing.

FIGURE 5.2.

Choose a type of special fold, and the Preview shows how it works.

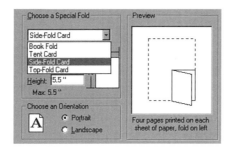

Special Sizes

If you have chosen Special Size as your layout, the box shows a list of sizes you can choose. Whichever size you choose, the pub is still designed to be printed on the paper selected for your printer.

When you choose a pub size that is smaller than the paper, Publisher marks in gray the parts of the paper that will be trimmed away after printing.

If you choose a size that is larger than one sheet of paper, Publisher automatically breaks the pub into pieces to be printed on separate sheets you can paste or tape together after printing.

Labels and Envelopes

For the Labels and Envelopes layouts, the box shows a list of standard label sheets in various sizes, or standard envelope sizes. You can purchase sheets of labels and all standard envelope sizes at any stationery or office supplies store (to print these on your own printer), or you can instruct your printing service which kind of label or envelope to use.

The Labels and Envelopes layouts are great companions to *mail merge*, a Publisher feature that enables you to easily generate address labels, pre-addressed envelopes, and personalized form letters for mass mailings (see Hour 20, "Beyond Publisher: Exploring Other Desktop Publishing Tools").

Choosing Orientation

For the Normal, Special Fold, and Special Size layouts, you can choose the page *orientation*.

I introduced orientation in Hour 4, but just in case you missed it or didn't quite catch on, orientation is the way the paper is turned when the words are upright. When the page is taller than it is wide (see Figure 5.3) it's in *portrait* orientation; when the page is wider than tall, it's in *landscape* orientation.

FIGURE 5.3.

Orientation determines the overall shape of the pub when upright.

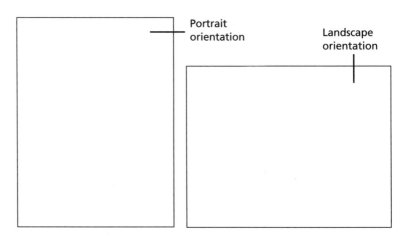

Portrait orientation

Landscape orientation

Which orientation to use for which pub? Well, your decision should be guided first by common practice, and second by personal taste.

Most newsletters are printed in portrait orientation, for example; that's at least in part because it is easiest to handle a multipage pub and turn its pages if it is in portrait orientation.

Books that include mostly text are usually printed portrait, although books containing a lot of artwork or photography—so-called "coffee table books"—are often printed landscape to present the artwork better.

With some kinds of pubs, such as flyers or brochures, choosing orientation isn't so simple. Here are some ideas to feed your choice:

- *What's the content like?* If you will show large amounts of text in columns, portrait is usually preferable because it's easier to read a few long columns than more, shorter ones (which is what you would get in landscape). If many pages are given over to artwork, and that artwork tends to have a landscape orientation, however, you may have more success working it into the layout if the layout is also landscape.

- *What are others doing?* Of course, check out similar pubs by your competitors and/or idols. But don't feel you must match them—if your competitor's brochure is in portrait, maybe yours should be landscape, to stand out.

> When creating a full-page ad for publication in someone else's magazine or other publication, your ad should match the orientation of the pub or pubs in which it will appear.
>
> Most magazines are printed in portrait orientation, for example, so most magazine ads are too—you don't want your reader to have to turn the magazine or twist a neck muscle to read your ad.

Setting the Print Area and Guides

After choosing a layout, options, and orientation on the Page Setup dialog, you may open the Layout Guides dialog (Arrange | Layout Guides; see Figure 5.4) to further define the *print area* for your pub and to begin mapping out the way elements on the page will be arranged.

NEW TERM   The *print area* describes the part of the paper within which your pub will appear. The margins on each side of the paper, therefore, are considered to be outside the print area.

On the dialog, you control the following two kinds of layout guides:

- *Margin Guides*. These lines mark the *margins* of the page, the area around the perimeter in which you don't want anything to print.

- *Grid Guides*. These lines divide your page horizontally and vertically into a grid of two or more parts. The grid organizes your page and helps you line up objects on it neatly.

5

Figure 5.4.

Use the Layout Guides dialog to set up your margins and divide your page with grid guides.

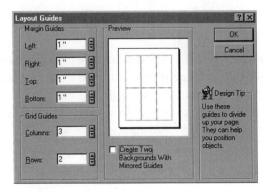

The layout guides appear as blue and pink lines onscreen, but do not show up in print; they're sometimes called *non-printing guides*.

To hide the guides onscreen (to more accurately judge the printed appearance of your pub), choose View | Hide Boundaries and Guides.

> You don't have to change the guides, or really pay any attention to them; as long as you stay within the printable area of the paper, you can position text frames and picture frames anywhere you like, and create your layout that way.
>
> But using the guides helps you neatly align objects on the page, and usually results in a sharper, more professional look. In this hour you will learn how to add and manipulate the guides, and in Hour 6, "Arranging Frames and Columns," you will learn how to use the guides to align objects.

Changing Margin Guides and Grid Guides

On the Layout Guides dialog, the margins are always preconfigured for you, but you can change them. To choose the width of the margins, use the up and down arrows next to each margin measurement to dial the measurement up or down. Each click on the up or down arrow changes the margin width by one-tenth of an inch (0.1 inches).

> Most home and office printing equipment—including all laser and inkjet printers—cannot print all the way to the edge of the paper. Most require that you leave a margin of at least 1/4 inch (sometimes more) on the top, bottom, and each side, which the printer requires for paper handling.

If your pub size and paper sheet size are the same, and you attempt to use margins that are smaller than your printer allows, Publisher displays a warning message. It does permit you to go ahead and use those margins, however, which you may do if you intend to change printers but haven't gotten around to it (see Hour 8).

If your pub size is smaller than the paper, you can set the margins to 0 to print all the way to the end of the print area. When the excess paper is trimmed away after printing, the print area will extend all the way to the edge of the page with no apparent margin.

Printers call a print area that runs to the edge of the paper a *bleed*.

To add grid guides, choose a number of columns (to divide the page vertically) and/or rows (to divide the page horizontally).

When you add grid guides, the page is automatically divided into equal-size sections; however, you can adjust the grid guides to make some sections larger or smaller than others. See the section titled "Fine-Tuning Grid Guides," next.

Fine-Tuning Grid Guides

You can fine-tune your grid guides right on the pub, and immediately see the results. First, however, you must tell Publisher that you want to work with the *background*.

NEW TERM Every page has a *background*, which holds the grid guides that control page layout and also text, pictures, or other objects that appear on every page of the pub. You will learn more about backgrounds in Hour 7, "Planning for Multiple Pages: Headers, Footers, and Backgrounds."

To switch to the background, choose View | Go to Background. (To switch back to the foreground, choose View | Go to Foreground.)

When on the background, to adjust a guide, point to it very carefully so that the very tip of the pointer rests on the grid line (don't click). Then press and hold the Shift key. The pointer changes to the Adjust pointer.

While still holding the Shift key, move your mouse; the grid line moves along. When the line appears where you want it to stay, release the Shift key.

5

In addition to the margin and grid guides—which affect the layout of all pages in a pub—you may optionally apply *ruler guides*.

Unlike grid guides, ruler guides affect only one page at a time. Within the general layout established by your grid guides, you may use the ruler guides to align objects on a page to give that page its own, special style.

You learn how to use ruler guides in Hour 6.

To Do: Set Up Some Grid Guides

1. Start with Unsaved Publication, or create a new, blank pub like it by clicking on the New button on the Standard toolbar.

2. Choose Arrange | Layout Guides to open the Layout Guides dialog box.

3. Under Grid Guides, choose 3 columns, 2 rows, and then click on OK. Guides divide the pub into six equal sections.

4. Choose View | Go to Background to switch to the background.

5. Point carefully to the one horizontal grid guide.

6. Press and hold the Shift key (the pointer changes to the Adjust pointer) and pull your mouse toward you to pull the line down. Pull it down to about 1/3 from the bottom of the page, and then release.

7. Choose View | Go to Foreground to switch to the foreground again.

Using "Special Paper"

For your projects, you can purchase paper that is preprinted with a particular design, pattern, or image. Publisher calls such paper stock "special paper" because you must incorporate into your layout the preprinted design. In effect, your layout must be empty in the spots where the paper's design is meant to show through.

Figure 5.5 shows a pub being designed for special paper. None of the background design you see will actually be printed from the Publisher file; it is preprinted on the paper stock. If you were to print this pub on ordinary white paper, the design would be missing.

Publisher helps you use special paper in two ways:

- Some of Publisher's templates are prebuilt for special paper. All the special paper templates have "special paper" in their name; you can see them all by choosing the Special Paper category on the Catalog's Publications by Design tab.

FIGURE 5.5.

The design you see on this "special paper" business card won't be printed—it's already in the paper. Only the text here prints.

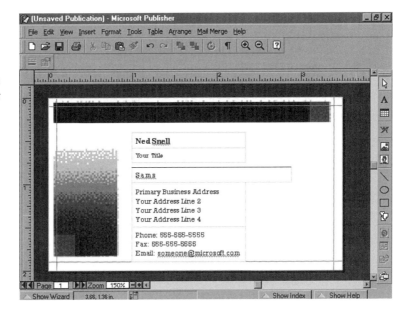

• You can choose to make any pub into a special paper pub by opening or creating the pub, and then choosing View | Special Paper to display the Special Paper dialog box (see Figure 5.6). From the list provided, you can choose from among dozens of special paper designs widely available from office suppliers and service bureaus.

Before basing an important pub on special paper, purchase the paper from your office supply store (to be sure you will have it when you need to print), or check that your service bureau can get the exact paper you have selected.

FIGURE 5.6.

Use the Special Paper dialog box to choose special paper for a pub.

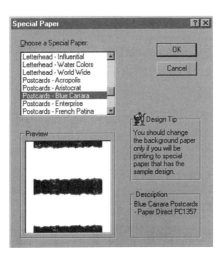

5

Summary

Now you can determine the size and shape of your pub, whether the pub folds (and how), and even the basic organization of elements on that page (although you retain the freedom to arrange items any way you like). You know how to set up a pub, and are ready to move on to choosing the size, shape, and organization of the parts of the page that will contain the text, tables, and pictures—the *frames*.

Workshop

The following workshop helps solidify the skills you learned in this lesson.

Q&A

Q When dealing with a blank sheet on my screen, it's a little hard to envision where to start with choosing grid guides and such. How do I know where to put my guides before I start putting content in the page?

A That's always a little tricky. The most important thing to keep in mind is that layout in Publisher remains flexible all the way through the process.

At any time, even after you have filled pages with content, you can change your paper size, orientation, margins, the works. Changing those things late in the game usually forces you to make a lot of other changes—so it's still smart to try to choose a workable layout early. But you're never stuck with any layout choice.

Choosing the right template is one good way to start a layout off right. When working from scratch, it is often useful to think in thirds, not halves. Designs where the page is split in equal halves or in four parts—vertically or horizontally—tend to look clunky and rigid; a page divided by thirds often looks better.

Try using a grid guide to split a page (vertically or horizontally) in two parts: one large part that takes up about 2/3 of the page, and the other part taking up about 1/3. You will see that basing a page on this "rule of thirds" usually produces a pleasing layout.

Quiz

Take the following quiz to see how much you have learned.

Questions

1. Paper size and publication size must match. (True/False)

2. To define the overall way each page in a pub will be divided up, add

    a. Grid irons

    b. Waffle irons

    c. Tour guides

    d. Grid guides

3. On the Page Setup dialog box, which type of publication layout might you select to create a greeting card with print on all sides?

    a. Normal

    b. Special fold

    c. Hallmark fold

    d. Special sauce

Answers

1. False. You can create publications that are smaller than the paper they're printed on, or larger (to be assembled out of multiple sheets after printing).

2. (d) Grid guides divide your page.

3. (b) Any of the Special fold choices might make a nice card.

Activities

Think about folding. How is a pub created by printing on a sheet one way, and then folding that sheet into its final form? From the Catalog, create a new pub from any of the Brochure templates to see how multiple pages or panels work together on a folded sheet.

5

HOUR 6

Arranging Frames and Columns

Words, pictures, and tables are mere content—grist for the mill. Your pub is formed out of an assortment of boxes, *frames*, that define where and how each object in your page appears.

This hour gives you the rundown on frames, including techniques that you can use without regard to what's *in* the frame, or what will be. At the end of the hour, you will be able to answer the following questions:

- What's a frame, and what does it do?
- How do I add new frames to my pub?
- How do I define my layout by moving, sizing, and shaping the frames in it?
- Can I overlap frames?
- How do I create text columns?
- How can I easily add to my pub prefilled frames from Publisher's Design Gallery?

What's a Frame?

Everything in a pub that will show up in print (or online) is an object, whether it is text, a picture, or a table. And each object in your pub must be contained in its own frame. A frame is just a rectangular box that defines the space within the layout occupied by its object.

While you edit your pub, the frame appears as a pale, gray box around the object (see Figure 6.1), but that box does not print—it is just there to show you where the frame is. (To hide the frame outline so that you can better evaluate your pub's exact printed appearance, choose View | Hide Boundaries and Guides.)

The final appearance of any page in your pub is ultimately determined by the following:

- The number of different frames on the page and their content
- The size, shape, and position of each frame
- The order of frames when they overlap—which frame is on top, which frame is partially covered by another

FIGURE 6.1.

Each of the boxes is a frame, and together they comprise a layout. All that's needed now is the frame contents: words, pictures, and so on.

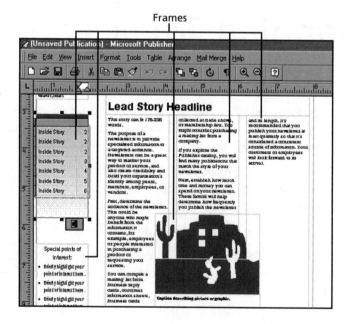

If you want to, you can make the outline of a frame actually print by applying a *border*, as you learn to do in Hour 15, "Snazzing Up Frames with Effects and Fine-Tuning."

There are different types of frames, each containing a different type of object; there are text frames, picture frames, table frames, and so on.

Working with the content of each type of frame is different, but working with the frame's role in the layout—its position, size, and so on—is done the same way regardless of the frame's type or contents.

Adding New Frames

The Objects toolbar contains five buttons that add frames:

 Text Frame Tool

 Table Frame Tool

 WordArt Frame Tool

 Picture Frame Tool

 Clip Art Gallery Tool

To add a frame to the current pub, just click on the button for the type of frame you want to add. Then point to your pub, click and hold the mouse button, and drag the mouse.

As you drag, you "draw" a box in the pub. When the box appears to be the rough size and shape you want, release the button. Note that you need not try to be too perfect about the frame's size and position. You can fine-tune the size and position later.

When you release the mouse button in the final moment of creating a frame, what happens next depends on the type of frame you add. When you add a text or picture frame, you're done as soon as you release the mouse button—the frame appears in your pub, ready for use.

But with other types of frames, when you release the button a dialog appears to help you select or create the table, WordArt, or Clip Gallery object. You will learn how to use these dialogs in the hours that cover these objects.

6

To Do: Add Frames

1. Start with a blank pub (Unsaved Publication is fine).

2. On the Objects toolbar, click on the Text Frame Tool button.

3. Point to a spot near the top-left corner of the page, and click and hold.

▼   4. Drag the mouse diagonally to the center of the page. A box appears, filling roughly the upper-left quadrant of the page.

     5. Release the mouse. You have a frame.

     6. Click on the Text Frame Tool button again, and point to the lower-right corner of the page.

     7. Drag the mouse diagonally to the center of the page. A box appears, filling roughly the lower-right quadrant of the page.

▲   8. Create one more frame to fill the upper-right quad.

> After clicking a frame tool on the Objects toolbar, instead of dragging to draw your frame, you can just point to your pub and single-click.
>
> Doing so creates a new frame of the type you selected, in a standard size. You can then choose the size, shape, and position of the frame (after the fact).

Changing Frames

The beauty of frames is that you can manipulate them—changing their position on the page, their size, their shape, and other aspects—to make them fit perfectly within the layout where you want them. Note that you can change the size, shape, and position of any frame at any point in the evolution of your pub—before you put an object in the frame, after the frame already contains an object, and so on.

Selecting a Frame

Before you can change a frame in any way, you must select it. A frame is selected automatically right after you have created it; you can tell it is selected if it is studded on all sides and at all corners by little black squares, called *handles* (see Figure 6.2).

NEW TERM   *Handles* are the little black squares that appear along the frame outline when the frame is selected. You drag a handle to change the size and/or shape of a frame.

- To select a frame, use the regular mouse pointer (don't click any Objects button first) to point anywhere in the frame, and click.

- To deselect a frame, click on the scratch area (the gray area of the workspace outside the pub), or select any other frame.

FIGURE 6.2.

*When you click on a
frame to select it, the
handles you can use to
manipulate it appear.*

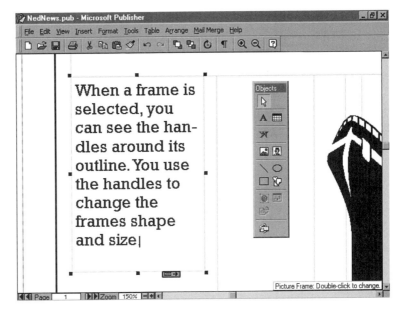

Moving a Frame

To move a frame, select it, and then point to any part of the frame outline other than a handle. (Don't point to a handle; the handles are used for changing the size of the frame.) The pointer changes to the Move pointer.

When you see the Move pointer, click and hold the mouse button, and drag—you will see the frame outline move wherever you drag to. When you have moved the outline to the spot where you want the frame, release the mouse button.

Changing the Size or Shape of a Frame

To change the size or shape of a frame, you select the frame, and then point to one of its handles. When you point to a handle, the Resize pointer appears, to indicate that clicking and dragging the handle changes the size and/or shape of the frame.

Note that you drag different handles for different kinds of changes, as described next.

Changing Height or Width

To change only the height of the frame (without changing the width), point to any handle along the top of the outline (whether in the corners or center), click and hold, and then drag straight downward (to shorten the frame) or upward (to make it taller).

6

To change only the width of the frame (without changing the height), point to any handle on either side of the outline, click and hold, and then drag directly away from the center of the frame (to widen the frame) or toward the center (to narrow it). (See Figure 6.3.)

FIGURE 6.3.

Click on a handle and drag to change the size of a frame.

Changing Height and Width Together

To change the height and width together (changing size, and usually also changing shape), point to any corner handle, and then drag diagonally, adjusting the angle at which you drag to control the shape.

> Sometimes it is important when changing the size of a frame to preserve its *aspect ratio,* the ratio of height to width that determines the shape of the frame. If you stretch a perfect square into a rectangle, you change the aspect ratio, which may dramatically affect the appearance of the frame contents (as you will see in Hour 16, "Controlling Color").
>
> To change the size of a frame while maintaining its aspect ratio, imagine a diagonal line running between the corner you will drag and its opposite corner. Drag along that line, either away from the center (to enlarge the frame) or toward it (to shrink the frame).

To Do: Move and Size Frames

1. Begin with the pub you created in the preceding To Do, with three frames in it.
2. Point to the frame at upper left and click. Its handles appear to show it is selected.
3. Point near the outline of the selected frame (but not to a handle) until the Move pointer appears.
4. Click and hold, and drag the frame to the empty area of the pub.
5. Select another frame.
6. Click and hold on any corner handle and drag inward, toward the center of the frame. The frame shrinks.

Deleting an Object

To delete a frame (including any object in it), select the frame, and then press your
Delete key.

> Text frames that have some text in them delete a little differently:
>
> To delete the text in the frame (but keep the frame), select the frame and
> press Delete.
>
> To delete the frame and its text together, select the frame, and then choose
> Edit | Delete Object.

Adjusting Frame Properties

You will learn more about frame properties as you work through this tutorial. For now
just note that each type of frame has its own "properties" dialog, on which you can
change options to change certain aspects of the frame. Figure 6.4, for example, shows
the properties dialog for a text frame.

On the Text Frame Properties dialog box, you can choose the number of text columns in
the frame (see the section titled "Making Columns," later in this hour) and also control
the frame *margins*, the measurement of the space between the text in the frame and the
top, bottom, and sides of the frame. By increasing or decreasing margins, you increase or
decrease the amount of *whitespace* around the text in the frame.

Whitespace is defined as any area on a page not completely covered by something—text, a picture, or color. Whitespace can appear in a lot of places: around
the page margins; around text as the frame margin; between columns; around pictures;
and even where a line of text stops short, before reaching the right margin.

FIGURE 6.4.

*Use a frame's proper-
ties dialog to choose
from among options
for that type of frame.*

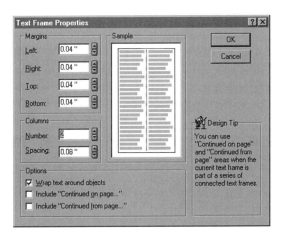

6

To open the properties for any frame, select the frame, and then choose Format to open the Format menu. On that menu, you will see an item for opening the properties dialog for the selected type of frame.

If a picture frame is selected, for example, the item Picture Frame Properties appears on the menu; if you've selected a table, the menu shows an item for Table Frame Properties.

Guiding Page Positioning with Ruler Guides

In Hour 5, "Fitting Page to Paper," you learned to create grid guides to define the overall organization of the pages in your pub. But what if you want to give a particular page its own look, or add guides in one place on one page and in different places on others?

The answer is *ruler guides*—green, wholly optional, non-printing guidelines you can add to a page to help determine its layout. Unlike grid guides, ruler guides affect only one page at a time, and you work with them in the foreground.

You can create vertical ruler guides or horizontal ones, as follows:

- To create a vertical guide, point anywhere on the vertical ruler, press and hold the Shift key, and then move the mouse a tiny nudge to make the Adjust pointer appear. Click and hold, and then drag to the right, straight across your pub to the place where you want the guide to appear.

- To create a horizontal guide, point anywhere on the horizontal ruler, press and hold the Shift key, and then nudge the mouse to make the Adjust pointer appear. Click and hold, and then drag down through your pub to the place where you want the guide.

After adding ruler guides, you can adjust their position at any time. Point to a ruler guide, press and hold Shift to display the Adjust pointer, click and hold, and then drag the guide wherever you want it.

To delete a ruler guide, point to it, press and hold Shift to display the Adjust pointer, click and hold, and then drag it off the pub into the scratch area.

Making Frames "Snap To" Ruler and Grids

You can use the grid guides on the page background or any ruler guides you have added as visual guidelines, by which you will manually line up objects in whatever way suits you. But if you want an easy way to make objects line up perfectly, try the "snap to" options (see Figure 6.5).

When you switch on the snap to options, any frame that gets fairly close to a guide automatically "snaps" right to the line. This saves you from having to delicately position the object to get it on the line—just drag it toward the line, and when it gets close enough, it snaps into place. You can even snap an object into a corner, at the junction of a vertical and horizontal guide.

- To switch on snapping to grid guides, choose Tools | Snap to Guides.
- To switch on snapping to ruler guides, choose Tools | Snap to Ruler Marks.

Note that you can turn on snapping for both together, or for either separately.

FIGURE 6.5.

When the "snap to" options are switched on, you can align frames to guides in a snap.

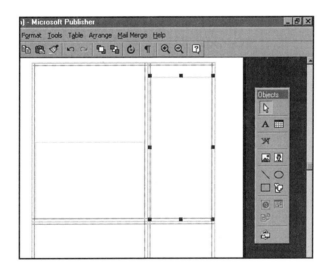

Layering Objects

You can *layer* frames so that they overlap (see Figure 6.6).

Why would you do that? Well, suppose you want to put some text on top of a picture, either as a caption or so that the text looks like part of the picture. Or suppose you want to insert a picture in the middle of some text, and allow the text to "wrap" around the picture. Both these techniques—which you will discover in greater detail later in the tutorial, along with other overlapping tips—require layering.

Just laying one object atop another is no great feat: Just drag one object over another, and you're finished. But often when layering, you find yourself in situations where you need to reshuffle the order of the frames in the stack. You want the object in back (the one that's partially covered) to move to the front so that it is on top now, or vice versa.

FIGURE 6.6.

You can overlap frames and control the order of objects in a stack of overlapped frames.

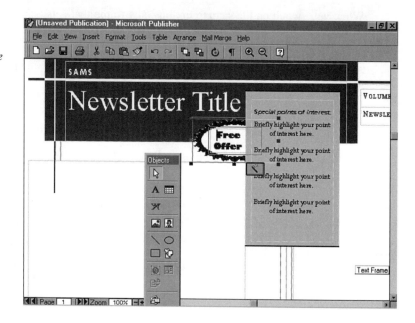

When fiddling with the organization of frames, and especially when layering, it is often useful to move one or more frames off the pub temporarily to get them out of the way. That's what the scratch area is for.

You can drag any frame into the scratch area to get it out of your way. While it is there, you can change its size, shape, or properties; you can drag it back into the pub whenever you want to.

Items on the Arrange menu enable you to change the stack order of layered objects. You begin by choosing the object whose order you want to change, and then you choose an item:

- Arrange | Bring to Front brings the selected object to the top of the stack.
- Arrange | Send to Back sends the selected object to the bottom of the stack.

When there are three or more objects, you have two more options:

- Arrange | Bring Forward brings the object one position closer to the top. If the object was the bottom of three objects, it moves up to the middle position.

- Arrange | Send Backward sends the object one position farther from the top. If the object was the top of three objects, it moves down to the middle position.

To Do: Layer Objects

1. Begin with the pub you have been using in this hour, or any pub with multiple frames in it.

2. Move any frame on top of another (but not completely covering it).

3. Move a third frame on top of the others, again not covering completely.

4. Click on an exposed spot on the bottom frame in the stack, and choose Arrange | Bring to Front. The frame comes to the top of the stack.

Making Columns

You can divide up text on a page into multiple, newspaper-style columns in a couple of ways. The most obvious is to create several text frames on the page, each of which forms a column.

But when text will need to *snake* from one column to one or more adjacent columns, it is often easier to divide a single text frame into multiple columns.

When a single story or article is set in multiple columns, it usually begins in the leftmost column. When the text reaches the bottom of that column, it continues at the top of the next column to the right.

NEW TERM   The curvy path the text follows down and up the columns is snakelike, so the text is said to *snake* through the columns, and the columns are sometimes called snaking columns.

To divide a text frame into columns, create the text frame, and then open its properties dialog (Format | Text Frame Properties). In the dialog's Columns box, change the Number to the number of columns you want.

After you add and format text in the frame (as you learn to do in Hour 8, "Printing Proofs"), you may feel there is not enough whitespace (or too much) between columns. To adjust the whitespace, you can return to the Text Frame Properties dialog and increase or decrease the Spacing, which determines the amount of space between columns.

6

Inserting Design Gallery Objects

Publisher includes a Design Gallery of predesigned objects—mostly the same ones you see in pubs you create with wizards—you can conveniently insert into a pub. When you're not sure where to start, these objects can give you a headstart on dressing up a pub.

To insert a Design Gallery object, begin in the pub in which you want the object to appear, but don't bother creating a frame for it—the Gallery takes care of that.

On the Objects toolbar, click on the Design Gallery Object button. The Gallery opens, as shown in Figure 6.7.

FIGURE 6.7.

Choose fabulous pre-fab objects from the Design Gallery.

Like the Catalog, the Gallery groups objects two ways:

- The Objects by Category tab groups objects by type, to help you find a particular type of object—a calendar, a coupon, and so on.
- The Objects by Design tab groups objects by style to help you use together different objects that share a basic appearance.

To insert an object, choose it from a tab, and then click on the Gallery's Insert button.

Most Design Gallery objects are made up of multiple text and picture objects "grouped" so that they can be moved and sized as if they were a single object, in a single frame. (You will learn how to group objects this way in Hour 15.)

In a way, that is handy. In your pub you can click on a text part of a Design Gallery object to select the text frame so that you can edit that text. You can also remove or reposition some parts of the object, making it your own.

But when moving or sizing the object, you must be careful to point only to frame outlines and handles on the farthest outside edges of the whole grouped object. Otherwise you may accidentally move or size only one part of the object, and scramble its appearance.

Summary

It is like doing a jigsaw puzzle, this layout gig. You make pieces of a particular size and move them around on a page until you get a fit that looks nice. But unlike a jigsaw puzzle, you can choose the size and shape of the pieces, and create new pieces to fill any holes.

Workshop

The following workshop helps solidify the skills you learned in this lesson.

Q&A

Q You brought up "whitespace" in this hour. How do I know how much whitespace in a pub is right?

A The simple answer is this: A page with too little whitespace looks crowded; a page with too much whitespace may look incomplete. Your job is to find what you consider an attractive balance between ink coverage and whitespace. As you move through this tutorial, I will alert you to ways you can increase or decrease whitespace.

The not-so-simple answer is that whitespace is something professional designers fuss over, and finding the right balance is very much a matter of experience, personal taste, and the personality of the pub. A pub intended as serene and simple tends to have more whitespace than one intended to be efficient and energetic. Trends play a part: Every few years, all the designers seem to start using more whitespace; then the pendulum swings back again.

6

For what it's worth, most first-time designers err on the side of too little white-space; they feel their pub will look unfinished unless there's ink on every millimeter of it. So watch out for excess whitespace, but don't be afraid to leave a little either.

Quiz

Take the following quiz to see how much you have learned.

Questions

1. To enlarge a frame without changing its shape,
    a. Drag a corner handle in any direction
    b. Drag a corner handle diagonally away from the opposite corner
    c. Move your eyes closer to or farther from the screen
    d. Zoom in or out
2. To make frames automatically align perfectly to grid guides, choose
    a. Tools | Snap to Ruler Marks
    b. Tools | Automatically Align Perfectly with Grid Guides
    c. Tools | Snap Snap Snap
    d. Tools | Snap to Guides
3. You can put a table in a text frame. (True/False)

Answers

1. (b) Dragging a corner handle diagonally away from the opposite corner enlarges the frame but preserves its shape, or aspect ratio.
2. (d) Easy, no?
3. False. Tables go only in table frames, text goes only in text frames, pictures go only in picture frames, and so forth.

Activities

Starting with a blank pub, create five text frames, and move and size them so that they all fit together on the page. Then change their position around. How many different looks can you achieve with the same five frames? Try two large frames over three smaller ones, or three columns sandwiched between a frame across the top of the page and another across the bottom.

Hour 7

Planning for Multiple Pages: Headers, Footers, and Backgrounds

Everything you explored in the first six hours had to do with one page of a publication. But what about a pub with two pages, or 12, or 400? Well, creating a publication like that isn't much different. Designing a page is designing a page, whether it's one page out of one, or one out of 100. Still, there are just a few techniques and tips you'll need when the page count busts the Big 1. You'll learn them all in the next 60 minutes or so.

At the end of the hour, you'll be able to answer the following questions:

- How do I add new pages to my pubs?
- How do I move from page to page?
- How can I view two facing pages together and fine-tune their appearance?
- How can I add headers, footers, and page numbers?

Making a Multipage Pub

How do you make a one-page pub into a multipage pub? Well, all you really do is add pages—pretty simple, huh? There's a little more to it than that. You'll need to know not only how to add pages, but also how to move among the pages you create, and how to view two facing pages at once to evaluate the look of a *spread*.

 When you open a book or magazine so that you see two pages at once—one on the left, one on the right—you're looking at a *spread*.

Adding Pages

To add one or more new pages to any pub, choose Insert | Page. The Insert Page dialog opens (see Figure 7.1) so you can choose the number of pages to add, plus a few other options about what should appear on the new pages.

FIGURE 7.1.

Choose Insert | Page to add pages.

 For example, among the special fold layouts (see Hour 8, "Printing Proofs"), the book fold layout creates four separate pages on one sheet of paper, separated by folding. Thus the number of pages in a book fold pub must always be a multiple of four: 4 pages, 8 pages, 12 pages, and so on.

If you attempt to add several pages to such a pub that would make the total number of pages a multiple that's not allowed by the layout, Publisher displays a dialog offering alternative numbers of pages that will fit.

On the Insert Page dialog, choose the number of new pages to add, then click a radio button to choose whether the new pages should follow the current page or be inserted before the current page.

In the Options box on the Insert Page dialog, you can choose what to include automatically on the new page. Depending on where you stand in the development of your pub, these options can give you a head start on working with the page's layout.

Remember that any grid guides you've added to your pub to help guide layout (see Hours 5, "Fitting Page to Paper" and 8) will appear automatically on any new pages you add, because grid guides—like anything else in the background—affect all pages in a pub.

In the Options box, choose from the following:

- *Insert Blank Pages*. This option makes the new pages completely blank (except for any grid guides).

- *Create One Text Frame on Each Page*. This option adds one large text frame filling the print area to all new pages, as a head start on getting the text into the page.

- *Duplicate All Objects on Page*. This option automatically copies all objects from the page number you specify onto all added pages to let you carry over a layout or object you like from one page to others. After inserting the pages, you can edit each new page any way you like, individually altering the appearance of each new page while retaining any copied objects you want to keep.

Moving from Page to Page

When your publication has multiple pages, you must know how to move among them. You might be tempted to press your keyboard's Page Down (PgDn) and Page Up (PgUp) keys, as you would in a word processor, but you'll find they don't cut it. Instead, you use the tiny left and right arrows you see in the Page and Zoom tools in the lower-left part of the Publisher window (see Figure 7.2). The tools are

- *First Page*: Jumps from any page to page 1.
- *Previous Page*: Moves backward one page.
- *Next Page*: Moves forward one page.
- *Last Page*: Jumps from any page to the last one in the pub.

FIGURE 7.2.

The Page and Zoom tools are your controls for moving among the pages of a multipage pub.

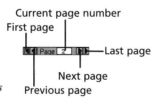

Current page number
First page
Last page
Next page
Previous page

7

When you're already on the very last page of the publication, clicking the Next Page button adds a new last page.

Sometimes a pub has so many pages that it would be tedious to go from, say, page 1 to page 17: You'd have to press the Next Page button over and over. The Go To Page dialog (see Figure 7.3) is the answer.

Choose View | Go to Page to open the dialog, and then type the page number where you want to go and click OK. Note that when a publication has only one page, this option is unavailable—and unnecessary, of course.

FIGURE 7.3.

Use the Go To Page dialog to easily jump directly to any page, by number.

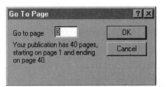

To Do: Add Pages and Move Among Them

1. Start with a blank, one-page pub (Unsaved Publication is fine).
2. Choose Insert | Page to open the Insert Page dialog.
3. In Number of New Pages, type 10 and click OK.
4. In the Page and Zoom tools, click the last page button. You land on page 11.
5. Click the Previous Page button three times. You're at page 8.
6. Click First Page to go to page 1.

7. Click Next page to go to page 2.

Viewing Two Pages at Once

Even when your publication has many pages, most of the time you'll work on one page at a time—if for no other reason than you can see only one page, or part of one page, at the zoom level you usually need to do most work in Publisher. Still, when working on a multipage pub that will be printed on both sides of the paper, you must account for the fact that the finished pub will have spreads—right-hand and left-hand pages that face each other. Because the reader will see both together, you must consider the appearance and composition not simply of each page in the spread, but of the spread itself, which forms a composition of its own. You want the two sides of a spread to harmonize and balance each other, to work together.

To see the spreads in your pub, choose View | Two-Page Spread. Publisher shows two pages at once, side by side (see Figure 7.4). As you page through the pub, you'll see all facing pages as a spread, just as a reader would.

FIGURE 7.4.

You can view a spread to see how pages will look as a reader would see them, side by side.

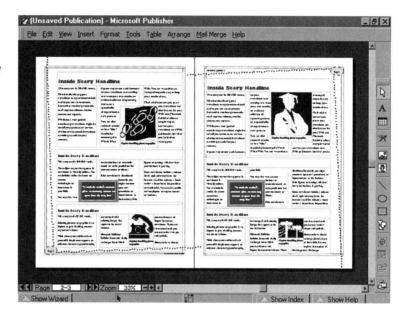

When a page has no other page facing it, Publisher shows just one page. For example, the very first page in a pub has no other page facing it, so you'll see page 1 alone, even in Two-Page Spread view. Click Next Page to move ahead, and you'll see pages 2 and 3 together as a spread.

Creating Mirrored Spreads

The grid guides and margins you set up on the Layout Guides dialog provide the basic layout of your pub and impose the same basic structure on every page. That's a problem with spreads. You see, spreads often look best not when the two pages have identical layouts, but when they have *mirrored* layouts—when the page on the right is a mirror image of the one on the left (see Figure 7.5).

7

FIGURE 7.5.

Use mirrored guides to compose spread layouts in which the facing pages balance and complement one another.

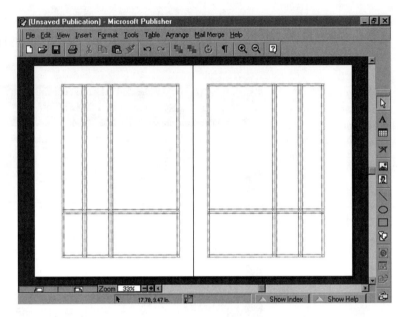

Mirroring not only makes the spread look better and more balanced, but it has practical purposes, too:

- Instead of having just left and right margins applied the same way to every page, mirroring enables you to choose one width to the outside margin of each page, and another for the inside margin, the one between the spread (called the *gutter*). You can make the inside margin extra wide to account for the way pages pinch together in the binding (so that no printed material gets buried there), and you get attractively even, matching whitespace on the outside margins of the spread.

- Page numbers and header and footer text (which you learn to add later in this hour) can appear always at the outside end of the paper (as the page numbers do in this book): on the left side of a left-hand page, and on the right side of a right-hand page.

To create mirrored guides, open the Layout Guides dialog (Arrange | Layout Guides), and check the check box at its bottom, labeled Create Two Backgrounds with Mirrored Guides. After you do:

- The Left and Right margin settings on the dialog are relabeled Inside and Outside. You can adjust the measurements and see the results in the Preview.

- Any grid guides you add divide each page into equal, symmetrical parts, so no mirroring of grid lines is apparent at first because there's no visible difference between a symmetrical layout and its mirror image. However, if you later adjust grid guides on the pub, any change you make to a vertical grid line on one page has the opposite effect on its mirrored page. On the left-hand page, drag a grid line to the left, and you'll see the same line move right on the right-hand page to keep the pages mirrored.

Don't forget that any changes you make to grid lines affect all pages in your pub. You always have the freedom to ignore the grid lines on selected pages to vary the layout (you can use ruler guides to help you do this), but you cannot change the grid page to page.

If you don't intend to apply a consistent layout for most spreads within the pub, then you might not need to bother with mirrored grid guides.

To Do: Mirror Grid Guides

1. Start with a blank, one-page pub with three or more pages (the pub from the previous To Do is fine).

2. Choose View | Two-Page Spread to switch to Two-Page Spread view. (If you don't see a spread, click Next Page or Previous Page to reveal a spread.)

3. Choose Arrange | Layout Guides to open the Layout Guides dialog.

4. Make sure the Number of Columns is 2 or greater.

5. Check the Create Two Backgrounds with Mirrored Guides check box; then click OK.

6. Choose View | Go to Background.

7. Point to a vertical grid guide, press and hold Shift, and then click and hold on the line and drag it right or left. The corresponding vertical grid line on the facing page moves in the opposite direction.

▲

Adding Stuff to the Background

Every pub has a background, whether you use it or not. Anything on that background appears on every page in the pub. For example, suppose you want a particular colored pattern or company logo to appear in the same spot on every page. Put it in the

7

background, and that's taken care of. (You'll practice this in Hour 15, "Snazzing Up Frames with Effects and Fine-Tuning.")

You add objects to the background exactly as you do to the foreground. The only difference is that you must switch first from foreground to background:

- To switch to the background, choose View | Go to Background. You then can add to the background any object you want, or adjust the grid guides there.
- To switch back to the foreground, choose View | Go to Foreground.

Okay, I lied.... The stuff in the background doesn't have to appear on every page. For selected pages, you can hide the background so that nothing on it shows through. This is a handy option, for example, if you want to hide background objects on the first page of a pub but allow them to appear thereafter.

To hide the background, go to the page on which you want to hide it, and choose View | Ignore Background. If you're viewing a single page, you're finished. If you're viewing a spread, a simple dialog appears with check boxes for Left and Right. Check the check box for the page of the spread (or both pages) on which you want to hide the background.

Creating Headers and Footers

NEW TERM   In most multipage pubs, *headers* and *footers* appear. A *header* is material that appears automatically at the very top of every page, and a *footer* is material that appears at the very bottom. Headers and footers are often used to carry the pub title, chapter name, or page numbers on every page to tie the pub together and provide a visual boundary to the top and bottom of the page.

To create headers and footers, all you must do is put the objects—text or pictures—you want at the top or bottom of the background. That material will appear on every page throughout the pub.

You can really dress up headers and footers by mirroring them. To create mirrored headers and footers, change to Two-Page Spread view, then switch to the background. Add objects separately to the right and left page, in mirrored positions. (If you want to, you can use the mirrored grid guides to help you do this.)

> You can use this technique to apply a different header or footer on each side of the spread. Look at the spreads in this book: The Hour number appears on the left, and the Hour title appears on the right. You can achieve these effects just by putting different objects in the left and right side of the background, in Two-Page Spread view.

Adding Page Numbers

You can add page numbers to a multipage pub anywhere you want them. Traditionally, they're put in the header or footer, but you can position them anywhere in the background, in a spot where they won't be covered by anything you'll put in the foreground.

To add page numbers, go to the background and create a text frame where you want the page numbers to appear on every page. Then choose Insert | Page Numbers. A pound sign (#) appears, to indicate that's where page numbers will go.

> To add page numbers to both sides of a spread, change to Two-Page Spread view, switch to the background, and insert page numbers separately in the right and left page—in mirrored positions, if you want.

Using the text-entry techniques you'll pick up in Hour 9, "Getting the Words Into Your Publication," you can add text before or after the pound sign (add "Page" to make "Page #") and apply character formatting to it to control the size and style of the type in which the page number appears (see Hour 10, "Dressing Up Your Words").

Summary

A page is a page is a page, and designing a page is your main job in Publisher. But when you use Insert Page to create a multipage pub, several techniques are available to you— viewing spreads, mirrored guides, and adding objects (including headers, footers, and page numbers) to the background—that give your pub a professional appearance.

7

Workshop

The following workshop helps solidify the skills you learned in this lesson.

Q&A

Q I want to create a book that has multiple chapters. How can I make the header change for each chapter so that I can put the chapter number and title there? And will the page numbers continue all the way through?

A To change the header, footer, or anything else in the background for each chapter, create each chapter as a separate pub—that way, you can use different background objects in each. The chapters can be printed separately, then assembled and bound together. In fact, multichapter pubs are almost always created this way.

That technique does create a problem with page numbers, though, because the page numbers will automatically start at 1 for each chapter, or pub. To make the numbers carry through in order from one pub to the next, you must first finish all the pubs in the book, so that you can see how many pages are in each chapter. For each pub, open the Options dialog (Tools|Options), and on the General tab change the number at the top (next to Start Publication With Page) to the page number at which that chapter begins.

If you want each chapter to begin on a right-hand page (as they do in this book), be sure to make the starting page number the next available odd number. For example, If Chapter 1 ends on page 9 (a right-hand page), make 11 the starting page for Chapter 2 so that Chapter 2 begins on a right-hand page and page 10 is left blank.

Quiz

Take the following quiz to see how much you've learned.

Questions

1. To move forward one page in a multipage pub:

   a. Press the PgDn key.

   b. Choose Flip|One Page.

   c. Scroll right.

   d. Click the Next Page button in the Page and Zoom tools.

2. Objects in the background:

    a. Appear on the first page.

    b. Come out fuzzy, like a watermark.

    c. Stay there until you choose Tools | Background | Reveal Background.

    d. Appear on every page.

3. Spreads look dressier when

    a. The left and right page layouts mirror one another.

    b. Headers and footers put a top and bottom on each page.

    c. Page numbers are mirrored in the header or footer.

    d. All the above.

Answers

1. (d) Use the Page and Zoom tools to get around a multipage pub.

2. (d) Anything in the background shows up everywhere.

3. (d) All three choices make a multipage pub look slick.

Activities

Become spread-savvy. Open a magazine and hold it at arm's length. Try to not focus your eyes so that you see a blurry spread instead of focusing on any object in it. How do the facing pages work together to create a balanced whole?

7

HOUR 8

Printing Proofs

A whole hour about printing? Well, maybe not quite. Maybe you and I can quit early this hour and have snack time. We've earned it.

Even though this will be an easy hour, don't underestimate the importance of understanding printing where Publisher is concerned. The techniques and issues surrounding printing in Publisher are more important, and more complicated, than what you might know from other programs.

At the end of the hour, you'll be able to answer the following questions:

- What's the difference between "local" printing and using a printing service, and why does it matter now?
- How do I configure Publisher to print my pubs on my printer?
- How do I print?
- How do I control printing options, such as those that help me print pubs that are larger or smaller than the paper?
- How do I improve my success when using a color printer?
- How can I obtain quick answers to common printing problems?

Where's the Printer?

There are really just two places you can print your pub:

- On a local printer. By *local*, I mean *your* printer—the one to which your PC is attached, one that probably prints pretty well but might or might not print in color and that probably can't print well enough for a truly professional, magazine-quality appearance.

- At a printing service. By *printing service* I mean any company that will print your publication files for you on better equipment than what you own. That company might be your local copy shop or a big service bureau.

Most folks print draft copies locally while developing a publication, then take their files to a printing service when finished for high-quality, final output. You therefore must deal with two different kinds of "printing": In this hour, you'll learn all about local printing (for draft or final print purposes), and in Part V, "Publishing on Paper," you'll learn all about using a printing service.

Setting Up to Print Locally

To select and configure your local printer, choose File | Print Setup to open the Print Setup dialog (see Figure 8.1).

FIGURE 8.1.

Use the Print Setup dialog to configure options for a printer and publication.

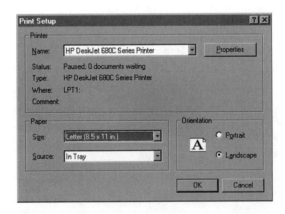

At first, the printer shown in Name is always your default Windows printer, the one configured in Windows 95 to be used whenever you don't specify otherwise. If your PC has access to several different printers (as it might if it's connected to a network), you can select the printer you want to use from the Name list.

If the printer listed in the Name box isn't the printer that's connected to your PC, your problem isn't in Publisher, but in Windows. You must close Publisher, open My Computer, click the Printers icon, and then open the Add Printer icon to install the correct printer driver for your printer.

Often when a particular printer driver is hard to come by, folks make do with a "close match"—for example, they use a driver that's for a different printer by the same manufacturer. With Publisher, however, it's important to use the correct driver for your printer so Publisher can take advantage of everything your printer can do, such as its paper-handling options.

If the correct driver doesn't appear on the list you'll see after opening Add Printer, you must acquire the right driver file. Contact your printer's manufacturer, or visit the manufacturer's Web site, where you can usually download the latest drivers.

The Properties button next to your printer's name on the Print Setup dialog opens a special dialog (or series of dialogs) on which you can select from options that are specific to your make and model of printer. With many printers, you can select from such options as image darkness (intensity) and color saturation.

Even if you don't intend to change anything, you should check out this dialog to learn what features of your printer you can control.

The options under Paper and Orientation in the Print Setup dialog are often selected automatically, based on the pub layout and your particular printer. For example, if the pub is in Labels layout, the Paper Size and Source are set automatically to the size of the label sheet and the paper tray or feed slot (Source) from which your printer model accepts labels. Although these settings are automatic, always check to make sure Publisher's print settings match what you intend.

After setting up the Print Setup dialog for a pub, you don't have to do so again for that pub unless you want to change something. Publisher "remembers" the settings for a pub, and changes you make for one pub don't affect the Print Setup settings for any other pub.

If you change the paper Size on the Print Setup dialog to a size that's different than the size for which your layout was composed (on the Page Setup dialog), Publisher automatically adjusts your pub's layout to fit the new paper.

Even though the adjustment is automatic, you'll probably find that it forces you to go back and do some cleanup work. To avoid this problem, check early in the development of a pub that Paper Size on the Page Setup dialog and Size on the Print Setup dialog match.

Printing Locally

After the Print Setup dialog has been properly configured, you can print at any time by choosing File | Print to open the Print dialog (see Figure 8.2).

FIGURE 8.2.

The Print dialog lets you choose from among a few last-minute options, such as the Number of Copies to print this time.

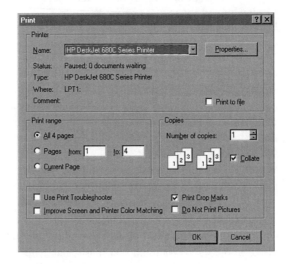

Before printing, make sure the printer is switched on and that it is loaded with paper—of the correct size and in the printer tray or slot specified in Source on the Print Setup dialog.

When you choose File | Print, the Print dialog is preconfigured to print one copy of all pages in your pub—just click OK, and the pub prints. But when you need to, you can choose among various options on the Print dialog, such as

- *Print Range*: To print only a specified range of pages, click the Pages radio button; then enter the first page of the range and the last in the From: and To: boxes. Or click Current Page to print only the page you were viewing before you clicked File | Print.

- *Copies*: Choose the Number of Copies of the pub (or page range) to print.
- *Collate*: Check this check box to collate when you print multiple copies. When you collate, the printer will print one copy of all pages of the pub (or range) in order, then begin the next copy. When you don't collate, the printer prints all copies of the first page, then all copies of the next page, and so on.

8

> On nearly all printers, printing pictures dramatically slows down printing. More important, on color printers, printing color pictures rapidly exhausts the printer's costly supply of color inks or dyes. When you're printing drafts to evaluate overall layout, text, or both, you can shut off picture printing to save time and money by checking the Do Not Print Pictures check box on the Print dialog.

To Do: Set Up and Print

1. Switch on your local printer.
2. Open any pub you want to print. (If you haven't already begun experimenting with your own pubs, quickly crank out any new pub from a wizard, and save time by clicking the wizard's Finish button to skip its questions. Save that pub, and you've got something you can print.)
3. Choose File | Print Setup, and examine the Print Setup dialog to ensure that the printer and options you want are selected.
4. Click OK to close the Print Setup dialog. You will not need to open the dialog again for this pub unless you want to change options.
5. Choose File | Print to open the Print dialog.
6. Under Copies, change the Number of Copies to 3, and make sure the Collate check box is checked.
7. Click OK. Three collated copies print.

What to Do When Paper Size and Pub Size Differ

As you know from Hour 5, "Fitting Page to Paper," you can create pubs that are larger or smaller than the paper on which they'll be printed. Options on the Print dialog can help you control how Publisher handles oversize or undersize pubs. When the pub size and paper size differ, in the lower-left corner of the Print dialog you'll see a large button whose name changes, depending on whether your pub is larger or smaller than the paper:

- If smaller, the button is labeled Page Options, and it opens a dialog on which you can control the way a smaller pub (or multiple instances of the pub, as with labels) is printed.

- If larger, the button is labeled Tile Printing Options, and it opens a dialog (see Figure 8.3) in which you can control the way multiple pages are tiled after printing to create one large pub. For example, the dialog lets you increase or decrease the width of the area in which the sheets will overlap when you tape or paste them together.

FIGURE 8.3.

Click the Tile Printing Options button on the Print dialog to customize the way Publisher prints a pub that's larger than the paper.

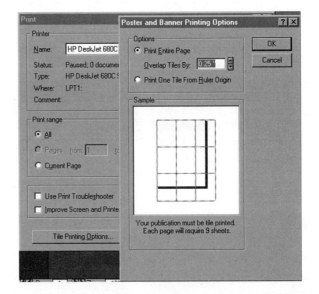

Another helpful option for undersized pubs is the Print Crop Marks check box on the Print dialog. When this option is checked, crop marks are printed at the outside corners of the pub to indicate the part you must trim away (the part that has always been displayed in gray as you've worked with the pub onscreen. After printing, you can just cut the paper along the lines indicated by the crop marks.

Improving the Match Between Screen and Printer

If you will print final output at a printing service, you needn't bother dealing with the match between what you see onscreen and what you can print—you'll deal with that when you deal with your printer, as you learn to do in Part V. However, if you'll print final output on your local printer, Publisher can help you in an important way.

Unless you have a very high-end PC and monitor (like the ones DTP professionals use), your screen cannot accurately display all the colors and shades possible from electronic press equipment. But if you have a typical home or office color printer, your screen might actually be capable of displaying colors that cannot be accurately printed on your printer. You might spend a lot of time perfecting a pub onscreen that will never look good in print because it includes colors your printer can't produce well.

To prevent this, choose Tools I Options to open the Options dialog, and check the Improve Screen and Printer Color Matching check box.

The Improve Screen and Printer Color Matching option doesn't support all printers. If your printer is incompatible, Publisher displays a dialog telling you so when you check the check box.

The Improve Screen and Printer Color Matching option has three important effects:

- When you print, Publisher will attempt to optimize the match between colors you see onscreen and the way those colors look when printed by your printer. The match is never perfect because colors of light (on your screen) and colors of ink are fundamentally different. But the match might be better than it would be without the option enabled.

- A check box for Improve Screen and Color Matching is added to the Print dialog, so you can selectively shut off this feature when you print by clearing the check box.

- A check box is added to the Colors dialog (see Hour 16, "Controlling Color") that enables you to instruct Publisher to strike a big fat X through any color in the dialog (see Figure 8.4) that might not print well on your printer. This doesn't prevent you from using any color—it simply helps you limit your choices to those that will look best on your equipment.

FIGURE 8.4.

When you apply colors, the Mark Colors that Will Not Print Well on My Printer option does what it claims, with big Xs.

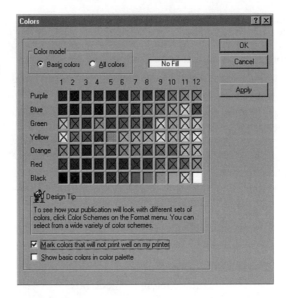

Letting Publisher Help You Solve Printing Problems

Publisher's Help system includes a Print Troubleshooter that can be called into action when printing is *troubling* you (or when you feel like *shooting* your printer). To use the Print Troubleshooter, check the Use Print Troubleshooter check box on the Print dialog. When you print, the Troubleshooter displays a list of common complaints (see Figure 8.5) in the Help Contents box, all related to printing problems.

If you experience any trouble, find the best general match for your printing complaint in the list, and click it. You'll be led through a series of more specific complaints until you arrive at a solution—or explanation—for your problem. The Troubleshooter includes help for most common problems, but you might experience unique printing problems not covered there.

To Do: Shoot Trouble (*Printing* Trouble, That Is...)

1. Switch on your local printer.
2. Open any pub you want to print.
3. Choose File | Print to open the Print dialog.
4. Check the Use Print Troubleshooter check box.

▼ 5. Click OK. The pub prints, and the Troubleshooter opens.

6. Pretend your pub wouldn't print, and click the Troubleshooter question "I cannot print my publication." Two more complaints pop up.

▲ 7. Click Hide Help in the Status bar to close the Troubleshooter.

8

FIGURE 8.5.

The Print Troubleshooter responds to your printing complaints.

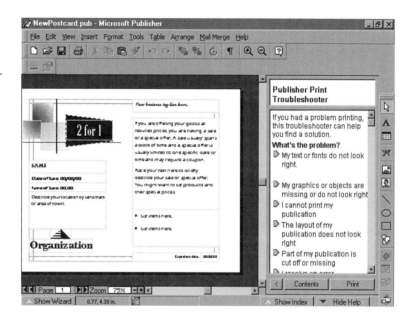

Summary

After you've got all the options set up right, printing a pub locally is pretty easy—choose File | Print, click OK, and you're finished. Most printing problems are caused by not setting up correctly in the first place. A little time spent on the Print Setup dialog can save you a world of trouble later.

Workshop

The following workshop helps solidify the skills you learned in this lesson.

Q&A

Q Hey! I've been looking at that little printer icon in the Standard toolbar for eight hours. And you didn't even mention it!

A Okay, okay… (I guess it really is time for that snack.) The Print button on the Standard toolbar prints your pub without displaying the Print dialog—it just goes ahead and prints, using all the Print dialog options—number of copies, page range and so on—you used the last time you printed.

The Print button is a handy shortcut, sure. But use it only when you're sure you want to use the exact same printing options you used last time. And if you're not sure, then you have to open the Print dialog anyway to find out, in which case there's no point in using the Print button.

So I wasn't really dodging the Print button—I just think it's usually better to choose File | Print, and that method demands just two clicks more than the button method.

Quiz

Take the following quiz to see how much you've learned.

Questions

1. When multiple copies are *collated*, they print
   a. One copy of all pages at a time
   b. All copies of each page at a time
   c. One copy of one page

2. If your printer isn't listed in the Name list on the Print Setup dialog, your best course of action is to
   a. Choose another model from the same manufacturer.
   b. Use a printing service.
   c. Leave Publisher, install the correct printer driver for your printer, and then return to the Print Setup dialog and select your printer from the Name list.
   d. Go buy one of the printers that's already listed in the Name list.

3. True or False: After setting up and printing successfully once, you needn't open the Print Setup dialog for that pub again unless you want to change settings.

Answers

1. (a) Collating assembles each copy of your pub, instead of printing multiple copies of each page you must then assemble yourself.

2. (c) is the best option, although (d) would work!

3. True. Unless you want to change options or fix a problem, you needn't open the Print Setup dialog again if you've previously done so for that pub.

Activities

Using the Catalog, quickly produce some proto-pubs (you can skip all the wizard questions by clicking Finish as soon as the wizard opens), and then print them. How do their text and pictures look when printed on your printer? Is there anything you want to change in the Print or Print Setup dialogs, or in the Properties dialog for your printer, that might improve the results?

8

PART III
Text and Type

Hour

HOUR 9

Getting the Words Into Your Publication

Your publication really includes just two things: style and content. And the plain truth is that you can't think of these as separate. They're interdependent—what you say affects how you say it, and vice-versa.

But as a practical matter, you deal with content and style separately in Publisher. Take your words, or *text*. Getting those words into your publication is one job; choosing the visual style for those words is another. You'll deal with the style of text in Hour 10, "Dressing Up Your Words." In this hour, you'll focus on content—getting the words into your pub where you can shape them.

At the end of the hour, you'll be able to answer the following questions:

- How do I select text so I can work with it?
- In what ways can I put text in my pub?
- How do I edit text in a frame?
- How can I fix any typing or editing mistake with one click?
- How do I make one story flow across multiple frames?

While working with text, don't forget that you can zoom in (see Hour 3, "Tools, Views, Menus, and Measures") when you need to, to make text appear larger. At zoom factors of 100% and lower, only very large text will be easy to read and edit accurately. It's customary to work at very high zoom factors when focusing on text work, temporarily ignoring the overall pub.

After getting the text close to its final appearance, you lower the zoom factor to return to evaluating the role of the text and its frame within the layout.

Selecting Text

NEW TERM Many of the activities in this hour and in Hour 10 require *selecting* text, highlighting one or more characters so that the next action you perform affects the entire group of highlighted characters—the *selection*.

You'll select text to copy it, move it, replace it, and change its appearance. If you have experience editing text in any Windows word processor, you already know how to select. But just in case...

When you've just started your pub from a template, any sample placeholder text in the new pub knows it's there only to be replaced by your words. So you'll find that if you point anywhere in a frame containing placeholder text and click, all the text in the frame is instantly selected, so that anything you type (or copy or import into the frame) replaces it. You'll learn more about replacing selected text later in this hour.

Selecting by Dragging

The simplest and most natural way to select text is to use your mouse. First click once in the text frame to select the frame itself. Point to the very beginning of the block you want to select, and click and hold the left mouse button. Drag the mouse to the right (to select only part of a line) or down (to select multiple lines). As you drag, you highlight all text in the pointer's path (see Figure 9.1).

9

FIGURE 9.1.

Drag across text to select it, so that whatever you do next affects only the highlighted portion.

When you reach the end of the block you want to highlight, release the mouse button. The block remains highlighted, ready to accept whatever action you choose to perform on it.

After you've selected a block, if you decide that you don't want to make any changes to that block, you can *deselect* it (remove the highlight) simply by clicking your mouse button once anywhere on the pub or by pressing any of the arrow keys.

After text is selected, don't press any key or click anything with the mouse except to perform the specific action you want to perform on that text. For example, if you type anything—even a single character—while text is selected, the selected text is instantly deleted and replaced by what you type. That's actually a handy editing feature, as you'll learn later in this hour, but you don't want a careless keystroke to wipe out text you intended to format, not replace.

If you accidentally replace or delete selected text—or do anything else to text that wasn't intended—you can use Undo to fix it, as described later in this hour.

Other Ways to Select

Besides dragging your mouse, you can select text in a variety of other ways, including the following:

- Double-click a word to select the word.
- Choose Edit | Highlight Entire Story to select all the text in the story (including the current frame and any connected frames; see "Connecting Frames So a Story Flows Through the Pub," later in this hour).
- Press and hold the Shift key; then press and hold an arrow key (left, right, up, or down) to highlight a selection that begins at the position of the edit cursor and ends wherever you release the arrow key.

NEW TERM   The *edit cursor* is a bold vertical bar that's a little taller than the letters that surround it and also flashes on and off, so it's easy to see. The edit cursor marks ground zero, the hot spot, the place where anything you do on the keyboard happens within the document.

Adding a Story to a Text Frame

When folks begin working with Publisher, their first projects often involve upgrading an existing document—a resume, a newsletter, an ad—from another program (such as a word processor) to Publisher. So before learning about typing text into frames and editing it there, it makes sense to show you how to save typing by pulling existing text from other programs into text frames, where you can then edit and shape it to your heart's content.

After you learn how to get existing text into a pub, you'll learn how to type new text, and then how to edit and manipulate that text—your *stories*—regardless of where the text came from.

NEW TERM   Publisher describes each discrete chunk of text—a particular article, sidebar, and so on—as a *story*. All the text in a frame is one story, and a single story can continue across multiple frames when those frames are connected (see "What If the Story Doesn't Fit in the Frame?" later in this hour).

Importing Text from Another Document

In Hour 3, you learned that you can take an existing document—usually a word processing file—and convert it to a publication. But when all you want to do is use the text of an existing document—and not its layout—as a story, Publisher's Insert Text File tool is a better option.

In your Publisher pub, click in the text frame where you want the story to appear; then choose Insert | Text File. The Insert Text File dialog opens, as shown in Figure 9.2. Use the dialog to import text as demonstrated in the following To Do.

FIGURE 9.2.

You can import all the text from another document straight into a text frame.

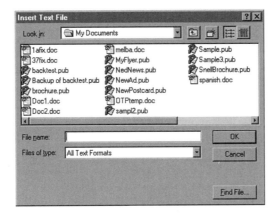

When you add more text to a frame than can fit (as often happens when you import text), Publisher displays only the text that fits and moves the remainder of the story into a netherworld called the *overflow area*.

An *overflow indicator* (A...) appears at the bottom of the frame to indicate that the frame contains more text than it can fit, and a dialog opens automatically to ask whether you want to automatically move the overflow text into another frame.

You have a variety of options for making text fit the frame, as you learn later in this hour. If you see the dialog in the meantime, just click No.

To Do: Import Text into a Frame

1. Start with a new, blank pub. (Unsaved Publication is fine.)

2. Create a large text frame (click the Text Frame Tool on the Objects toolbar; then click, hold, and drag in the pub). Leave it selected.

3. Choose Insert | Text File. The Insert Text File dialog opens.

4. Use the dialog's Look In list to navigate to a folder where you store word processing or text files. The dialog lists all documents in the selected Look In folder from which Publisher is capable of importing text.

5. Select the file from which you want to import text, and then click OK.

> If the document you want to use doesn't show up in the Import Text File dialog even though you know it's in the current folder, that document is stored in a file format from which Publisher cannot import text.
>
> No problem—if the document is from a Windows program, you can still use Copy and Paste to copy its text into your pub, as you learn later in this hour.

Copying Text from Another Document

Another way to pull existing text into a pub is to use Windows Copy and Paste features. Within nearly any Windows program that produces some sort of document—a word processor, spreadsheet, or presentation program, you can select text and copy it to a temporary storage location called the Windows Clipboard. You then open your pub and paste the Clipboard's contents into a text frame.

Note that Windows programs support a variety of different methods for using Copy and Paste, but I'll show you just one method—the one that's most reliable and usually easiest.

Part 1: Copy the Text

You always begin in the document from which you want to copy text—call it the *source* document, displayed within the program used to edit that type of file. Using the same text selection techniques described earlier in this hour, highlight the text you want to copy and then choose Edit | Copy to copy the selection to the clipboard. Switch to Publisher so you can paste the selection into a pub.

> When switching between pubs to perform a copy operation, it doesn't really matter how you do it. You can close the source program and then open Publisher, or you can begin with both programs open and switch between them from the taskbar.
>
> If your PC has 16MB of memory or less, it might behave unreliably if you keep both programs open while copying and pasting. In such cases, it's smarter to open the source program, copy the selection, close the source program, and open Publisher to paste.

Part 2: Paste It in Your Pub

In Publisher, after copying a selection in another program, click in the text frame where you want to paste the selection, and then click the Paste button on the Standard toolbar (or choose Edit | Paste).

> When you use Paste in a move or copy operation, the text is always inserted at the edit cursor position—it doesn't overwrite nearby text, even if you are in Overtype mode. However, if you select text in the frame right before pasting, the text you paste replaces the highlighted text.

Typing New Text

9

To enter text in a pub, click in the frame where you want to add text, and type away. That's it. As you type, the edit cursor moves to the right and jumps down to the beginning of the next line automatically when you reach the end of a line. Keep going. Let the genius fly from your fingertips.

In case you're a little new to Windows text entry, here's a few keyboarding tips:

- To type a blank space, press the spacebar.
- To break a paragraph and start a new one, or to insert a blank line, press Enter.
- To type an *uppercase* (capital) letter (or the upper character that appears on a key that shows two characters) press and hold the Shift key; then press the letter key.
- To fix a mistake, use your arrow keys or pointer to move the edit cursor to the mistake, then press the Backspace key or Delete (Delete) key. Backspace deletes the character to the left of the edit cursor; Delete deletes the character to the right of the edit cursor.

> As you begin to add or edit text, you'll see that some of your words or phrases appear to be underlined by jaggy, red lines. The zigzag underlines don't appear in print—they're just an indication that Publisher's built-in, automatic spell-checker thinks you might have misspelled the underlined word or words.
>
> You'll learn how to fix your spelling—and to get rid of the zigzags—later in this hour.

Undoing Typing and Editing Goofs

When you're working with text in frames, the Undo button is your best friend (see Figure 9.3).

The principle behind the Undo button is simple: When you click Undo, the very last thing you did is undone, as if it had never happened. You'll find Undo (and its partner Redo) on the Standard toolbar.

FIGURE 9.3.

Undo and Redo are your saviors when you type and edit; they are the easiest way to get out of a jam.

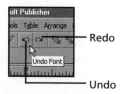

Redo

Undo

Doing Undo

If you click Undo immediately after performing some action to text, the text instantly returns to its exact state before you performed the action. For example, if you select text and then press the Delete key, you delete the text. If you then click Undo, the text is restored and still selected—ready for the correct action.

Redoing (Undo Redux)

In those really confused moments, you might undo something and then decide that you liked it better before you undid it. For those occasions, the Redo button is available, right next to the Undo button.

Predicting what Undo will do is pretty simple when what you're undoing is a deletion (the deletion is restored) or any action to selected text (the text reverts to the way it was before the last action). But Undo is a little trickier when it comes to typing.

When you click Undo after typing something, undo deletes everything you've typed *since the last time you did something besides typing.*

In other words, if you type three paragraphs in a row without stopping to format something or perform some other nontyping activity, clicking Undo deletes all three paragraphs; it undoes the last uninterrupted typing session. If you type three paragraphs, then go back to fix a mistake, *then* type one more sentence, Undo deletes only that last sentence.

Redo reverses the action of Undo—restoring, essentially, the changes that you thought were mistakes when you clicked Undo. Note that Redo does nothing unless you've already used Undo; without an undo, there can't be a redo.

Editing Text

After you have your raw, basic text in place, you will inevitably need to edit it, not only to fix mistakes, but also to adjust it for other reasons, such as making it fit properly in the frame (more about that later).

If you use Microsoft Word, you can edit your Publisher stories from within Word without any importing, exporting, copying, and such. This enables you to take advantage of editing features included in Word but not in Publisher, such as Word's grammar and style checking.

Begin in Publisher, in the text frame containing the story you want to edit. Then choose Edit I Edit Story in Microsoft Word. Word opens, showing the text of the story. If the text you selected was placeholder text from a template, the Word file appears empty—Publisher doesn't count that text as real text. However, you can type the new text into that blank Word page, and it will automatically replace the placeholder text.

Edit or expand the story any way you want, and then close Word (or just close the story). In your pub, the story shows any changes you made to it in Word.

Replacing Text

To replace any text, select that text and then type new text, or paste text you've previously copied to the Clipboard. Whatever you type or paste instantly replaces all the selected text.

Deleting Text

To delete text, select that text and press the Delete or Backspace key on your keyboard.

Inserting Text

Unlike a word processor, Publisher has no Overtype mode. It's always in Insert mode, meaning that any new text you type appears at the edit cursor location and doesn't overtype, or erase, any text in its way.

- To insert one or more characters anywhere in a story, click the desired spot to put the edit cursor there; then type or paste.
- To overtype a character or characters, select the characters you want to overtype; then type their replacement.

Copying or Moving Text Within a Pub

Using Copy and Paste—or its cousin, Cut and Paste—you can copy blocks of text to use the same text in different spots, or you can move text from one spot to another.

Begin by selecting the text you want to copy or move. Then do the following:

- If you intend to copy the selection, click the Copy button on the Standard toolbar (or choose Edit | Copy).

- If you intend to move the selection, click the Cut button on the Standard toolbar (or choose Edit | Cut).

Click in the spot where you want to copy or move the text. Note that this can be anywhere in the pub: in the same frame as the selection, in another frame, in a new frame, or on a frame on another page. To complete the move or copy operation, click the Paste button (or choose Edit | Paste).

When you use Paste in a move or copy operation, the text is always inserted at the edit cursor position—it doesn't overwrite nearby text. However, if you select something immediately before pasting, the text you paste replaces the selection.

Copying or Moving Text Between Pubs

What about copying or moving blocks of text from one Publisher pub to another? Well, you can do that, too. Just open the pub from which you want to copy or move text, click Copy or Cut, then open the pub in which you want the text to go, and paste it.

Finally, you can use drag and drop to move text between pubs—but doing so can get a little tricky, and it isn't any easier than using copy and paste. Because Publisher can have open only one pub at a time, to drag and drop you must open Publisher twice; so you have two Publisher windows open at once, each containing a different document (see Figure 9.4).

Opening multiple Publisher windows for drag and drop takes a lot of memory, especially if the pubs are large. If your PC has less than 16–24MB of memory, you might be better off sticking with regular copy and paste techniques.

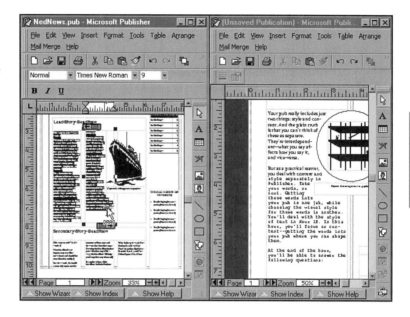

FIGURE 9.4.

To drag and drop between Publisher windows, you must tile them so they share the screen.

Begin by closing all folders and programs (except Windows, of course). Open Publisher and open one of the pubs, as usual. To open the second pub, choose the pub's File icon from a Windows folder or from the Documents menu; the pub will open in a separate Publisher window.

Next, right-click an empty spot on your Windows taskbar to display its pop-up menu, and choose Tile Windows Vertically from the menu. The two Publisher windows will be displayed side-by-side.

- To move text, select it, click and hold on the selection, drag it to a text frame in the other pub, and release.
- To move a whole frame, click it to select it, point to the frame border (so that the Move pointer appears), click and hold, drag to the other pub, and release.
- To maximize either window so it fills the screen again, double-click its title bar.

What If the Story Doesn't Fit in the Frame?

When you created your layout, you built into it frames of a certain size to accommodate your text. Inevitably, of course, the text doesn't perfectly fit inside the frame. You might have too much text for the frame (pushing some into the overflow area) or too little, leaving too much whitespace in the frame. That's when *copyfitting* comes into play.

NEW TERM *Copyfitting* is a publishing term that describes any of the techniques you might apply to make a story fit within its space in the layout. Copyfitting techniques include such obvious actions as shortening or lengthening the story or reworking the layout to make the frame larger or smaller. But there are other, subtler copyfitting techniques, too.

Here's the full run of ways you can copyfit (note that copyfitting often requires applying two or three of these techniques in order to get everything just right):

- Edit the story to make it longer or shorter as necessary.

- Adjust the size or spacing of the characters or lines, as you learn to do in Hour 10.

- Resize the frame (and also rework the layout, if necessary).

- Select the frame and choose Format I Text Frame Properties to open the Text Frame Properties dialog (see Figure 9.5). Decrease the size of the margins to fit more text in the frame, or increase margins to make short text fill out the frame.

- Use Publisher's Copyfit Text feature, or connect frames, as described in the next two sections.

FIGURE 9.5.

You can change the margin measurements in the Text Frame Properties dialog to increase or decrease whitespace around the text in the frame, and to help copyfit.

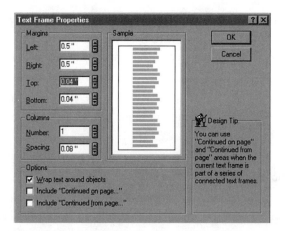

Fitting Copy to a Frame

Publisher includes a feature called *automatic copyfitting* that automatically adjusts the size and spacing of all the text in a frame to make it fit that frame perfectly. If there's overflow, the text is made smaller until it can all fit in the frame. If the text doesn't completely fill the frame, it's expanded until it does.

To use automatic copyfitting, click the frame, then choose Format | Copyfit Text. A sub-menu opens with three choices:

- *None*. This choice applies no automatic copyfitting. You can use it to switch off automatic copyfitting if you've switched it on previously.
- *Best Fit*. This choice automatically adjusts the size of the text to fit the frame. If you later cut some of the text, resize the frame, or change its margins, the text size will be adjusted again so that it's always a perfect fit. If you add text to the frame, however, no adjustments are made, and any text that doesn't fit goes into the overflow area.
- *Shrink Text on Overflow*. This choice does everything the previous choice does. But when you add text to the frame, this option also reduces the size of all the text in the frame to maintain the fit with no overflow.

Automatic copyfitting can be a handy feature, and can save a lot of time when you care more about quickly fitting text than about how that text looks. But I see automatic copyfitting as a tool of last resort. You'll usually get better results by applying the other copyfitting techniques so that the text not only fits the frame, but also looks just the way you want it to.

Connecting Frames So a Story Flows Through the Pub

Publisher calls all the text within a frame a *story*. But in a real pub, a real story often spreads through multiple columns, parts of a page, or pages. To accommodate that, Publisher lets you connect text frames together so that a single story can run through multiple frames.

When you've split a single frame into multiple columns (see Hour 8, "Printing Proofs"), you don't need to connect frames just to make the text flow through the column; it does so automatically.

The great thing about connected frames is that they automatically accommodate any changes to the length of the story. For example, when a story flows through two connected frames, if you add a few lines to the first frame, a few lines at the bottom of that frame jump to the top of the second frame. You can edit and develop your story without having to fiddle all the time with how changes affect each frame.

Connecting While Creating a Layout

You don't have to wait for overflow to connect frames. If you plan in your layout to have a story flow across two or more frames (as you would if a picture frame or table frame interrupts the flow of text, or if the story spreads across pages), you can simply connect those frames from the start.

That way, when you insert, paste, or type a story starting in the first frame, it will automatically flow through all the frames you plan for it to inhabit.

> To be connected to other frames, a frame must have automatic copyfitting switched off (choose Format | Copyfit Text | None).

Begin by creating the frames you will connect to each other. Select the frame where the story will begin; then click Tools | Text Frame Connecting. A floating Connect toolbar appears.

On the toolbar, click the Connect Text Frames button, and then point to the next frame to which the story will flow (the pointer becomes a pouring pail to show that any overflow from the first frame will be poured into the next frame you click). Click, and the frames are connected.

> You can easily add a "Continued on..." message at the bottom of any frame whose story will be continued in another, connected frame. The message automatically shows the correct page number where the reader must turn to find the rest of the story. And at the top of a frame containing a story that began elsewhere, Publisher can display an automatic "Continued from..." message, telling the reader where the story began.
>
> To add these messages, click in the frame and choose Format | Text Frame Properties. In the dialog, check the Continued On Page check box or the Continued From Page check box.

Auto-Connecting on Overflow

Any time you put so much text in an unconnected frame that you go to overflow, the overflow indicator appears and the dialog shown in Figure 9.6 pops up. If you click Yes on the dialog, Publisher leads you through connecting as many frames as are required until all overflow has a place to go.

FIGURE 9.6.

When you go into overflow, Publisher offers you an easy way to connect frames to give the overflow a place to go.

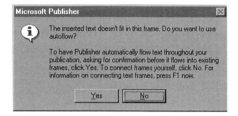

9

After you click Yes, Publisher jumps to the next available frame in the pub and displays a dialog asking whether you want to Autoflow To (connect to) that frame. Click Yes to connect or No to instruct Publisher to move ahead to another frame.

If Publisher runs out of frames before taking care of all the overflow, it asks whether you want to create a new frame. Click Yes, and a new frame is created and automatically connected to the preceding frame.

Disconnecting Frames

Any time you click a connected frame, the Connect toolbar appears. To disconnect that frame from any to which it's connected, click the Connect Text Frame toolbar's Disconnect Text Frames button.

Summary

You know how to get your own words into your pub now, to replace placeholder text or to build a new pub from scratch. Given what you've learned so far, you know now—after just nine hours—how to create a completely finished pub based on a template whose text you've replaced with your own. From here on, you'll be learning how to put your own personal stamp on a pub by controlling every aspect of its appearance.

Workshop

The following workshop helps solidify the skills you learned in this hour.

Q&A

Q **I've noticed that when text is displayed very small (because it's small text or because my zoom factor is low) it looks like a garble of garbage characters, but when I increase the zoom, the text reads fine.** *Que pasa?*

A When the text is so small, or zoom factor so low, that the text cannot be displayed clearly, Publisher *greeks* it.

A trick for improving Publisher's performance, *greeking* means to display nonsense characters in place of real ones when the text is displayed too small to read anyway. When you increase the zoom to a level that makes the text large enough to read, the greeking is replaced by the actual text.

Note that greeking happens only onscreen. When you print, the real text is always printed, no matter how small.

Quiz

Take the following quiz to see how much you've learned.

Questions

1. Which of the following is a way you can get story text into a frame?
    a. Type it there.
    b. In another program, copy text to the Clipboard, and then switch to Publisher and paste it in a text frame.
    c. Choose Insert | Text From File to import all the text in another document or pub file into a text frame.
    d. All the above.

2. The overflow indicator tells you that:
    a. There's more text in the frame than can fit there.
    b. There are too many frames in your pub.
    c. There are too many pubs on your PC.
    d. All the above.

3. To replace placeholder text from a template, click it once to select it and then type or paste its replacement. (True/False)

Answers

1. (d) Choices (a), (b), and (c) are all ways you can get text into a frame.
2. (a) The overflow indicator tells you some of the frame's text is hidden because it can't fit within the space allotted.
3. True. To replace placeholder text, just click and go.

Activities

If you've been using a word processor on your PC, review the documents that are stored on your PC. See any you might want to remake in Publisher, beginning by importing or copying the text from doc to pub.

HOUR 10

Dressing Up Your Words

The printed word is an art form. We sometimes don't look at it that way because we think of words as content and pictures and color as art. But *typography*—the creation and application of different styles of type—is a true art form.

In this hour, you'll deal with typography in your publication, controlling not just the *fonts* (typefaces) you use, but also other aspects of text formatting that affect the text's appearance and its role in the layout. At the end of the hour, you'll be able to answer the following questions:

- How do I choose the font and size of text?
- How can I emphasize text with bold, italic, and other effects?
- How can I change character and line spacing to control text's appearance and the amount of space it occupies?
- How do I type special characters and graphical symbols?
- How do I start a story with a fancy, "big" first letter—a *drop cap*?

> There's one important way to create cool-looking text you won't hear about here: WordArt. That's because WordArt makes text that's really a picture.... Except it's not, it's still text.... Except...
>
> Heck, WordArt makes dressed-up, graphical text, but you'll have to learn more about working with graphics first. Hang on until Hour 14, "Creating WordArt and Drawings," when you'll make words into art.

Fun with Fonts

A *font*, as you probably already know, is a particular typeface, the general style in which your words appear both onscreen and when printed. Every font has a name, such as Arial, Courier, or Bookman (see Figure 10.1).

FIGURE 10.1.

The Formatting toolbar's Font list, from which you examine and select fonts.

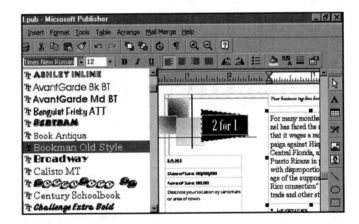

Although the font determines the style of your text, you must also choose a size for the text in that font. The size of text is expressed in *points*.

NEW TERM   A *point* is the unit of measurement for characters in typography. One point equals 1/72 of an inch and describes the height of the capital letters. In 12-point type, a capital I is 1/6 of an inch high.

You can choose the font and size for any text in your document. You can even change fonts in the middle of a frame or paragraph, or even in the middle of a word. Of course, you may choose to use a single font throughout a document, as well. It's your pub.

Professional-looking documents generally use at least two fonts; one for big type (headline, titles, and so on), and one for the general-purpose text, sometimes known as *body text*.

Use fonts creatively but sparingly. A document that incorporates four or five different fonts usually appears sloppy and disorganized. Try choosing two or three fonts that look good together and apply them consistently throughout the document; for example, use font A for all headings, headlines, and other large type, and font B for all body text. Special elements, such as boxes or sidebars, can have their own, unique fonts to set them apart.

Look at the page you're reading now. There's a font for headings (in several sizes), a body text font, and a different, smaller font for text inside boxes like this one. These fonts are applied consistently to the same kinds of text elements throughout the book.

In your font list, you'll see a few extra-fancy fonts whose names appear in ALL CAPITAL LETTERS. Note that these fonts have no lowercase letters—anything set in the font will always appear in all caps.

These fun fonts are really appropriate only for headings and other large, short chunks of text and should be used sparingly.

10

To Do: Check Out Your Font List

To Do

1. Click in any text frame, so that the Formatting toolbar shows tools for text formatting.

2. Drop down the Font list. Each font's name is displayed in the font itself, so you can choose a font by its appearance in the list.

3. Scroll through the list to see which fonts you have.

Stylistically, fonts are divided into two basic groups:

- In a *monospaced* font, such as Courier, every character occupies the exact same amount of space; the letter i is given as much space on the line as m. Monospaced fonts have a typewriterish look to them.

- In a *proportional* font, the space *between* the characters remains consistent, although each character takes up only as much space as it needs—letters i and l get a little space, m and w get a lot.

Proportional fonts are dressier and are used much more often in printed pubs the monospaced fonts. Most of the fonts you probably see on your Font list—including Arial, Bookman, Century Schoolbook, and Times New Roman—are proportional.

Types of Fonts

Most of the fonts you'll see in your font list are *TrueType* fonts (in the list, TrueType fonts have a TT before them). TrueType fonts are specially designed for Windows programs to achieve a very close match between what you see on your screen and what you'll get on paper.

In addition to the TrueType fonts, you might also see a few *printer fonts* (in the Font list, printer fonts have a printer icon next to them). Printer fonts are built into the printer currently selected for the pub.

> Use printer fonts only when the currently selected printer in Publisher is the one on which this pub will be printed in its final form (see Hour 8, "Printing Proofs").

Other than TrueType and printer fonts, there is one more type you might discover in your font list: PostScript fonts. PostScript fonts are fonts that you can print only on a PostScript-compatible printer. Nearly all printing services can print PostScript fonts.

Although your PC probably has a good selection of fonts to get you started, note that you can add fonts any time you want. Windows font files are available in commercial software packages, in shareware, and from professional font houses.

> TrueType, PostScript, and other fonts are widely available for download from the Web. Check out Appendix A, "Internet Resources for Publisher Users," to learn the addresses of Web sites where you can pick up great new fonts for your pubs.
>
> When you get a new font file, you add it to Publisher (and all Windows programs) by opening the Font icon in the Windows Control Panel, choosing File | Install New Font, and then using the dialog that appears to navigate to and select the new font file.

Choosing Fonts and Sizes

To change the font and size of text, first select the text you want to format. Then choose a font from the Font list on the Formatting toolbar, and choose a size from the Size list.

Font and Font Size work completely independently of one another. If you select a chunk of text that contains text in several different fonts and sizes—for example, some text in 12-point Arial and some in 10-point Courier—and then choose Bookman from the font list, all the text in the selection changes to Bookman, but the sizes remain unchanged. You wind up with some 12-point Bookman and some 10-point Bookman.

Conversely, if you highlight a multifont, multisize selection and change only the size, all text in the block changes to the size you selected, but the fonts don't change.

To Do: Apply Fonts and Sizes

1. Open (or quickly create from a template) any pub containing text.
2. Select a whole paragraph.
3. From the Formatting toolbar, drop down the Font list, and choose any font that looks interesting.
4. Drop down the Size list, and choose 14. The paragraph is set in 14-point text, in the font you selected.
5. In the same paragraph, select only one word or sentence.
6. Apply to that selection a different font than the one you chose in step 3.
7. Reselect the whole paragraph, and change the size to 16 points. The whole paragraph changes to 16-point type, but the fonts remain unchanged.

10

Applying Attributes: Bold, Italic, and Underlining

On the Formatting toolbar, to the right of the Font Size button, appears a bank of three buttons. These buttons change the look of text, but don't actually change the font. What they do is change the *attributes*, or style, of selected text. The following buttons are available:

- Bold. Makes text **bold**.
- Italic. Makes text *italic*.
- Underline. <u>Underlines</u> text.

These buttons all work the same, doing their bit to selected text. To apply an attribute to text, select the text, then click the desired button. To remove an attribute, highlight the text, then click the attribute button again.

> You can combine attributes. Highlight a word, click the Bold button, then click the Italic button, and the text becomes ***bold and italic***. **Bold and underlined**, *italic and underlined*, and ***bold, italic, and underlined*** are also possible.
>
> However, combining attributes in this way is generally considered overkill. A little emphasis—a single attribute—goes a long way.

Applying Special Underline Styles and Text Effects

To apply character formatting beyond what the toolbar offers, select the text you want to format and then choose Format | Font to open the Font dialog (see Figure 10.2).

On the Font dialog, the top row of three items—Font, Font Style, and Size—duplicate precisely the font-control activities you have performed with the toolbar. But below the top row you'll find ways to do things you can't do on the toolbar.

> Observe that the bottom of the Font dialog features a preview pane. Immediately after you make any choice in the dialog, the preview pane shows the formatting that will be applied to the selection if you click OK.

For example, the Underline button on the toolbar simply applies a solid, unbroken underline under the selected text (including all words and the spaces between them). By choosing an option from the Underline list (see Figure 10.2), you can achieve a wide variety of underlining effects.

> The Color list (on the Font dialog to the right of the Underline list) controls the color of text. Using color in your documents requires balancing many considerations, such as where and how the document will be published. These issues—including the use of the Color list—are covered in Hour 16, "Controlling Color."

Figure 10.2.

Use the Font dialog to apply text formatting that's not available on the Formatting toolbar.

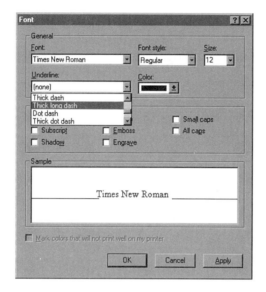

The set of Effects check boxes above the preview pane enables you to apply a wide variety of special text effects, including ^{Superscript}, Subscript, and ALL CAPS.

Many of the effects can be used in combination. But when working with effects, keep in mind that such effects are notorious for looking much worse on paper than they do on your screen. Any time you choose to get fancy with text effects, be sure to evaluate their printed appearance carefully. You might wind up simplifying your text formatting after you see its effect on paper.

Controlling Character Spacing

The Character Spacing dialog (see Figure 10.3) enables you to make minute adjustments to the spacing between characters in each line of selected text. Don't confuse character spacing with *line spacing*—changing the space between lines of text (that's covered next).

The Character Spacing dialog lets you alter three aspects of character spacing: scale, tracking, and kerning.

FIGURE 10.3.

The Character Spacing dialog lets you control how much space characters take up in a given width.

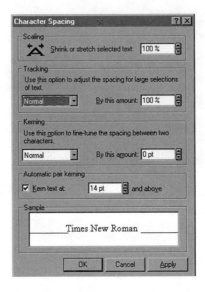

Before fiddling with spacing, keep in mind that font designers set the spacing for a font carefully, to achieve an eye-pleasing effect. Unless you're a type designer yourself, you might diminish the beauty and readability of the text if you alter the character spacing needlessly.

Still, you might choose to change the spacing to achieve a special effect. For example, you might want to

s p r e a d   o u t

some words in a title or heading to give it a unique appearance. Advertisers do that a lot these days with product names and slogans, to catch your eye.

You might also choose to squeeze characters closer together or spread them slightly apart to make the text fit better within a frame.

Scale

Scale has no effect on the amount of space *between* the characters; instead, scale stretches or squeezes the width of the characters themselves.

The default choice, 100%, leaves the characters at their normal width, as set by the font's designer. Percentages greater than 100% make the characters wider, and percentages below 100% narrow the characters. Stretching characters can create interesting, strong headlines.

Tracking

Tracking adjusts the space between the characters. When the default choice, Normal, is in place, the characters are spaced normally, and no entry is necessary in the By This Amount box. Instead of Normal, you can choose from the list:

- One of the two "tight" options (Tight, Very Tight) to squeeze characters closer together

- One of the two "loose" options (Loose, Very Loose) to spread characters farther apart.

After making a choice, you can fine-tune the amount by which the characters are respaced by choosing a percentage in the By This Amount box. Increasing the percentage in the box makes text looser; decreasing the percentage tightens the text.

Automatic Pair Kerning

When font designers design a proportional font, they carefully select the uniform spacing between characters for the best overall effect. However, when text is set at larger sizes, an optical illusion makes some character combinations begin to look like they're too far apart. For example, lowercase f and lowercase i can begin to look too far apart because of the way they're shaped; your eye naturally wants to see the little i tucked under the f's arm, so to speak.

Font designers compensate for this phenomenon with *kerning pairs*. The designer picks out the particular pairs of letters, like f and i, that begin to look oddly spaced at larger point sizes, and builds special spacing for those pairs into the font design.

By checking the check box next to Kern Text At, you instruct Publisher to automatically apply any kerning instructions that are built into the font. From the list to the right of the check box, choose the size at which kerning should start; all text set at that size or larger will be kerned.

The box above Automatic Pair Kerning, Kerning, enables you to manually adjust the kerning for a particular pair. You select the pair before opening the Character Spacing dialog, then use the controls in this box to create a special effect by expanding or condensing the spacing for the pair.

But again, type designers know what they're doing when they build specific kerning instructions into a pair. Your type will generally look best if you trust the designer and leave the Kerning box alone.

Controlling Line Spacing

When absolutely necessary, you can adjust the space between each line in selected text, or the space between paragraphs.

Designers sometimes subtly increase or decrease line spacing to make text fit properly in a frame (although changing the font size or editing the text are usually preferable ways to make text fit). Sometimes designers increase the spacing to make text look less dense and crowded (particularly with small text or wide columns) and to increase whitespace.

To adjust line spacing, select the lines of text for which you want to change the spacing; then choose Format | Line Spacing to open the Line Spacing dialog (see Figure 10.4). Increase the spacing between lines, before paragraphs, or after paragraphs to achieve the effect you want.

FIGURE 10.4.

Use the Line Spacing dialog to control the vertical spacing between lines and paragraphs.

Typing Special Characters (Symbols)

From time to time, you'll need to type characters that appear nowhere on your keyboard, such as the following:

- Characters used in languages other than English, such as the accented letters used in Romance languages
- Mathematical or musical notations
- Greek and Cyrillic characters
- Trademark and copyright symbols
- Fractions

Such characters are known collectively as *symbols*, and although they don't appear on your keys, you can still get them into your pubs. You use the Symbol dialog (Insert | Symbol; see Figure 10.5) to choose and insert symbols, as shown in the following To Do.

FIGURE 10.5.

*If you can't find a
character on your key-
board, get it from the
Symbol dialog.*

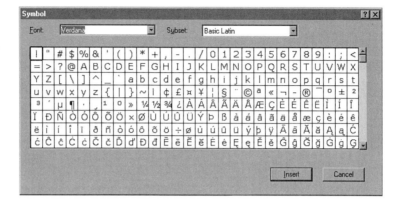

To Do: Insert a Symbol

1. Position the edit cursor at the spot in your text where you want the symbol to appear.

2. Choose Insert | Symbol to open the Symbol dialog.

3. In the Symbol dialog, choose a font from the list. The dialog displays all the available characters for that font, including letters, numbers, punctuation, and any other special characters and symbols. (You can display alternative sets of characters and symbols for some fonts by choosing a different character set from the Subset list.)

4. Click and hold any symbol to enlarge it for a better look.

5. To insert a character, click it, and then click the Insert button.

After choosing a symbol from the Symbol dialog, be very careful to check the symbol if you change fonts later. In such cases, changing the font often changes the symbol, too.

Adding a Big First Letter (or Drop Cap)

In books, magazines, and newsletters, the very first letter of the first word of a chapter or story is often set in a huge, fancy font to kick off the text with style (see Figure 10.6). That big letter is called a *drop cap*, and it's easy to make in Publisher.

FIGURE 10.6.

Drop caps dress up the beginning of a chapter or article.

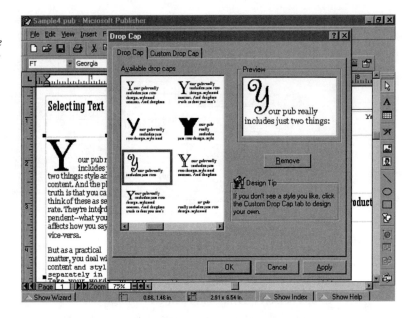

Begin by locating the edit cursor anywhere within the paragraph you want started with the drop cap. (It doesn't matter where in the paragraph you put the cursor; Publisher automatically makes the first letter of that paragraph the drop cap.) Then choose Format | Drop Cap to open the Drop Cap dialog. From the options presented, choose the drop cap you like, and click OK.

To change or remove a drop cap later, click in the paragraph and choose Format | Change Drop Cap. Pick a new drop cap from the list, or click the Remove button to remove the drop cap and restore the regular text formatting.

Summary

Words are art, and by applying the text formatting techniques in this chapter—particularly fonts and text attributes—you both enhance the look of your publication and lend authority and readability to your words.

Workshop

The following workshop helps solidify the skills you learned in this lesson.

Q&A

Q **In my font list, especially near the bottom, I see some fonts that appear to be made up of little pictures and symbols instead of letters and numbers. What are these all about?**

A Dingbat! No, wait…. I'm not making fun of you. Those funky fonts contain *dingbats*—little pictures—instead of the regular letters, numbers, punctuation, and other symbols used by regular fonts. You use dingbats to add graphical touches with the ease of adding text. For example, it's customary in magazines and newsletters to put a dingbat at the very end of a story, to mark it with a flourish.

You can change the size of a dingbat just as you would a character typed in any other font. But knowing which key to press to type a particular dingbat is tricky; that's why it's often easiest to use the Symbols dialog when you want to type a dingbat. Just choose a dingbat font from the dialog's Font list, then choose any little graphic you like.

If you use dingbats, be careful when changing fonts later. If you change the font of a selection that contains a dingbat, you will change the dingbat to a different-looking character than the one you originally selected.

Quiz

Take the following quiz to see how much you've learned.

Questions

1. The height of type is generally measured in _____, 72nds of an inch.

   a. Gallons

   b. Bytes

   c. Eensies

   d. Points

2. Kerning adjusts the space

   a. Between lines of text, to make them more even

   b. Between all characters, to make lines l o n g e r

   c. Between selected pairs of letters, to make them look better together

   d. Between a drop cap and text that follows it

3. To insert a trademark symbol:

    a. Choose Insert | Symbol, then choose the symbol from the dialog.

    b. Choose Insert | Trademark.

    c. Press and hold T, then press and hold M, then get a friend to come to the keyboard and press Ctrl+Alt+PgDn.

    d. Any of the above.

Answers

1. (d) Points measure type height.

2. (c) Kerning cleans up spacing for designated kerning pairs only.

3. (a) You choose trademarks and other symbols from the Symbol dialog.

Activities

Study type. Look at magazines or ads you find appealing. How do they use type? How many fonts appear within a page? How and when do they use effects, such as attributes or special spacing?

Hour 11

Shaping Text in Its Frame

Most of what you discovered in Hour 10, "Dressing Up Your Words," has to do with the style and appearance of text characters, but what about the overall shape and organization of the text within the frame? That's the other half of formatting text—the half you'll discover in this hour.

At the end of the hour, you'll be able to answer the following questions:

- How do I control the way text aligns along the sides of the frame?
- How can I use tabs to control the position of text?
- How can I indent whole paragraphs?
- How can I quickly format great-looking lists?
- How do I create tables?

Selecting Paragraphs

Most formatting techniques in this hour—including alignment, indents, tabs, and list formatting—could be called *paragraph formatting*, because they always affect one or more full paragraphs. You cannot apply paragraph formatting to only part of a paragraph.

When you select text to which you'll apply paragraph formatting, the rules are different than the selecting steps you've used before:

- You need not select the whole paragraph. Just place the edit cursor anywhere within the paragraph, then choose your formatting. The formatting is automatically applied to the entire paragraph, even though you didn't highlight anything.

- To format multiple paragraphs at once, hold down and drag your mouse to highlight anywhere within the first paragraph to anywhere in the last one (see Figure 11.1). All parts of all paragraphs that have any part of them selected will take on the formatting—including unselected portions of the first and last paragraph.

FIGURE 11.1.

Applying paragraph formatting to multiple paragraphs.

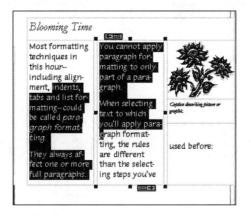

Aligning Paragraphs

NEW TERM *Alignment* describes the way the lines of a paragraph are lined up along the sides of the frame.

On the Formatting toolbar when a text frame is selected, you'll see four alignment buttons, each of which aligns selected paragraphs in a different way. Figure 11.2 shows the different alignments.

- *Align Left*. The lines align evenly on the left side (*flush left*), while the right ends of the lines run unevenly, or *ragged*. In a left-aligned paragraph, the first line is often indented by a tab (see "Working with Tabs," later in this hour), and might not line up exactly with the lines that follow.

NEW TERM On a side of a paragraph where the lines of text align evenly, they are said to be *flush* on that side. Where lines are allowed to end at natural break points between words (creating an uneven pattern), the text is said to be *ragged* on that side. For example, left-aligned text is flush on the left side and ragged on the right.

FIGURE 11.2.

The alignment buttons control the way the lines of a paragraph line up.

- *Center.* Each line of the paragraph is perfectly centered; both sides of the paragraph run ragged. Except for special effects—such as poems or short ad copy—center alignment is rarely used for body text paragraphs; instead, it is used for centered titles, headings, or other text elements less than a full line long.
- *Align Right.* Lines align flush on the right side, and the left side runs ragged. Right alignment fights the reader's eyes—which are trained to always jump back to a consistent left side to start each new line—and is thus used sparingly, for effect.
- *Justify.* The spacing between words in the paragraph is automatically adjusted so that each line spreads completely across the frame. Both left and right sides are flush, and no side is ragged. (If the very last line is shorter than a full line it is aligned left, to avoid spreading it out unnaturally.) Justified alignment can create a dressy look, but with certain fonts and within narrow columns, some lines in justified text can appear unnaturally spaced out or squeezed together.

To Do: Align Paragraphs

1. Locate the edit cursor anywhere within a paragraph.
2. On the formatting toolbar, click Align Right. Observe how the paragraph's appearance changes.
3. Now click Justify. What do you think?

Besides the regular horizontal alignment types you just learned, you can also control how the text in a frame aligns to the top and bottom margins—the *vertical alignment.*

▼

> By default, the text in a frame is top-aligned: It begins at the top and leaves whitespace at the bottom (if it doesn't fill the whole frame). You can also choose the following:
>
> - Format I Align Text Vertically I Center to vertically center all text in the frame so that an equal amount of whitespace appears above and below it.
> - Format I Align Text Vertically I Bottom to drop all text in the frame to the bottom, so that all whitespace appears in the top of the frame.

▲

Working with Tabs

Tabs play many parts in Publisher. They can indent the first line of a paragraph, line up items in a list, or automatically align a column of numbers. Like indenting, tabs can push text away from the margins, but unlike an indent, a tab affects only one line of text. A tab at the beginning of a paragraph indents just the first line, not the entire paragraph.

Every time you press the Tab key while working in your document, you insert a tab character into your text. Like a space or paragraph break, a tab is a nonprinting character. A tab pushes the characters next to it in a particular direction.

> Ordinarily, you don't see the actual tab character in your document; you just see its effect. But sometimes you might want to see exactly where your tabs (and other nonprinting characters) are actually placed in your document.
>
> To display all nonprinting characters in the document, click the Show/Hide Special Characters button on the Standard toolbar.

Setting Left Tab Stops

NEW TERM   A tab character aligns the text it precedes to a preset point, called a *tab stop*. You can set different tab stops for each frame in your pub to customize exactly what the tab characters do there.

Tab stops come in four different types. The most commonly used, a left tab stop, does exactly what you expect from tabs: The tab pushes the text away from the left frame margin, aligning the character following the tab with the tab stop.

In a frame that has no specific tab stops set, Publisher assumes *default tab stops*—all left tab stops—at every half inch from margin to margin. Each time you press Tab, the text to the right of the edit cursor is pushed half an inch to the left. Press Tab three times, and you push the line to the right by 1.5 inches.

To create a left tab stop, click in the frame for which you want to set tab stops. On the horizontal ruler, point to the place where you want a left tab stop, and click. The symbol for a left tab stop appears there (see Figure 11.3). That stop will be visible on the ruler only when that frame is selected.

FIGURE 11.3.

A marker for a left tab stop appears on the ruler.

Using Special Tab Types

Besides left tabs, there are three other types:

- Right tab stop. Pressing Tab when the next tab stop is a right tab pushes the text away from the right margin, aligning with the tab stop the character following the tab.

- Center tab stop. Pressing Tab when the next tab stop is a center tab centers around the tab stop the text following the tab character.

- Decimal tab stop. Pressing Tab when the next tab stop is a decimal tab stop pushes a number following the tab until its decimal point (or its presumed decimal point, if it doesn't contain one) aligns with the tab stop. Decimal tabs are used to align a column of numbers properly.

To create one of these tab stops, click in the frame for which you want to set tab stops, then open the Tabs dialog by choosing Format | Tabs (see Figure 11.4). Then define and set specific tab stops, one by one.

1. In Tab Positions, enter the distance from the left frame margin (regardless of the tab type you're creating); for example, enter 2.5 to create a tab stop 2.5 inches from the left frame margin.

2. In Alignment, choose the type of tab stop.

3. Click the Set button. The position of the new tab appears in the box beneath Tab Positions.

FIGURE 11.4.

Use the Tabs dialog to create right, center, or decimal tab stops.

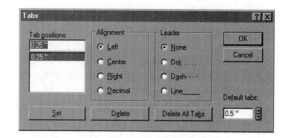

The Tabs dialog lets you optionally select *leader characters*. Leader characters fill any empty space on the line created by the tab with a dotted line, dashed line, or solid line. (The default choice, None, inserts no leader character.)

The most common use of leader characters is to run dotted lines in a table of contents—an effect you can achieve by aligning page numbers to a right tab stop and using a dotted leader character. If you choose to use leader characters on the Tabs dialog, you make the leaders appear in your pub by following each tab character with a single space.

Indenting Paragraphs and Making Lists

Indenting paragraphs and creating lists might seem like two very different jobs, but they're actually interrelated because most lists are indented. Perhaps that's why Publisher groups these activities together on the Indents and Lists dialog (see Figure 11.5), which you open by choosing Format | Indents and Lists.

FIGURE 11.5.

This one dialog takes care of all your indenting and list-making needs.

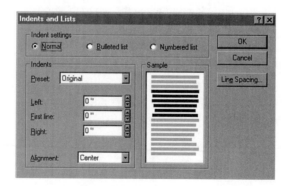

Pushing Paragraphs with Indents

When you *indent* a paragraph, you push it away from the frame margin on one side (see Figure 11.6), making it a little narrower than text in the frame that's not indented.

FIGURE 11.6.

Indents push text in from the frame margin.

Most formatting techniques in this hour—including alignment, indents, tabs and list formatting--could be called *paragraph formatting*, since they always affect one or more full paragraphs. You cannot apply paragraph formatting to only part of a paragraph.

When selecting text to which you'll apply paragraph formatting, the rules are different than the selecting steps you've used before:

Most formatting techniques in this hour—including alignment, indents, tabs and list formatting--could be called *paragraph formatting*, since

Most indents are *left indents*, which push the paragraph in from the left frame margin. Although the left side of the paragraph is pushed in, the right frame margin prevents the right end of the paragraph from moving to compensate; indenting makes the paragraph narrower, and usually longer.

Besides a regular left indent, you can create the following indents:

* First-line indent. Not really an indent, a first-line indent pushes in the left end of the first line but leaves the rest of the paragraph un-indented. The effect is the same as typing a tab at the beginning of a paragraph.

* Hanging indent. A hanging indent—used mainly for lists—pushes the entire paragraph in from the left, except for the top line, which is allowed to "hang" to the left of the rest of the paragraph. Hanging indents enable the bullets or numbers on list items to jut smartly to the left.

* Quotation. The paragraph is indented not only from the left, but also from the right so that it forms a narrow, centered column, customary for paragraph-length quotations.

* Custom. By entering measurements for left or right indenting, you can create a custom indent of any shape you like.

When you use a quotation indent to format a quoted paragraph, you need not surround the quotation with quotation marks. The indent alone serves to indicate that you're quoting.

11

To Do: Indenting Paragraphs

To Do

1. Select one or more paragraphs.
2. Choose Format | Indents and Lists to open the Indents and Lists dialog.
3. Under Indent Settings, choose Normal.
4. Next to Left, use the up arrow to dial up the left indent measurement to 0.5 inch. Observe that the Sample preview pane shows the effect of the left indent you're creating. Observe also that the Preset list has changed automatically to Custom, because you're entering a custom measurement.
5. Click OK. Observe the effects in your pub.
6. Now return to the Indents and Lists dialog, and choose a different option from the Preset list. How does that choice affect the paragraph?

Making Lovely Lists

Lists come in two basic types, distinguished by the way the beginning of each item is marked:

- Bulleted. Each list item is preceded by a graphical character called a *bullet* (you can choose among several different bullets). In a bulleted list, the order of items is not important.
- Numbered. Each list item is preceded by a numeral or letter, and the numerals (or letter position in the alphabet) increase as you move down the list. In a numbered list, the order of items is important, showing an ordered sequence of steps or a ranking.

To make a bulleted list in a snap, type the list items (pressing Enter between each item to make each a new paragraph). Then select all the items and click the Bullets button on the Formatting toolbar.

A list of bullet styles drops down from the button. Click a style you like, and you've got a list.

To Do: Create a List

To Do

1. In a text frame, type your list items, each in its own paragraph (press Enter once between each item). Don't bother trying to create any bullets or numbers; Publisher takes care of that.

▼
2. Select the list items you want to format. (It's sufficient to run a highlight from any-where in the first list item to anywhere in the last; doing so selects all paragraphs that make up the list.)

3. Choose Format | Indents and Lists to open the Indents and Lists dialog.

4. Under Indent Settings, choose Bulleted List or Numbered List.

5. Customize the options shown for the type of list you selected (or leave the defaults in place, which usually work best):

For a bulleted list, you can choose a bullet type, the size of the bullet, and the indent and alignment.

For a numbered list, you can choose among different numbering styles (1 2 3, ABC, and so on), a separator (the character between the number and the list item text), the number at which to begin the list, and the indent and alignment.
▲

Making Tables

Using a table is a great way to format text when short bits of information fall naturally into groups or categories. Publisher includes a built-in table maker that helps you build beautiful tables quickly. Note that here you'll get just the basics of creating tables; in Part IV, "Pictures, Backgrounds, and Color," you'll learn more about dressing up a table.

Creating a new table is almost as easy as creating a text frame: You just draw the table frame, choose a few options, and you're finished, as the following To Do demonstrates.

11

To Do: Draw a New Table

▼ To Do
1. On the Objects toolbar, click the Table Frame tool.

2. In your pub, click and drag to draw a table frame of the rough size and shape you want, in the position you want. (As with any frame, you can adjust a table frame's size and position later.) When you release the mouse button, the Create Table dialog appears (see Figure 11.7).

FIGURE 11.7.

Create a new table by choosing among the many great-looking table formats.

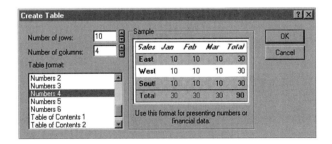

▼

3. On the dialog, specify the number of columns and rows that will make up your table. (Don't forget to include an extra row and column for any row or column headings you plan to use.)

4. Choose a table format from the list. As you choose a table format, the sample shows how that format will appear (but not at your selected number of rows and columns). Try several until you find one you like.

> After creating a table, you can choose a new table format any time by clicking in the table and choosing Table | Table Autoformat.

5. Click OK, and Publisher creates the table. You can now enter information in your table or change its appearance any way you like.

Adding Text to a Table

After you set up your table, point to a cell and click to begin supplying that cell's contents. Note that when you select a cell by clicking it, a thick border appears around it to show that it's selected.

NEW TERM A *cell* is the box in a table formed by the intersection of a row and column.

You can type in a cell to enter text there. If the content you provide requires it, the height of the row automatically increases to accommodate a large amount of text. Format the text in cells exactly as you would format text anywhere else in the document, including applying fonts, font sizes, attributes, and symbols.

You may apply paragraph formatting to text in a cell, but it works a little differently than it does outside a cell. For paragraph formatting purposes, a cell acts like a whole frame. For example, if you position the edit cursor within a paragraph in a cell, then click the Align Center button on the Formatting toolbar, the paragraph is centered within the cell. The other alignment buttons, and the Indents and List dialog, all do their regular thing, too, but relative to the cell, not the table frame.

Moving Among Table Cells

To move to another cell, click in the cell you want to go to, or press Tab to jump from the current cell to the next one to the right.

Cells can hold not only text, but pictures, too. See Hour 13, "Getting Graphics."

Selecting Tables and Cells

By selecting a group of table cells, you can conveniently perform a variety of actions that affect all cells in the selection. The most natural way to select table cells is to click in a cell and drag across other cells until all the cells you want are selected.

You can also select cells by clicking in the cell, row, or column you want to select, then choosing Table | Select. That displays a list from which you can choose Table (to select the whole table), Rows (to select the row in which you clicked), and so on.

After you've selected the cells to work on, you can

- Apply any kind of text formatting to format the text in all selected cells the same way.
- Choose Table | Merge Cells to change two or more cells into one.
- Apply borders or shading to the selected cells. (See Hour 15, "Snazzing Up Frames with Effects and Fine-Tuning.")
- Select a row or column of cells, and choose Table | Delete to remove a portion of the table and all its contents.
- Choose Table | Cell Diagonals to open the Cell Diagonals dialog (see Figure 11.8), in which you can divide cells diagonally so that you can enter content both above and below the divide.

Cells have their own margins, like little text frames. You can adjust the margins of a cell to create more or less whitespace around the text. To change margins, select the cell or cells and choose Format | Table Cell Properties.

11

FIGURE 11.8.

Cell Diagonals lets you divide one cell into two slanty ones.

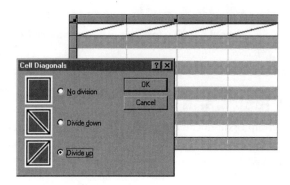

Adjusting Column Width and Row Height

As you develop your table and add its contents, you'll inevitably want to adjust the column widths. The row heights change automatically to accommodate your cell entries, but you might decide to adjust row heights manually, as well.

- To adjust column width, point very carefully to the very top of the vertical grid line until the pointer changes to the Adjust pointer. Click and drag the line left or right.

- To adjust row height, point very carefully to the left end of the horizontal grid line until the pointer changes to the Adjust pointer. Click and drag the line up or down.

Summary

Now that you know how to shape text in your layout by applying paragraph formatting and list formatting (and cramming text into tables), you know pretty much all you need to work with text in Publisher. All that's left are a few handy, optional tools, such as spell-checking, that you can use to make working with words quicker and easier. That's coming in Hour 12, "Text Tools: Spell-Checking, Personal Information Sets, and More."

Workshop

The following workshop will help you solidify the skills you learned in this lesson.

Q&A

Q For body text, how do I choose when to use left alignment and when to justify?

A Are you asking me for a justification for justification? (Just kidding.)

The choice is largely a matter of taste and experience, both of which you gain by paying attention to the alignment applied in pubs you think look good. In layouts with a lot of text (and not enough built-in whitespace), left alignment is often preferred because the nooks and crannies created by the ragged right side create a little natural whitespace.

Look at the pages in this book. Regular body text paragraphs, paragraphs in boxes, the steps in a To Do, and even this Q&A are all left-aligned. Headings and subheadings are also left-aligned, while text in the page headers is centered.

So here columns made narrower by indenting are left-aligned. That makes a pretty good rule of thumb: The narrower the text, the more likely it is to look best when left-aligned—or rather, the more likely it is to look lousy if justified.

Quiz

Take the following quiz to see how much you've learned.

Questions

1. On a side of a paragraph, if the ends of the lines of text align evenly they're _____; if uneven, then they're _____.

    a. cool, yucky

    b. flush, ragged

    c. rigid, free-form

2. When a paragraph is formatted with a hanging indent, the first line

    a. Is indented farther right than the rest of the paragraph.

    b. Is indented the same as the rest of the paragraph.

    c. Is preceded by a drop cap.

    d. Is indented less than the rest of the paragraph, so it hangs back to the left.

3. You can't choose the font and size of text in a table cell. (True/False)

Answers

1. (b) Even alignment is flush, uneven alignment is ragged.

2. (c) In a hanging indent the first line hangs out to the left, as on a list item.

3. False. You can format table text any way you want.

Activities

Take any publication you've been working on, and change the alignment of all the body text. How does that change affect the overall look of the pub? Would you want to keep that alignment? Does it look good some places, but not others? If so, undo the change everywhere but the places it looks good. Now what do you think?

HOUR 12

Text Tools: Spell-Checking, Personal Information Sets, and More

You might be using Publisher for stuff that doesn't have all that much text to it: a one-page ad, business cards, simple flyers, and so on. When the text is short and simple, you might not need any of the tools in this hour. The more words you use, the easier it is to miss a mistake and the more drudge work you must do to type and edit it. The tools you discover in this hour not only help you conveniently find and fix goofs but also help you enter and edit text more quickly and accurately.

At the end of the hour, you'll be able to answer the following questions:

- In what ways does Publisher help me find and fix spelling mistakes?
- How can I change all instances of one word or phrase into another, without doing a lot of hunting and typing?
- How do I control the way hyphens are automatically used to break words at the end of a line?
- How can I save time by making Publisher type text I use often, such as my name or today's date?

Fixing Text as You Go

Sure, you can always finish your text and then run Publisher's spell checker to clean it up, as you learn to do next. You might not need to, though. Publisher helps you clean up your words as you create them, through two facilities: an as-you-go spell checker and AutoCorrect.

What to Do About Those Zigzag Red Lines

Those jagged red lines beneath words you type are indicators that Publisher's spell checker doesn't recognize the word. The word might just be a name or other word that doesn't happen to be in Publisher's dictionary, in which case you can ignore the line. Unless the word marked by the jagged underline is a name, there's a good chance it's spelled wrong.

If you edit the word to fix its spelling, the underlining goes away. If you're uncertain of the correct spelling, Publisher can help you.

> The jagged red underlines appear only onscreen, never in print, so you can ignore them when they mark a name or other word you know you've spelled correctly.
>
> If you're confident in your spelling and don't want the jagged lines disrupting the onscreen appearance of your pub, you can hide the lines by choosing Tools | Spelling | Hide Spelling Errors.

To fix the spelling of the underlined word, point to the word and right-click.

At the top of the pop-up menu that appears (see Figure 12.1), Publisher lists any correctly spelled words it thinks might be the word you really want. (If Publisher can't come up with a guess, it displays No Suggestions at the top of the menu.)

FIGURE 12.1.

Right-click a word with a jagged underline to see Publisher's suggestions for the correct spelling of that word.

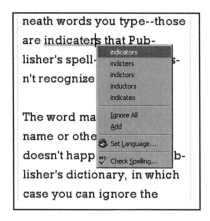

- If one of the words at the top of the pop-up menu is the word you intended (but misspelled), click it. That word instantly replaces the one that was underlined, and the underline disappears.

- Alternatively, you can choose Check Spelling from the pop-up menu to start the spell checker (described later in this hour). From the spell checker, you can perform more powerful spell-checking operations; for example, you can not only fix the word in question but also automatically fix that same error anywhere else it appears.

To Do: Try to Spell as You Go

1. In a text frame, type the word compooter, followed by one space. (Publisher does not flag misspelled words until you type a space or punctuation symbol to indicate that the word is finished.) A red zigzag line appears beneath it.

2. Right-click the word. At the top of the pop-up menu that appears, a list of alternatives appears, including computer, composer, and compote.

3. Click composer. The menu closes, compooter has been replaced by composer, and the zigzag line is gone.

How Publisher *AutoCorrects* You

Publisher's AutoCorrect facility makes a variety of useful fixes for you as you go along. It doesn't ask your permission; it just does its thing. Try typing a sentence without capitalizing the first letter of the first word, and you'll see AutoCorrect make that cap for you.

12

▼ To Do

▲

The changes AutoCorrect makes fall into three general groups:

- *Advanced typography*: Dressy looking pubs use characters that don't appear on your keyboard. For example, an *em dash* (the long, solid dash) doesn't appear on your keyboard. Any time you type two regular dashes together (- -), AutoCorrect changes them to an em dash. Other typography changes include

    Smart Quotes: Plain straight quote marks ("") are automatically replaced with typographically fancier ones, called *smart quotes*, in which the right and left mark mirror one another ("").

    Symbols: Trademark and copyright symbols are created automatically from their typed equivalents; type (tm), and AutoCorrect swaps it for a real trademark, ™.

- *Common capitalization errors*: AutoCorrect can automatically fix your text when you forget to capitalize a sentence or a day of the week and when you type two initial capital letters at the beginning of a word (LIke THis).

- *Common spelling errors*: AutoCorrect keeps a list of common mispellings and punctuation errors and applies corrections automatically. Type youve and it automatically becomes you've.

Customizing AutoCorrect

AutoCorrect is automatic, but you're still in control. Using the AutoCorrect dialog (see Figure 12.2), you can switch on or off any of AutoCorrect's instructions to enable or disable anything it does. To open the dialog, choose Tools | AutoCorrect.

> When you change settings on the AutoCorrect dialog, AutoCorrect begins applying those changes to whatever you type from then on. However, it does not go back and undo anything it did before you changed the dialog.
>
> For example, if you switch off smart quotes, any quotes you type from then on will not be changed to smart quotes. However, quotes you typed *before* switching off smart quotes will remain smart quotes, unless you go back and replace them manually.

On the AutoCorrect dialog, use the check boxes at the top of the AutoCorrect tab to enable or disable correcting of capitalization errors, and use the check boxes on the AutoFormat As You Type tab to enable or disable smart quotes and dashes.

FIGURE 12.2.

Change the AutoCorrect dialog to control which mistakes Publisher fixes automatically.

On the AutoCorrect dialog, use the Replace With list at the bottom of the AutoCorrect tab to control automatic spelling fixes:

- To disable all fixes, remove the check mark next to Replace Text As You Type.

- To add a new entry (to fix a typing mistake you tend to make often), type the mistake in the Replace box, type its correction in the With box, and then click Add.

- To remove an entry (so that AutoCorrect stops making that correction), click it in the list; then click Delete.

12

Making Exceptions to the AutoCorrect Rules

You might encounter situations in which AutoCorrect's zealousness prevents you from typing something you really need to type.

For example, suppose your company calls itself *ABco, Inc.* to play on the fact that it makes exercise machines. AutoCorrect would always change *ABco* to *Abco*. Also, when using abbreviations, you might need to use a period in the middle of a sentence. You need a way to prevent AutoCorrect from forcing the word following the abbreviation to be capitalized because it thinks that the period marks the end of a sentence.

You can deal with both these exceptions to the rules on the AutoCorrect Exceptions dialog. To open the dialog, open the AutoCorrect dialog and click its Exceptions button.

The Exceptions dialog has two tabs:

- *First letter*: Here you can add or remove words that end in a period but don't necessarily mark the end of a sentence, to prevent AutoCorrect from forcing any word following these words to be capitalized.
- *INitial CAps*: Here you can add any word that must begin with two capital letters, to prevent AutoCorrect from fixing it.

Spell Checking

Even if you use AutoCorrect and spell as-you-go to full advantage, it's always smart to run the spell checker early and often (and again after any time you make changes to text).

To spell check, click the text frame containing the story you want to check. If you want to check all stories in a pub, just click any text frame—Publisher will ask you later whether you want to check the whole pub.

Choose Tools | Spelling | Check Spelling. The Check Spelling dialog opens (see Figure 12.3) and displays the first word it finds that does not appear in the dictionary.

FIGURE 12.3.

Spell checking is a snap, thanks to the suggestions the Check Spelling dialog offers.

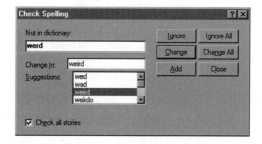

Again, Publisher can't tell the difference between a misspelled word and a word that's spelled properly but isn't in the dictionary (like many surnames, especially *Snell*).

To play it safe, the spell checker will bring to your attention some words that are not misspelled. That's okay—what matters is that it finds the ones that *are* misspelled. By calling names and other such words to your attention, the spell checker helps you make sure—with your own eyes—that you've spelled them properly.

At each word the spell checker chooses, you can do any of the following. As soon as you perform any of the actions described next, the spell checker moves ahead to the next word it doesn't recognize.

If the word is truly misspelled:

- The Suggestions box shows words Publisher thinks might be the one you intend. If one of the suggestions is correct, click it, and then click the Change button (to change just this one instance of the misspelled word) or Change All (to make this change both here and anywhere else in the story).

- Edit the word in the Change To box until it's spelled the way you want it to be; then click Change or Change All.

If the word is spelled correctly (and isn't in the dictionary):

- Click the Ignore button (to ignore just this one instance of the word but to continue to stop on it as a misspelling if encountered elsewhere) or Ignore All (to ignore this word both here and anywhere else it appears in the story).

- Make absolutely sure the word is spelled correctly, and if it is, click the Add button to add it to the dictionary so that the spell checker (and those spell-as-you-go zigzag lines, described earlier in this hour) will never question it again.

> The first time the spell checker stops on words you'll use often—your name, your company name, and so on—take the opportunity to add them to the dictionary so that Publisher knows from then on that they're not mistakes.
>
> Besides saving time, this saves you embarrassment. If your name is in the dictionary, and the spell checker stops on it anyway, you must have misspelled it in the pub—so read it carefully.

12

If the pub contains more than one story, when the spell checker has finished with the current story, it displays a dialog asking whether you want to spell check the remaining stories in the pub. Click Yes to check the rest of the pub or No to close the spell checker.

To Do: Check Your Spelling

1. Open a new text frame and type in it the following words: `fanci`, `fastulous`, and `Snell`.

2. With the edit cursor at the very beginning, choose Tools | Spelling | Check Spelling.

3. The Check Spelling dialog shows `fanci` and offers as suggestions `fancy` and `Fanuc`. (What's a *Fanuc*?)

▼ To Do

▼

▼   4. In the Suggestions box, click `fancy` and then click Change. The word is changed, and the spell checker moves ahead to `fastulous`.

5. The Suggestions box offers `fistulas`, but you know you meant `fabulous`. Edit the word in the Change To box to `fabulous`, and click Change. The spell checker moves ahead to `Snell`.

▲   6. The Suggestions box offers all kinds of ideas for `Snell`, all wrong and some unpleasant. Click Ignore.

Always remember that the spell checker can determine only whether a word is misspelled, not whether the word is the right word or is used correctly. For example, if you type *to* where you mean *too* or *two*, the spell checker ignores it because *to* is still a correctly spelled word.

Any spell checker is an aid to proofing, not a replacement for it. Before and after spell checking, read your pub carefully to check for mistakes, and whenever possible, have someone else read it, too, to double-check.

Putting Hyphens Where You Want `Em

Publisher automatically applies standard rules of hyphenation at the end of a line of text. If the last word in the line is too long to fit, Publisher breaks the word at the proper break point and adds a hyphen to the end of the line to indicate that the word continues on the next line.

By selecting a story and then choosing Tools | Language | Hyphenation, you can use the Hyphenation dialog (see Figure 12.4) to customize how and when hyphens are applied in the selected story.

FIGURE 12.4.

Choose Tools | Language | Hyphenation to customize the way Publisher breaks words at the end of a line.

> Almost any changes you make to text or layout tend to affect where lines of text break, which affects where hyphens will appear. Because of this, it's generally a waste of time to fiddle much with hyphenation until your pub is nearly finished. Consider hyphenation one of your final clean-up steps.

On the dialog, add or remove the check mark to switch automatic hyphenation on or off. (If you switch it off, lines are always broken between words.) You can also modify the measurement for the *hyphenation zone*.

NEW TERM The *hyphenation zone* is a measurement for the width of the area between the right margin and the point at which an automatic hyphen will be applied. For example, if the hyphenation zone for a story is 0.25 inches, any word that comes within a quarter-inch of the right margin, but can't fit completely, will be broken and hyphenated.

Why change the hyphenation zone? Well, if too many words are being broken and hyphenated (see Figure 12.5), it makes the story harder to read. You could just switch off automatic hyphenation, but that might leave the right side of the text looking more ragged than you want it to. Hyphens make the right side more even; that's their job.

Instead of switching off hyphenation, you can increase the size of the hyphenation zone, which tends to make the right margin more ragged but might result in fewer words being hyphenated.

If you think your right margin looks *too* ragged, and few words are hyphenated, you might try reducing the size of the hyphenation zone, which tends to reduce raggedness by breaking more words.

12

FIGURE 12.5.

More hyphens or a more ragged right side: your choice.

Narrower Zone	Wider Zone
Why change the hyphenation zone? Well, if too many words are being broken and hyphenated, it makes the story harder to read. You could just switch off automatic hyphenation, but that might leave the right side of the text looking more ragged than you want it to. Hyphens make the right side more even; that's their job.	Why change the hyphenation zone? Well, if too many words are being broken and hyphenated, it makes the story harder to read. You could just switch off automatic hyphenation, but that might leave the right side of the text looking more ragged than you want it to. Hyphens make the right side more even; that's their job.

If you can't achieve results you like by adjusting the hyphenation zone, try using the Manual button on the Hyphenation dialog. Publisher leads you through the story and stops at each word it wants to hyphenate, giving you the option of accepting or rejecting the hyphens on a case-by-case basis.

Find and Replace

When working with longer stories and pubs, finding specific words or phrases you need to work with can be tricky. It's also tricky to make so-called *global* changes—changing every instance in the pub of a particular word or phrase, as you might do if the name of the product covered by an ad or brochure is changed unexpectedly.

Publisher features find-and-replace tools to help you. Begin by selecting the story and then Find or Replace:

- To find any particular word or phrase, choose Edit | Find. On the Find dialog that appears, type the word or phrase in Find What?, and click Find Next.
- To make a global change, choose Edit | Replace. On the Find dialog that appears, type the word or phrase in Find What?, and click Find Next.

Making Publisher Do the Typing

Way back in Hour 4, "Starting a New Publication," you saw that Publisher's wizards sometimes prompt for your personal information set, from which they can automatically add to your pubs your name, company name, and other oft-typed information.

The only problem then was that you didn't really have personal information sets yet. In a moment, you will. You'll also discover another way Publisher saves you typing: automatic dates and times.

Using Your Personal Information Sets

It's one of those chicken-and-the-egg things: Before you can start using personal information sets in your pubs, you must start using personal information sets in your pubs.

You see, every time you attach a personal information set to a pub and then add personal information manually to that pub, you add to the personal information set. Thus, the best way to build up your personal information sets is to start using them.

Attaching a Personal Information Set to a Pub

Again, many wizards prompt to choose a personal information set for the pub. If you do, you'll probably notice that your name and company name appear in the pub; this information has been added to the set automatically, from a dialog you filled in while installing Publisher.

You can also choose a personal information set for any pub at any time by choosing Insert | Personal Information | Select to open a submenu of personal information sets (see Figure 12.6). You then choose one of your four sets: Primary Business, Secondary Business, Other Organization, and Home/Family. Note that you can maintain completely different information for each of these.

FIGURE 12.6.

Attach a personal information set to the current pub by choosing it from a menu.

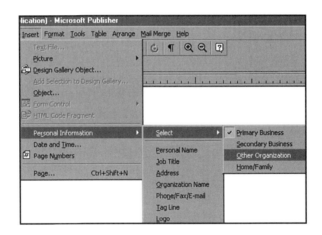

Using Information from a Set

After attaching a personal information set, you can insert into your pub, with a few clicks, any piece of information from that set. Note that the insertions come in their own text frames; creating a text frame first is not necessary.

Choose Insert | Personal Information to display a list of items (see Figure 12.6) that are available in the set that's attached to the current pub. Choose any item in the list, and that information is inserted in your pub, in a new text frame.

- If the set already contains the information, as it always will if you choose Personal Name from the menu, that information appears in the new frame.
- If you've not yet supplied the information, placeholder text appears (see Figure 12.7).

FIGURE 12.7.

Until you've added information, a personal information set inserts placeholder text.

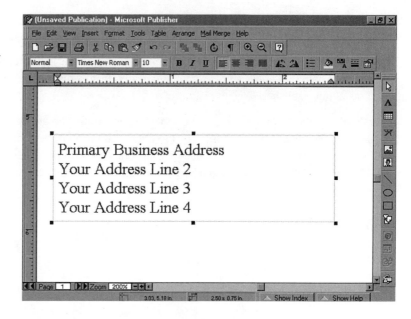

Adding Information to a Set

To add new information to a personal information set, attach that set to a pub, insert the item you want to add information for, and then replace the placeholder text with real text.

For example, suppose I've never entered my business phone number in the Primary Business set. If I attach that set to a pub and then choose Insert | Personal Information | Phone/Fax/E-mail, placeholder text appears in the pub for my business phone number, fax number, and email address.

If I replace the placeholder text with my real numbers, that information is automatically added to the set and from then on will be available for use in any other pub to which I attach the Primary Business set.

You have complete control of all information in your sets:

- You can change any information in a set, including your name.
- Changing information in one set does not affect the others. You're free to use a different name, address, and so on, for each of the four sets.

To Do: Use and Add to a Personal Information Set

To practice using sets and to begin building yours, try this:

1. Open the Letterhead category in the Catalog's Publications By Wizard tab, choose Arcs Letterhead, and click Start Wizard.

2. From the wizard's Welcome page, click Next three times to skip ahead to the question about personal information sets. Observe that the Primary Business Set has already been selected for this pub and will be attached to it (unless you choose a different set).

3. Click Finish to create the pub.

4. Zoom in to 100% to work more easily with the text at the top of the letter. Observe that it's mostly placeholder text.

5. Replace all the placeholder text with your real information.

6. Save the pub.

7. Create any new pub; then choose Insert | Personal Information | Select | Primary Business, to attach the Primary Business set to your new pub.

8. Choose Insert | Personal Information | Address. The address appears in a new text frame.

▲

Inserting the Date and Time

So often, you must type a date or time in a pub. Publisher can take care of that, too, and optionally update the information every day, every minute, so that it always shows the current date or time.

To insert the date and/or time, click a spot within a text frame where you want the date or time to appear; then choose Insert | Date and Time to open the Date and Time dialog (see Figure 12.8).

12

From the list, choose the format of date and time you want to insert. Then select one of the option buttons at the bottom of the dialog:

- *Update Automatically*: The date or time will change automatically to stay current. Whenever you print this pub, the date and time on it will show the date and time at which it was printed.
- *Insert as Plain Text*: The date and time will not be updated automatically, and you can edit them any way you like.

After choosing an option button, click OK to insert.

Summary

For simple pubs, you might not need the tools in this lesson. However, for any pub containing more than a paragraph or two, you'll find that AutoCorrect and the spelling tools do a great job of saving you from yourself, and the personal information sets can help you quickly, accurately insert often used information with a few clicks.

Workshop

The following workshop helps solidify the skills you learned in this lesson.

Q&A

Q **You'd not never notice it, but grammar are my problem. Publisher helps me spell, but where at can I get help with my grammar and, as well, also my style, too?**

A If you struggle with grammar—and grammar is important in the pubs you produce—you really need to collaborate with a friend or coworker whose grammar is better than yours and ask that person to clean up your writing.

No software program can truly improve your writing, but some can help you fix grammar errors. Microsoft Word features a grammar and style checker. If you use Word, consider taking advantage of Word's capability to edit Publisher stories (Edit | Edit Story in Microsoft Word; see Hour 9, "Getting the Words Into Your Publication"), so you can apply Word's powerful checkers to your pub text.

If you use another word processor that features grammar checking, such as WordPerfect, consider perfecting your text in your word processor before importing it into your pub.

Keep in mind that different kinds of pubs require different kinds of grammar. A friendly, conversational piece can bend grammar rules that a formal proposal must adhere to…or, um, *to which a formal proposal must adhere*. That's better.

Quiz

Take the following quiz to see how much you've learned.

Questions

1. When Publisher has zigzag-underlined a word, you can obtain a list of suggested spelling corrections by

    a. Clicking the Pedant button on the Standard toolbar

    b. Publishing the thing anyway and waiting for your readers to write you letters to complain about your *speling*

    c. Pretending that you misspelled the word on purpose, just to be *kute*

    d. Right-clicking the word

2. To complete the information in your personal information sets, you must

    a. Apply the sets in pubs and replace any placeholder text.

    b. Complete the Personal Information Set Management dialog.

    c. Reinstall Publisher.

    d. All the above.

3. Your sorority friends named you SUzie, and it stuck. How can you stop AutoCorrect from changing your name to *Suzie* all the time?

    a. You can't. You need a grown-up name.

    b. Choose Tools | AutoCorrect, click the Exceptions button, and add *SUzie* to the list on the INitial CAps tab.

    c. Choose Tools | AutoCorrect; then check the check box next to Ignore Funky Names.

    d. Exchange your copy of Microsoft Publisher for the alternative version, MIcrosoft PUblisher. (It's available at *SEars*.)

12

Answers

1. (d) Right-clicking displays suggested corrections you can click to replace the underlined word.

2. (a) To use personal information sets, you must use personal information sets. Life is funny that way.

3. (b) Add to the exceptions lists anything you want AutoCorrect to leave alone.

Activities

You're finished with text, for now—in the next part, you begin working with pictures. To prepare, begin evaluating the pubs you've already created. How can pictures and color make them better? Where would those elements fit best within the general layout you've established?

PART IV

Pictures, Backgrounds, and Color

Hour

HOUR 13

Getting Graphics

Just recently, the *New York Times* finally caved and started putting a color picture on the front page, like every other major American daily. Readers like pictures, and they like them in color.

But pictures are even more important than that. At a practical level, they illustrate the text, showing things—car crashes, grassy fields, financial trends—that are difficult to describe fully in words. Aesthetically, they help break up the page into meaningful parts, and give the eye a rest from that sea of words.

In this hour, you'll pick up the basics of getting pictures into your publication and into place within the layout. (In Hour 15, "Snazzing Up Frames with Effects and Fine-Tuning," you'll learn more advanced techniques for working with pictures.) At the end of the hour, you'll be able to answer the following questions:

- What's the difference between vector and bitmap graphics, and why should I care?

- How do I find the perfect picture in Publisher's Clip Art Gallery and insert it in my page?

- How do I use pictures from other sources, such as paint or draw programs or my scanner?
- How do I crop a picture to trim away parts I don't want to see?
- How can I adjust a picture's size and shape?

All About Art

I don't want to make working with pictures any trickier than it has to be—and it really can be pretty simple. But just to help you avoid certain picture problems later on, I need to share with you a quick word now about the two basic types of picture files (see Figure 13.1):

- *Vector graphics*: Pictures whose file formats permit them to be easily sized, shaped, and even recolored while still retaining a quality appearance. Vector files—also known as *raster* or *draw* files—generally hold very graphical, nonphoto type stuff like cartoons, line drawings, abstract shapes, and logos.
- *Bitmap graphics*: Pictures—often photographs—whose file formats don't typically tolerate too much manipulation. You can alter the size and shape of a bitmap graphic, but the more you fiddle with it, the more its appearance can suffer. Bitmaps are sometimes called *paint* images.

> Programs you use to create and edit your own pictures generally come in two types: "draw" programs (CorelDRAW!, WordArt) and "paint" programs (Publisher's Paintbrush, Windows Paint accessory).
>
> Some programs can produce multiple file types, but as a rule, draw programs create vector graphics ("draw" files) and paint programs create bitmaps ("paint" files).

In a pub, you insert and manipulate either type of image in essentially the same way. But as you'll see in this hour and in several hours to come, the type of graphics files you use can play an important role in how you choose to manipulate the appearance of a picture, how you choose to print your pub, and how you make several other decisions.

FIGURE 13.1.

Vector graphics are more flexible; bitmaps are more realistic.

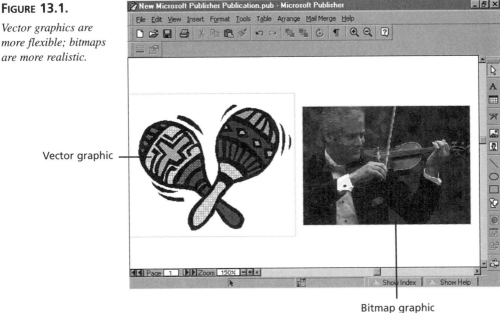

Vector graphic

Bitmap graphic

Borrowing Pictures from the Clip Gallery

The quickest, easiest way to get pictures into pubs is to use Publisher's Clip Art Gallery. From the Gallery's four tabs, you can add any of the following to a pub, all using the same basic steps shown in the next To Do:

- *Clip Art*: Colorful vector images in a wide range of styles and relating to a wide range of subjects. Clip Art lets you dress up a pub quickly, and offers the advantages of vector graphics—limitless flexibility in size, shape, and color.

- *Images*: Colorful bitmaps, mostly photos, related to a wide range of subjects.

- *Sounds*: Sound effects and music that play when the pub is viewed online or on the Web (see Hour 23, "Adding Links, Motion, and Other Web Goodies").

- *Motion Clips*: Animation and movie clips that play online or on the Web (see Hour 23).

13

Always insert your Publisher CD-ROM in your PC before using the Clip Art Gallery. Because the Clip Art Gallery is so huge, Publisher does not install most of its holdings on your hard disk when you install it. Instead, most of the clip art remains on the Publisher CD-ROM, where the Gallery can easily access it.

After you copy an object from the Gallery into your pub, you can remove the CD-ROM—the object has been copied to your hard disk.

To Do: Insert Clip Art

1. Start in any practice pub, and choose a spot for the picture.

2. Insert your Publisher CD-ROM (or Office CD-ROM, if you acquired Publisher bundled with Office).

If you have the AutoPlay option enabled in Windows (see Hour 1, "Setting Up Publisher 98"), Publisher might start to reinstall itself when you insert the CD. Just click Cancel (or No) on any dialog that appears, and continue to step 3.

3. On the Objects toolbar, click the Clip Art Gallery tool.

4. Click and drag in your pub at the rough spot where you want to put the picture. Don't worry about getting the size or position of the frame just right—you'll have to adjust these later.

When you release the mouse button, the Clip Art Gallery opens (see Figure 13.2).

Observe that the Clip Art Gallery includes a Clips From Web button. This button connects you to the Internet (if you have an Internet account configured in Windows) and provides access to more clips from a library at Microsoft.

The Clip Art Web page you'll see is divided into the same tabs as the Gallery (Clip Art, Images, and so on). Choose a tab and choose a file, and that file is automatically added to the Clip Art Gallery on your PC. You can then insert that file in any pub, at any time, right from the Gallery without connecting to the Internet.

5. From the Clip Art or Images tab, choose a picture. You can do this in several ways on either tab:

   - Scroll through all the available pictures.
   - In the left column, click a category to show on the tab only the pictures in that category.
   - Click the Find button to open the Find Clips dialog (see Figure 13.3). Type a keyword describing the subject to which the picture you want should relate; then click the Find Now button. The tab shows only pictures that match the keyword.

   When you see the picture you want, click it to select it. (A gray box appears around the selected picture.)

While exploring the Clip Art Gallery, you can get a better look at the selected picture by clicking the Magnify button.

FIGURE 13.2.

Use the Clip Art Gallery to add artwork in a snap.

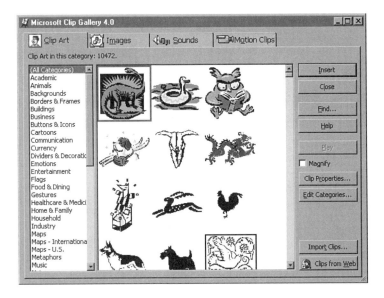

13

▼   6. Click the Insert button. The picture appears in the pub in its original size and shape; observe that the frame's size and shape might change to accommodate the picture. (You may remove the CD-ROM if you're finished with the Clip Art Gallery for now.)

FIGURE 13.3.

In the Gallery, you can search for artwork related to a keyword.

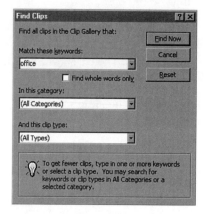

You may now fit the picture to your layout by editing its position, size, or shape as described later in this hour, or change other characteristics—such as its colors or
▲   rotation—as described in Hours 15 and 16, "Controlling Color."

Using Pictures from Elsewhere (Anywhere!)

Besides stuff from the Clip Art Gallery, you can insert picture files from almost any other source. After you have the picture file on your hard disk or on a CD-ROM, the steps for inserting it in a pub are the same, no matter where the file came from.

In addition to all the picture sources described next, you can also use Publisher's built-in art tools—WordArt and the Drawing tools—to create your own artwork and insert it in a pub. See Hour 14, "Creating WordArt and Drawings."

The following are some places to get picture files:

- *Other clip art collections*: Many word processing and graphics programs include libraries of picture files, and you can purchase CD-based clip art libraries at any software store.

- *Online*: The Web is a treasure-trove of picture files you can download and use in your print pubs and your Web pages. Appendix A, "Internet Resources for Publisher Users," shows the Web addresses of several great clip art libraries.

- *From a draw or paint program*: Using tools such as CorelDRAW! and others you'll learn about in Hour 20, "Beyond Publisher: Exploring Other Desktop Publishing Tools," you can create new artwork, save it in one of the file formats supported by Publisher (see Table 13.1), and then insert the file in a pub.

- *From your local photo lab*: When you bring a roll of exposed film into a growing number of photo labs, the lab can optionally supply not only prints or slides, but a disk or CD on which the pictures are stored as high-quality graphics files. The file format used most often, called PhotoCD, is returned to you on a special CD-ROM from which you can insert the pictures in your pubs.

- *From another document or pub*: Using the copy and paste techniques you learned in Hour 9, "Getting the Words Into Your Publication," (for copying text between pubs or from a word processing document into a pub), you can also copy a picture from any document displayed by a Windows program. Just select the picture, choose Edit | Copy, and then switch to your pub and choose Edit | Paste.

- *From a scanner*: You can scan pictures directly into a pub, as described later in this hour. If you've already scanned the picture and stored it as a file on your PC you can insert that file in a pub, just as you would any file.

Any time you use a picture you did not draw or photograph yourself, you run the risk of violating the copyright of the person who created it.

Clip art libraries—on disk or on the Web—all come with different copyright restrictions. Even clip art advertised as "free" usually has some restrictions, such as a prohibition against selling the clip art to someone else.

Always read and follow any copyright rules accompanying clip art, and never scan a photograph you did not take yourself, unless you have the photographer's express permission.

When you're unsure of the copyright status of a picture, just don't use it. There are too many alternatives to risk running over someone else's copyright.

13

File Types You Can Use

Picture files come in a surprising number of different file types. Fortunately, you can use most common file formats in Publisher, including those shown in Table 13.1. You can tell the type of a file by its extension, the period and three letters at the very end of the filename.

TABLE 13.1. TYPES OF PICTURE FILES YOU CAN USE IN PUBS.

Bitmap Files	Vector Files
.bmp (Windows bitmap)	.cgm (Computer Graphics Metafile)
.tif (Tagged Image File Format)	.wmf (Windows Metafile)
.pcx (PC Paintbrush)	.drw (Micrografx Designer/Draw)
.pcd (Kodak PhotoCD)	.eps (Encapsulated PostScript)
.jpg (Joint Photographic Experts Group)	.wpg (DrawPerfect)
.gif (Graphics Interchange Format)	.cdr (CorelDRAW!)

If you have a picture file you want to use and it is not stored in one of the file formats shown in Table 13.1, you might be able to convert it to one of those types.

For example, if you can open the file in your draw or paint program, open it there, and then use the program's Export or Save As feature to save the file in a type listed in Table 13.1.

Inserting a Picture

To insert a picture file, use the Objects toolbar's Picture Frame tool to draw a picture frame, select it, and then choose Insert I Picture I From File to open the dialog on which you choose the file.

When inserting a picture, you can first draw the frame and then insert a picture into it, or you can do both together (as the To Do shows).

Make sure no frame is selected (you can do this by clicking an empty spot on the scratch area); then choose Insert I Picture I From File. The picture will appear in a new frame, which you can then size and shape to fit in the layout.

To Do: Insert a Picture from a File

1. Start in any practice pub, and choose a spot for the picture.
2. Click in the scratch area to ensure that no frame is selected in the pub. (If a frame is selected, the new picture will replace its contents.)

▼ To Do

3. Choose Insert | Picture | From File to open the Insert Picture File dialog (see Figure 13.4). By default, the dialog shows at first the files in a folder where it keeps some of its clip art.

FIGURE 13.4.

Choose just about any graphics file from the Insert Picture File dialog.

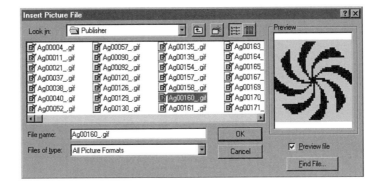

By default, the Insert Picture File dialog shows all files in the current folder that are in any of the file types shown earlier in Table 13.1. That way, you can see every picture file that you could use. But if you want to limit the display only to pictures of a certain file type, drop down the Files Of Type list and choose that type from the list.

4. Use the Look In list to navigate to the folder where your picture file is stored. (For practice, you can just stay in the current folder and finish this To Do using one of the clip art images.)

5. Click the filename of the picture. A preview of it appears in the Preview box (if the dialog's Preview File check box is checked).

6. Click OK to insert the picture. The picture appears in the pub in its original size and shape; observe that the frame's size and shape may change to accommodate the picture.

You may now drag the frame to its proper position on the page, and change its size or other characteristics as described later in this hour and in Hour 15.

13

Adding Pictures from a Scanner or Digital Camera

A scanner is a great way to get pictures—especially your own printed photos—into your pubs. Most scanners are compatible with a standard called TWAIN, which enables programs such as Publisher to control them. Many digital cameras are also TWAIN compatible, and give you a way to snap a photo and pull it straight into a pub.

> Nearly all scanners sold today are TWAIN-compliant. But if yours is not, you cannot scan directly from within Publisher.
>
> However, you can simply use the software packaged with your scanner to scan outside of Publisher, and save the picture in one of the file formats supported by Publisher. You can then insert the file in your pub as you would any other picture file (Insert I Picture I From File).

To use your TWAIN-compatible scanner or camera, make sure you have already attached the device to your PC and followed any steps required to set up the scanner and its software.

Load the picture into the scanner according to the scanner's instructions. Then open Publisher and the pub and page in which the scanned image should appear. Choose Insert I Picture I From Scanner or Camera. On the submenu that appears:

- If you have more than one scanner or both a scanner and digital camera, choose Select Device to open a dialog on which you can choose the device from which you'll insert a picture.

- If you have just one device, or have already selected the device, choose Acquire Image.

Publisher opens the TWAIN driver for your device (the TWAIN driver for my scanner is shown in Figure 13.5, but yours will probably be different). Set the options in the TWAIN driver as desired and start the scan. When the scan is complete, the image appears in your pub.

Working a Picture into the Layout

Before you can manipulate a picture to work it into your layout, you must select it. A picture is selected automatically right after you insert it; to select it later, point to it and click. Note that when a picture is selected, the tools in the Formatting toolbar change to tools for working with pictures.

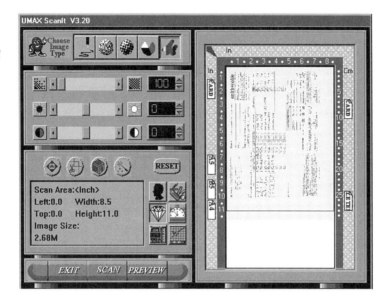

FIGURE 13.5.

The TWAIN driver for your scanner or digital camera offers you image options.

Except where I say otherwise, you manipulate pictures exactly the same way regardless of where they came from: Clip Art Gallery, file, scanner, or draw object (see Hour 14).

Deleting and Replacing Pictures

Deleting a picture (frame and all) is quite simple: select it, then press your Delete key. Note that this deletes the picture from the pub but does not erase the file from your hard disk or CD; you can still use the same picture in any pub.

Eventually, you'll need to replace pictures for any of the following reasons:

- You created the pub from a template and want to replace the placeholder pictures in it with more personal pictures, ones you've created or selected yourself.

- You change your mind.

- You're creating a new pub from an older one. For example, you needn't create a new layout for each issue of a newsletter; you can simply replace the pictures and text in their frames with new content.

13

To replace a picture with another of the same type (replacing one Clip Art Gallery picture with another or replacing one picture file with another), double-click the picture. The dialog from which you added the original picture (the Gallery or the Insert Picture File dialog) opens, and whatever you choose from that dialog replaces the picture you double-clicked.

To replace a Gallery picture with a regular picture file, or vice-versa, delete the picture; then insert its replacement in a new frame.

Cropping a Picture

 Cropping a picture means cutting off a slice of the image on one or more sides to remove an unwanted portion (see Figure 13.6).

FIGURE 13.6.

Cropping shaves portions of the image from the sides.

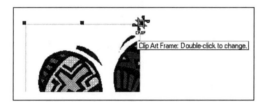

For example, if a scanned photograph shows both you and cousin Ruth, but you want to show only yourself, you can crop out Ruth. Cropping is also useful to remove extraneous space or objects around the sides of an image to improve its composition (bringing the most important parts to the center).

- To crop a picture, select it and click the Crop Picture button on the Formatting toolbar (or choose Format | Crop Picture). Then point to any handle on the picture. When on a handle, the pointer now turns into the crop pointer (instead of the resize pointer).

- To crop out part of either side, or the top or bottom, of the picture, point to a handle along the side you want to crop, click and hold, and drag up, down, left, or right to crop out as much as you want.

- To add whitespace around the picture, drag the crop pointer away from the center of the picture. Doing so enlarges the frame but not the picture in it, adding whitespace.

- To crop a side and the top or bottom together, point to a corner handle, click and hold, and drag diagonally toward the opposite corner.

▼ To Do

To Do: Crop a Picture

1. Select any picture you've inserted.

2. Click the Crop Picture button on the Formatting toolbar, or choose Format | Crop Picture.

3. Point to the handle that appears at the center of the bottom of the picture so that the crop pointer appears.

4. Click and hold, then drag straight up, halfway up the picture, and release. You have just cropped out the bottom half of the picture.

5. Click the Undo button on the Standard toolbar to restore the cropped portion.

> Note that when you crop a picture, the parts you crop out don't really go away; they're just hidden. You can recrop the picture at any time, dragging the Crop pointer away from the center of the picture, to restore any parts you cut out previously.

▲

Sizing, or Scaling, a Picture

You can *scale* a picture by dragging its handles to change the size of the picture frame, just as you would resize any other frame. But when the object at hand is a picture, there's more to consider.

NEW TERM Resizing a picture is called *scaling* it, and the term *scale* is also used to describe the percentage of the change. At its full original size, a picture is at 100% scale. Scaled down to half its original size, that picture is at 50% scale, or *half scale*.

If when scaling a picture you're not careful to preserve its original *aspect ratio*—overall shape, the relationship between the height and width of the frame—you distort the image, as shown in Figure 13.7. This would happen if you used the resize pointer to drag a side handle, or if you dragged a corner handle and were not careful to drag diagonally away from the opposite corner handle.

Of course, you might have situations in which you really want to distort the appearance of a picture in this way, especially when working with abstract shapes in vector files. For special effects, you can even distort bitmapped photos this way. For example, you can drag the top handle of a photo of people up, making them unnaturally tall and thin.

But when working with a picture where you'd typically want to preserve the aspect ratio—as you usually would in a photograph—you must be careful not to distort the aspect ratio. One way to do this is to drag only corner handles, and only on the diagonals. But a better way is to use the Scale Picture dialog, as shown in the next To Do.

13

FIGURE 13.7.

When you scale pictures without preserving the height-to-width ratio, you distort them.

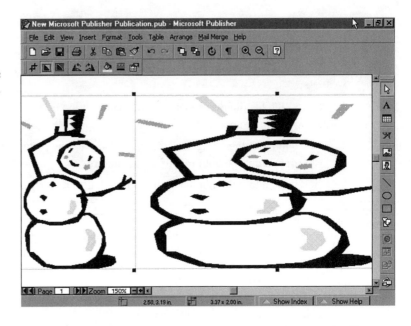

As a rule, you can change the size and shape of a vector file all you like, and it will still look pretty good. But bitmap files often respond poorly to scaling and very poorly to changes in aspect ratio, developing *artifacts*—odd geometric patterns, fuzziness, and other icky flaws.

I can't offer a reliable way to predict which files respond poorly to what formatting. A wide range of factors determines the effect of formatting on a picture, including not just its file type, but also its resolution and color depth, the presence of certain kinds of textures or line patterns, and the amount of scaling or other formatting applied (and in what combination).

To lessen the chances of artifacts developing, try to start with picture files that require as little formatting as possible—ones that are the proper size and shape to begin with. When you create a bitmap yourself with a paint program or scanner, perform any necessary scaling or other manipulation within the paint or scan program before inserting the file in your pub.

To Do: Scale a Picture

1. Select any picture.
2. Choose Format | Scale Object to open the Scale Object dialog.

3. Enter **200** in both Scale height and Scale width. You have scaled both height and width to 200%, doubling the image from its original size. As long as the percentages in Scale Height and Scale Width are identical, the image retains it original aspect ratio.

 If you've scaled or warped an image—possibly by dragging handles—and you don't like the results but are having trouble restoring the image, open the Scale Object dialog and click the Original Size check box (see Figure 13.8). The picture returns to its original size and shape.

FIGURE 13.8.

Enter equal height and width percentages in the Scale Object dialog to resize a picture without changing its shape.

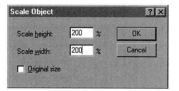

Summary

You have so many choices for adding pictures—the Clip Art Gallery, any common graphics file, scanners, and more—that its hard to know where to begin sometimes. Take it easy. Grab something simple from the Clip Art Gallery to start, and work your way up to pictorial masterpieces. Remember: One simple, well-chosen image on a page is far better than several sloppy, over-ambitious ones.

Workshop

The following workshop helps solidify the skills you learned in this lesson.

Q&A

Q When I scan, how do I know which settings to choose on my scanner's TWAIN Driver dialog?

A The main choices you'll have relate to the image area (the area to be scanned), the resolution, and the color depth. Get the scan area as correct as you can, but remember that you just need to capture the part you want, and if there's a little extra, you can crop that out in Publisher.

13

A scanner usually has a maximum scanning resolution, expressed in dots per inch (dpi), but can optionally scan at lower resolutions. The higher the resolution, the sharper, smoother, and more realistic the image.

A color scanner can scan at its full color depth, but can also scan in *grayscale* (photo-quality, shaded black-and-white with gray) and in *black-and-white* or *line art* mode (the image will be black-and-white only, with no shades of gray, for a poster-style, graphical look).

Choose the resolution and color depth that are appropriate for the way your pub will be printed and the look you want to achieve. As a rule, scan at the same resolution that you will print at (see Hour 17, "Setting Up for a Printing Service"); if you will print on a 600 dpi printer, scan at 600 dpi. (Commercial printers often express their printer resolutions in lines per inch, or *lpi*. Choose a scan dpi that's twice the lpi at which you will print.) There's no harm in scanning higher than the print resolution, but the resulting image file will be larger (in bytes) and harder to deal with for little or no visible improvement.

When the image needn't be magazine quality, you can keep the size of the image file smaller and speed up scanning and printing by choosing lower scan resolutions. Scan resolutions as low as 200 dpi can yield very good results.

Finally, you must consider scan resolution relative to any scaling you'll do to the image. If you will greatly enlarge the image in Publisher, you must increase your scan resolution somewhat to get the best results. If you will shrink the image, you might be able to get away with a lower resolution. Experiment.

Quiz

Take the following quiz to see how much you've learned.

Questions

1. Which of the following is least likely to look lousy when stretched out or otherwise manipulated?

    a. Me.

    b. A vector graphic, such as any choice from the Clip Art Gallery's Clip Art tab.

    c. A bitmap graphic, such as any choice from the Clip Art Gallery's Images tab.

    d. A scanned photo of me.

2. If a picture shows Santino, Fredo, and Michael in a row, and you want to cut out Santino, you can

    a. Crop the picture.

    b. Scale the picture.

    c. Delete the picture.

    d. Stretch the picture.

3. You can create artwork for your pubs in other programs. (True/False)

Answers

1. (b) Vector graphics take a licking and keep on ticking.

2. (a) Cropping can remove the side with Santino.

3. True, as long as the program you use saves files in one of Publisher's supported formats (refer to Table 13.1).

Activities

What's on your PC? With all the stuff that comes on new PCs these days, and other stuff that accumulates on a PC, you may have draw, paint, or other useful graphics programs you don't even know you have. Take a tour and explore whatever you find. At the very least, open your Start menu and choose Programs | Accessories | Paint to check out Windows built-in bitmap-maker, Paint.

13

Hour 14

Creating WordArt and Drawings

"I'm no artist," you say. (Okay, maybe it's just me who says that.) Anyway, Publisher's built-in art tools aren't necessarily for "artwork," and demand no artistic talent, experience, motivation, suffering, or tattered berets. What these tools really do is offer you an easy, fast way to add stylish text touches and simple, functional objects—such as lines, circles, and boxes—quickly and easily.

At the end of the hour, you'll be able to answer the following questions:

- How do I create "WordArt" to give a chunk of text all the graphical flair of a picture?
- How can I draw shapes—rectangles, ovals, and even custom shapes such as hearts and cartoon word balloons—right in my pub?
- How can I draw lines and arrows wherever I might need them?

Making Words into Art

Fonts are great, but they're not enough. Look at the incredibly stylized company or product logos you see in ads, and even at the style of text and headlines and slogans in some magazines. The words are shaped, bent, twisted, shaded, colored, and more (see Figure 14.1).

FIGURE 14.1.

WordArt lends the visual power of graphics to mere text.

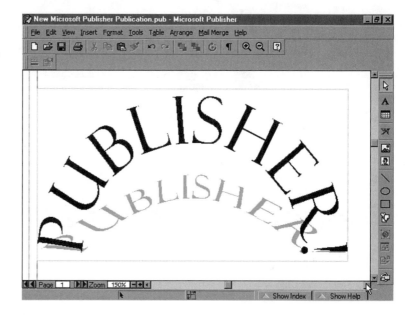

The letters and words in such creations are still legible, so the text still fulfills its primary mission to communicate its content. But the *style* in which the words are set adds another layer of communication, a graphical one that makes a statement about the style or personality of whatever those words describe. Such creations are both textual and graphical content in one.

Publisher's WordArt tool offers you a fast, easy way to create these word/art combos. You can create a logo or snappy-looking headline in seconds, or deploy an amazing range of different tools—in any combination—to style the text in an infinite range of ways.

Perhaps the best way to use WordArt is to create a logo, for yourself or your company, by making WordArt from the company name (or your name). If it's a logo you want, I ought to tell you that the Design Gallery (see Hour 6, "Arranging Frames and Columns") includes a Logo Creation Wizard you can use to create a logo. To start the wizard, choose Logos from the Design Gallery's Objects by Design tab, and then choose one of the logo templates shown.

However, I recommend using WordArt, or a separate draw program (see Hour 20, "Beyond Publisher: Exploring Other Desktop Publishing Tools"), to create logos rather than using the Logo Creation Wizard. The reason has to do with the copyright licensing on all graphics supplied with Publisher (including everything in the Clip Gallery and the Design Gallery). Microsoft gives you complete license to use these in your pubs, but *not* to copyright or trademark them for yourself.

That means a logo created from Publisher's Logo Creation Wizard might be impossible to trademark as a true logo. More important, the logo might in fact violate someone *else's* trademark. Microsoft says you should talk to a lawyer before adopting a logo created with the Wizard. I say save your money and create a new, original logo with WordArt or another tool.

Starting a New WordArt Picture

To create a new WordArt picture in your pub, click the WordArt Frame Tool on the Objects toolbar, and drag to draw a new frame as you would any other. When you release the mouse button, the small text-entry dialog shown in Figure 14.2 appears, and Publisher immediately changes its appearance to WordArt view, which has its own unique toolbar. You'll always see this view while working with WordArt.

The WordArt view appears automatically any time you create a new WordArt frame.

- To return to the regular Publisher view to work on other frames, click anywhere in the pub except on a WordArt frame.
- To bring back the WordArt view at any time to edit your WordArt, double-click the WordArt frame you want to edit.

14

Figure 14.2.

*You create and edit
WordArt in this
WordArt view.*

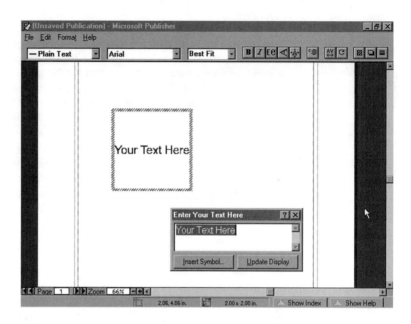

In the text-entry dialog, when you type your text it automatically replaces the words "Your Text Here" that first appear in the dialog. As you type, don't worry about how the words look yet, and don't even worry whether you've typed exactly what you want to (you can easily change the text later). Just get your basic word or words in place so you can move ahead to the "art" part of WordArt.

After typing your text, click the X button in the upper-right corner of the little text-entry dialog to close it.

> If you need to use special symbols that do not appear on your keyboard, click the Insert Symbol button on the text-entry dialog to open the Symbol dialog; then use that dialog exactly as you would for regular text.

Putting the "Art" in WordArt

Within the WordArt view, you have a huge selection of tools on the toolbar, most of which are also duplicated on the Format menu.

Choosing a Font and Attributes

Near the middle of the toolbar, you'll see a font list and a size list; they don't show you the actual style of the fonts named, but other than that you use them exactly as you would on any text, to choose a font and size. Other WordArt toolbar buttons you probably recognize (and already know how to use) include the Bold and Italic buttons.

> You cannot apply different fonts or attributes to different parts of the text within one WordArt frame. Any font, size, or attribute selections apply automatically to all text in the frame.

But beyond font, size, bold, and italic, the toolbar offers a whole batch of new buttons, each of which adds art to the words.

There's no way I can realistically demonstrate all the effects you can achieve by clicking these buttons and applying combinations of them—the possibilities are endless. Instead, I'll tell you what each does, and I encourage you to experiment with them to develop a better understanding of their effects. You'll have that chance in the next To Do.

> WordArt's toolbar buttons do not have ToolTips that display automatically to tell you their names (which means that they don't really *have* names).
>
> Use the following descriptions to learn what each button does by its appearance, and when in doubt, use the items on the Format menu instead of the toolbar buttons.

Makes all letters in the text—both uppercase and lowercase letters—the same height. This option can be useful in achieving a smooth look when you apply a shape to text (see "Molding Words into Shapes," next).

Makes text run vertically, top to bottom, instead of horizontally.

Expands the size of the letters so that the text fills the frame completely, top-to-bottom and side-to-side.

Displays a list of text alignment options, including the familiar Center, Left, and Right alignment, and three forms of justified alignment: Stretch Justify (adjusts the width of the letters), Letter Justify (adjusts the spacing between the letters), and Word Justify (adjust the spacing between words).

Opens a dialog on which you can adjust character spacing and pair kerning.

14

Opens a Special Effects dialog you use to adjust the rotation and slant of the text (see "Adding 'Special Effects'," later in this hour).

Opens a Shading dialog from which you can apply colors and shading for the text.

Opens a Shadow dialog from which you can choose a style of shadow to lay behind each letter to give the WordArt a 3D, floating-atop-the-page look.

Opens a Border dialog you can use to add an outline around the letters box.

Molding Words into Shapes

How much would you pay for a tool that does to words all the things I just described? Fifty dollars? A hundred? But wait…. Don't decide yet! There's more!

The leftmost list on the WordArt toolbar drops down a collection of shapes (see Figure 14.3). Choose a shape, and the WordArt text is warped into that shape. (To return text to its original, normal shape, choose the upper-left shape—the straight horizontal line.)

It's this shaping capability that really makes WordArt special and provides a very fast way to invent a new logo or other "shaped" text.

FIGURE 14.3.

Choose a shape to mold the text to match.

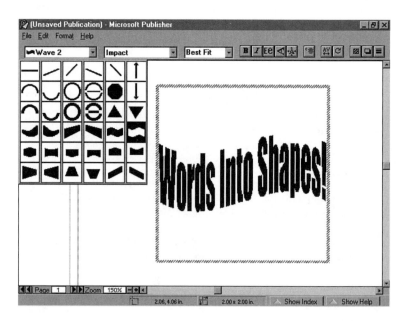

To Do: Play with WordArt

1. Start in any pub.

2. On the Objects toolbar, click the WordArt Frame tool.

3. Click and drag in your pub to draw a new frame. The WordArt view and the text-entry dialog appear.

4. Type your name, and then click the X corner on the text-entry dialog to close it.

5. Increase the zoom, if necessary, to see your WordArt name clearly.

6. Drop down the shapes list from the left end of the toolbar.

7. Choose one of the semicircle ("arch") shapes. Your name forms a semicircle.

8. Choose one of the irregular, black shapes (polygons) from the bottom row, and see what happens.

9. Click the toolbar button to the right of the italic button (Even Height). All the letters in your name become the same height.

10. Beginning with the next button to the right, try each button, and observe how it affects the WordArt.

11. When you're finished experimenting, click anywhere in the pub but on the WordArt. The regular Publisher view returns.

Adding "Special Effects"

Pretty much everything you do in WordArt is adding "special effects." But WordArt reserves that label for the things you can do from the Special Effects dialog (see Figure 14.4), which you open by choosing Format | Rotation and Effects or by clicking the toolbar button with the curved arrow on it. You can do the following in the dialog:

- Raise or lower the Rotation percentage to change the rotation angle of the WordArt. For example, Rotation of 0 degrees is upright; 90 degrees lays the words on their side and 180 degrees turns text upside-down. (For more about rotation, see Hour 15, "Snazzing Up Frames with Effects and Fine-Tuning.")

- Raise or lower the Slider percentage to slant or "skew" the letters to the left or right. Letters are vertical at a slider setting of 50%. Percentages above 50% skew the text to the right; below 50%, text skews left.

14

FIGURE 14.4.

Use the Special Effects dialog to rotate and skew the words.

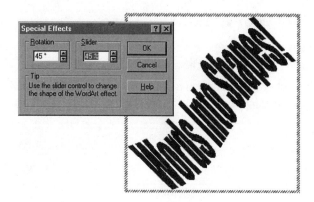

Choosing Shading, Line Thickness, and "Shadows"

When your WordArt is in its basic shape, you can add some terrific finishing touches through the options for shading, line thickness, and shadows.

Shading

The color choices for all objects in Publisher are affected by your selected color scheme (see Hour 16, "Controlling Color"), except for WordArt objects. This means you can choose any colors you like for WordArt, without the guidance of the pub's color scheme. It also means you must take care when choosing colors so that they work well with other colors in the pub.

To color and shade your WordArt from within WordArt view, choose Format | Shading, or click the button that also opens the Shading dialog (see Figure 14.5).

On the Shading dialog shown in Figure 14.5, you'll notice that you can choose separate colors for the foreground and background. Don't be confused by these terms—you cannot use the Shading dialog to choose a color for the entire background of the WordArt frame.

WordArt lets you add textured patterns, made up of two colors (foreground and background), to the letters themselves, and that's what you do on the Shading dialog in WordArt view. You choose a fill color or shading pattern for the frame background just as you would do for any frame in regular Publisher view (see Hour 16).

FIGURE **14.5.**

*Choose Shading to
color your WordArt.*

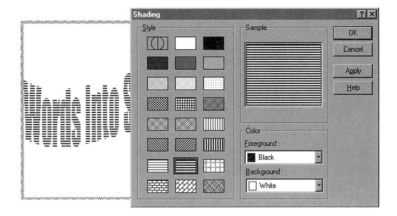

To choose shading for the letters, choose the following in the Shading dialog:

- *Style*: Choose a shading pattern from the options provided. The top three options have special uses:

 Makes the letters clear, so that anything in the frame beneath the WordArt frame shows through the letters. This option usually works best in combination with a border (see the section "Borders, [or Rather, Outlines]," next).

 Fills the characters with the solid background color and ignores the foreground color, creating no shading pattern.

 Fills the characters with the solid foreground color and ignores the foreground color, creating no shading pattern.

- *Foreground*: Choose the color for the foreground layer of the selected shading pattern.

- *Background*: Choose the color for the background layer of the selected shading pattern.

Borders (or Rather, Outlines)

Borders is another item where WordArt throws in its own terminology that differs from Publisher's. In Hour 15, you'll learn how to add borders—rectangular boxes around the frame boundary—to frames. But that's not what border means in WordArt.

14

NEW TERM In WordArt, a *border* is an outline that traces the contours of the letters. By adding a border, you can add extra definition to WordArt and make the words stand out better. You can also use borders to define the edges of the letters when you've used a light or clear shading pattern.

To add borders in WordArt view, choose Format | Border or click the toolbar button that opens the Border dialog. Choose a thickness for the outline, and a color, if you want to.

> Because borders hug the letters so closely, it can be hard to see the effects of a border. Choose a new color (different from the text color) on the Borders dialog, and you'll be able to see exactly what the border is doing.

Shadows

NEW TERM A *drop shadow* is a gray shadow layered behind an object to make the object appear to be "floating" slightly above the page. It's a nice touch, and in Hour 15, you'll learn how to add a drop shadow to any frame.

WordArt can add shadows behind letters, in the shape of the letters. Choose Format | Shadow to open the Shadow dialog (see Figure 14.6), then choose a Shadow style and color.

FIGURE 14.6.

Add shadows to WordArt to make it float above the page.

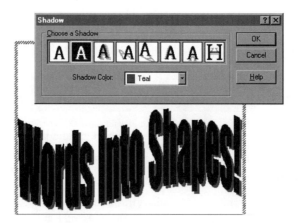

Changing the Words in WordArt

You can change the words and letters in a WordArt frame at any time, without affecting any of the art you've applied to the words. To edit the words, double-click the WordArt frame in your pub to switch to WordArt view, where the dialog for entering text appears automatically. In the dialog, edit or add to the text any way you like, and close the dialog when you're finished.

Drawing Shapes and Lines

To use Publisher's drawing tools to make shapes, lines, and arrows, you work from within the regular Publisher view, choosing your tools from the Objects toolbar.

When you draw a shape, what you get is an empty outline, through which the contents of any frame beneath the shape will show. You can optionally fill in the shape with a solid color or shading pattern; see Hour 16.

Drawing an Oval or Rectangle

You draw a shape—a rectangle, circle, or oval—exactly as you would draw a new frame in a pub. You begin by clicking the Oval or Rectangle tool. Point to the general spot where you want the shape to go (don't try to be perfect—you can move it later), click and hold, and drag to draw the shape.

As you drag, you can adjust the angle at which you drag to adjust the shape:

- Dragging at low, horizontal angles makes the shape shorter and wider.
- Dragging at high, vertical angles makes the shape tall and thin.

If you're very good with your mouse, you can drag at a perfect 45-degree angle to draw a perfect square (with the Rectangle tool) or circle (with the Oval tool). But there's an easier way.

After choosing your tool but before clicking in your pub, press and hold your Shift key. While still holding Shift, click and drag to draw the shape. You'll get a perfect square or rectangle every time, no matter the angle of your drag.

14

Adding a Custom Shape

There's more to life than rectangles and ovals. There are heart shapes, cartoon explosions, and triangles, of course. The Custom Shapes tool on the Objects toolbar gives you a fast and easy way to draw all the more important shapes of life.

Click the Custom Shapes tool to display a collection of shapes (see Figure 14.7). Click the shape you want to draw, point to your pub, and then do one of the following:

- Single-click to instantly create the shape, in its default size, in your pub. You can adjust its size and other characteristics later.
- Click, hold, and drag (as you would to draw a circle or rectangle) to draw the shape in a particular size.

FIGURE 14.7.

Choose a custom shape from the Objects toolbar to make a neat shape quickly.

Customizing Shapes

In practice, each shape you draw with the drawing tools is a frame. That means you manipulate the position, size, and shape of a drawing object exactly as you would any frame. That also means that you can apply to drawings all the advanced frame manipulation techniques, such as rotation or drop shadows, that you'll discover in Hour 15.

To select a drawing so that you can customize it, point very carefully to its outline so that the very tip of the pointer touches the line. (You must point to the line; you can't select a circle, for example, by pointing to the middle of it.) Single-click, and the familiar family of handles appears to show the shape is selected.

When a shape is selected you can do the following:

- To move it, point to it so the Move pointer appears, and then click, hold, and drag to its new position.
- To change its size or aspect ratio, drag a handle as you would to change the size of a frame.
- To change the thickness of the outline, click the Line/Border Style button on the Formatting toolbar (or choose Format | Line/Border Style) and choose a thickness from the menu of choices that appears. (For more about line thicknesses and borders, see Hour 15.)

- To fill the shape with a solid color or shading, click the Fill button on the Formatting toolbar (see Hour 16).

Drawing Lines and Arrows

Lines (and arrows, which are just lines with points) come in handier than you might think. You can use lines to connect the boxes in a flowchart or organizational chart, or dress up a headline with a fine line above or below it. Another popular use for lines and arrows is connecting callouts to the objects they refer to.

NEW TERM A *callout* is text used to identify only a part of a picture (unlike a caption, which describes the picture as a whole). Typically, a callout is layered above the picture, adjacent to the part of the picture it identifies, or the callout text appears outside the picture and an arrow connects the callout to its part of the picture. Multiple callouts are often used to call the reader's attention to key parts of a photo or diagram.

Drawing a Line

To draw a line (which can become an arrow, as you learn later), begin by clicking the Line tool in the Objects toolbar. Click and hold in your pub at the right spot for one end of the line, then drag to the spot where the opposite end of the line belongs. Until you release the mouse button, you can continue to fine-tune the angle and length of the line until you get it just right.

Customizing a Line

To select a line so you can customize it, point very carefully to the line, so that the very tip of the pointer touches the line, then click. A handle appears at each end to show the line is selected.

When a line is selected you can do the following:

- To move the line, point to it so the Move pointer appears; then click, hold, and drag it to its new position.
- To change the length or angle of the line, drag one of the handles.
- To change the thickness of the line, click the Line/Border Style button on the Formatting toolbar (or choose Format | Line/Border Style) and choose a thickness from the menu of choices that appears.

By choosing the More Styles item from the bottom of the Line/Border menu, you can choose a custom thickness for the line (see Hour 15), or choose its color (see Hour 16).

14

Adding Points to Lines to Make Arrows

Right after drawing a line, and any time a line is selected, you'll see on the Formatting toolbar new tools for making that line an arrow:

- Click Add/Remove Left Arrow to put an arrow point at the left end of the line.
- Click Add/Remove Right Arrow to put an arrow point at the right end of the line.
- Click Add/Remove Both Arrows to put an arrow point at both ends.

To remove a point, click the button you used to add it.

To Do: Add Callouts to a Picture

▼ To Do

1. Start in any pub with a picture in it, or quickly add a picture from the Clip Art Gallery. Zoom in to work closely with the picture.
2. On top of the picture, in its upper-right corner, draw a small text frame and type a word or two in it.
3. Click the Line tool on the Objects toolbar.
4. Point carefully to the lower-left corner of the text frame.
5. Click, hold, and drag to the center of the picture and release. A line appears from the corner of the text frame to the center of the picture.
6. Click the Add/Remove Left Arrow button on the toolbar to add an arrow pointing to the center of the picture.

▲

Summary

Often, WordArt and the drawing tools are handiest when you're stumped. Perhaps there's no picture available for a page, or no need for one, but you want to add some visual interest. A quick trip to WordArt, or a nice drawn shape to give the page a little geometry, can add just what the page needs.

Workshop

The following workshop helps solidify the skills you learned in this lesson.

Q&A

Q **Can I build complex drawings out of shapes and lines? Like, can I make a kitty-cat face out of various shapes used together?**

A *Absolutely*—go nuts. (I'm a dog person myself, but it's your pub.) But if you're going to go to all that trouble, you owe it to yourself to learn how to group multiple objects so that they can be manipulated as a unit (see Hour 15).

After you group all the parts of your kitty face into one object, you can move, scale, and manipulate the face in just about any other way as if it were a single picture, not a bunch of separate ones.

Quiz

Take the following quiz to see how much you've learned.

Questions

1. To make some WordArt text conform to a hexagon shape:

    a. Hold it up to a Stop sign and trim around the edges.

    b. Drag all six handles to the center.

    c. Crop off all corners.

    d. Open the list of shapes from the WordArt toolbar, and choose the hexagon.

2. To make a perfect circle, hold down _____ while using the Oval tool.

    a. Shift

    b. Prices

    c. da Noise

    d. Ctrl

3. You can't edit the words in WordArt after you've added the art. (True/False)

Answers

1. (d) Use that handy shapes list to fit WordArt to a shape.

2. (a) Hold Shift while drawing to make perfect squares or circles.

3. False. You can edit the words at any time, without affecting the art.

Activities

Look at company names, product names, titles, and headlines in pubs you're developing, and find some good candidates for WordArt. Try using WordArt to design a logo for a made-up (or real!) company, club, or theater group.

14

HOUR 15

Snazzing Up Frames with Effects and Fine-Tuning

Getting (or creating) your pictures and inserting them in publications is only the beginning of the ways you can refine the graphical appearance of your pub. You can also set off frames with borders, rotate frames, wrap text around irregular objects, and more.

Most of what you'll learn in this hour can be used on any type of frame— not just a picture, WordArt, or shape frame, but a text or table frame, too. So why did I cover it here among the graphics hours? Because all these techniques—regardless of the contents of the frame to which they're applied— affect your page in a graphical way. They're all graphics techniques, even when applied to text or tables.

At the end of the hour, you'll be able to answer the following questions:

- How can I add borders to the boundaries of a frame to box up its contents?
- Can I choose which lines within a table show up in print?
- How does BorderArt add fun, funky boxes to frames in a hurry?
- Can I tilt the angle of a frame, or even turn it upside-down?
- When multiple frames must work closely together, how can I connect them so they operate as a unit?
- How can I make columns of text align to the uneven contours of a picture, just because it looks cool?

Adding Borders

NEW TERM   A *border* is a rectangular box that can appear around any kind of frame, including not only picture frames but also text frames and tables. In Publisher, you can add two types of borders (see Figure 15.1):

- Regular line borders, which appear as a box on all sides of a frame or as lines only on selected sides.
- BorderArt—fun, frilly graphical boxes around frames that add an instant decorative touch.

FIGURE 15.1.

You can add clean, classy borders, or fun and frilly BorderArt.

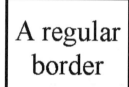

Adding a Simple Box Border

To quickly add a simple box border around all sides of a frame, select the frame, and then click the Line/Border Style button on the Formatting toolbar (or choose Format | Line/Border Style). The menu shown in Figure 15.2 appears. From the menu, choose

- *Hairline* to apply a box made out of extremely thin, classy-looking border lines.
- Any of the line thicknesses that appear below the Hairline choice, to add a box made up of thicker lines.
- *More Styles*, to add a better border as described next.

FIGURE 15.2.

Quickly adding a box border.

15

Adding a Better Border

You'll usually add a box border to a frame to visually separate it from other nearby objects and make it stand out. But you can also selectively apply border lines only to one or more sides of a frame, not to all, to achieve a particular effect.

For example, on a frame containing a header, you could add a border line only to the bottom of the frame to form a perfect dividing line between the header and the body of the page (like the line under all the headers in this book).

On the Line Border tab of the Border Style dialog (see Figure 15.3), you can not only choose which sides of the frame to add a border to, but you can also choose a color for the border, and choose among a wider range of options for the border thickness.

FIGURE 15.3.

The Border Style dialog.

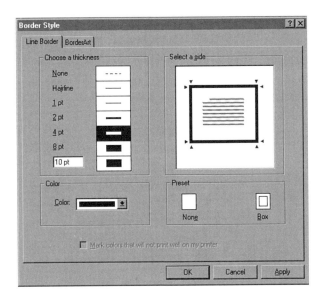

To open the dialog, select the frame and then click the Line/Border Style button on the Formatting toolbar (or choose Format|Line/Border Style) to open the menu. Choose

More Styles from the menu's bottom, and make sure the Line Border tab is selected. Then choose one of the following:

- In the Select A Side box, click a side to which you want to apply a border. You can also use the choices in the Preset box to quickly remove the border from all sides (None) or add it to all sides (Box).

- In the Choose A Thickness box, choose a thickness for the selected border line from the options presented. At the bottom of the Line Border box, you can enter a custom thickness in points (72nds of an inch).

- In the Color box, choose a color (see Hour 16, "Controlling Color").

> Using the Border Style dialog, you can optionally apply different thicknesses or colors of lines to different sides.
>
> In the Select A Side box, choose a side and then choose a thickness or color for it. Then click another side and choose a different thickness or color.

To Do: Add Borders

1. Choose any frame in a pub.
2. Click the Line/Border Style button on the formatting toolbar, and choose Hairline. A nice hairline box appears all around the frame.
3. With the frame still selected, click the Line/Border Style button again, and choose More Styles to open the Border Style dialog.
4. Under Preset, click None. The hairline border disappears from the sample under Select a Side.
5. Under Select a Side, click the top borderline in the sample.
6. Under Choose a Thickness, choose 8 pt. A very heavy, 8-point border appears at the top (only) of the sample.

7. Click OK to close the dialog and see the results in your pub.

Adding Gridlines to Tables

Border lines can appear on any or all of the four sides of a picture, text frame, or table. But a table has not only an outside border, but also *gridlines*—the inside lines between rows, columns, and cells. Using the Line Border tab of the Border Style dialog, you can not only apply border lines to selected outside borders of the table, but to selected gridlines, too.

When you add a new table, you select a table format for it. Some of the more stylish table formats already have carefully selected border and gridlines applied to them.

So another way to get great gridlines is to choose a new table format (see Hour 11, "Shaping Text in Its Frame"). If you choose to fiddle with gridlines, be sure to consider which gridlines already appear in the table.

To choose borders and gridlines for a table, select the parts of the table—cells, rows, columns, or the whole table (see Hour 11) to which you want to apply lines. Then open the tab as usual (Format I Line/Border Style I More Styles). Use the Select A Side box to click the border or gridlines you want to apply lines to, and choose a thickness or color.

To quickly add lines to all sides and gridlines in the selected portion of the table, choose Grid in the Preset box.

Adding a Drop Shadow

NEW TERM   A *drop shadow* adds depth to a frame, making it appear to float slightly above the paper. It is a gray shadow applied to the right side and bottom of a frame (see Figure 15.4) to add a 3D effect.

FIGURE 15.4.

Drop shadows make a frame float.

Drop shadows are a fast, easy way to add drama to your page, and you can add them to any frame (with or without a border). To add a drop shadow, just select the frame and choose Format I Shadow. (To remove the drop shadow, just choose Format I Shadow again.)

Drop shadows are so easy and effective that they're also easily abused. Watch out for using more than one drop shadow on a page, except where two or more small frames must match.

Adding a Really Cool Border

BorderArt runs neat little pictures around a frame to form a graphical border. BorderArt borders are more fun than regular borders, but they're not as flexible—BorderArt always forms a complete box around the frame and cannot be applied just to selected sides.

To apply BorderArt, select the frame and open the Border Style dialog (Format | Line/Border Style | More Styles). Then choose the dialog's BorderArt tab (see Figure 15.5).

FIGURE 15.5.

BorderArt is a fast way to put a frame inside a really wild box.

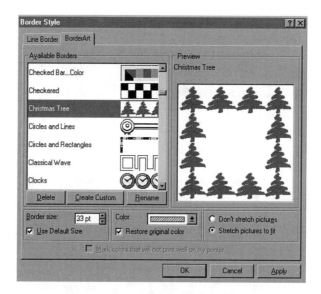

Choose a BorderArt style from the Available Borders list, and evaluate it in the Preview pane. You can also apply any of a number of options on the tab:

- *Border Size*: Increase or decrease the point size to make the border graphics larger or smaller.
- *Color*: Choose a primary color for the BorderArt (see Hour 16).

15

- *Don't Stretch Pictures*: Leave the pictures at their normal shape, which typically will also leave some small, evenly spaced gaps between them.
- *Stretch Pictures to Fit*: To minimize the gaps between the pictures making up the border, stretch the pictures (distorting their shape) so that they almost touch.

> If you've wrapped text around a picture, you cannot apply BorderArt to it. See "Wrapping Text Around Pictures," later in this hour.

Rotating Frames

NEW TERM You can *rotate* any frame, turning it right or left in relation to the page (see Figure 15.6). The obvious reason you might try this is to change the angle of a graphic, turning it sideways or upside down. But you can apply the same technique to rotate text or even a table, for all sorts of creative effects.

FIGURE 15.6.

Rotation lets you put a new spin on a frame.

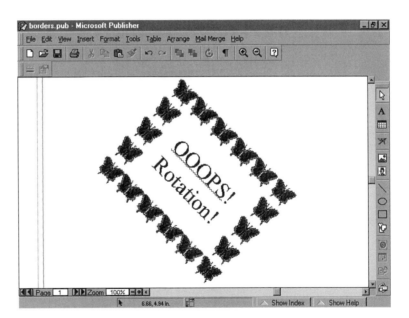

If you intend to print final output on your local printer, check proofs carefully after rotating objects. Older or lower-end printers can produce jagged-
looking, nasty results from rotated objects, particularly text.

If you decide after the fact that you don't want to rotate an object, an easy
way to restore it to its original state is to select it, click the Custom Rotation
button on the Standard toolbar, and then click No Rotation on the dialog
that appears.

To rotate a frame, select it and then choose one of the following:

- To rotate the frame exactly 90 degrees right or left, click the Rotate Left or Rotate
  Right button on the Formatting toolbar. (To turn the object upside-down, click
  either button twice.)

- To custom rotate the object to an angle other than 90 or 180 degrees, click the
  Custom Rotate button on the Standard toolbar to open the Custom Rotate dialog
  (see Figure 15.7). Click either of the large buttons with the circular arrows; each
  click rotates the object 5 degrees in the direction indicated by the arrow.

FIGURE 15.7.

*Use the Custom Rotate
dialog to rotate a
frame in increments of
5 degrees or to easily
undo any rotation.*

To get really tight control over rotation, select the frame, point to a handle,
and press and hold the Alt key. The pointer changes to the Rotate pointer;
while still holding Alt, click and hold the handle, and drag the outline of the
frame to any angle you like.

Grouping and Ungrouping Objects

15

Some objects are really made up of multiple frames. For example, suppose you lay a small text frame on top of a picture or snug up next to the picture frame, for a caption. Or suppose a column contains a table and a text frame containing that table's title or a paragraph introducing the table.

After creating such multipart objects, you want all the object's parts to stay together if you move, scale, or otherwise manipulate the object. You need a way to treat an object made of multiple frames as if it were a single frame.

To do that, you group the frames. When a set of frames are grouped, they act like a single frame or object. You can move that object, scale it, or rotate it, and all its parts stay together.

To group frames into a single object, click the Pointer tool on the Objects toolbar. Press and hold the Shift key, and while holding it click on each frame that belongs in the group. A puzzle icon appears on the object when it's selected (see Figure 15.8); when you've clicked all the frames that belong in it, release the Shift key and click the puzzle icon to group the objects (the puzzle pieces lock together to show that the objects are grouped).

FIGURE 15.8.

The puzzle icon indicates grouped objects.

Caption goes here

To ungroup the object later so that you can manipulate just part of it, click the puzzle icon or choose Arrange | Ungroup Objects.

Most of the Design Gallery objects are made of grouped frames. To customize an object you've inserted from the Design Gallery, you can ungroup the object and rearrange it, adding or deleting objects if you want, and then regroup when you're finished.

Wrapping Text Around Pictures

NEW TERM When text *wraps* around an object, the lines of text break at points that follow the contours of the object (see Figure 15.9). Text wrapping lends a professional appearance to newsletters, ads, and other pubs where there might be a close relationship between words and pictures.

To wrap text, you must first position a picture on top of a text frame. Then right-click the picture and choose Format | Picture Frame Properties to open the frame's Picture Frame Properties dialog (see Figure 15.9).

FIGURE 15.9.

Use a picture frame's Picture Frame Properties dialog to control how the text in a frame beneath it wraps around the picture.

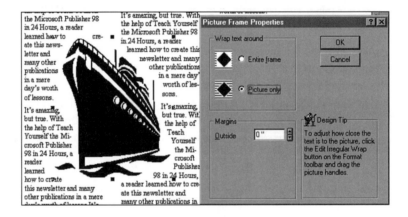

- To make text wrap around the outside of the rectangular frame holding the picture, click the top option button, Entire Frame.
- To make text ignore the boundaries of the picture frame and instead conform to the contours of the picture itself, click the Picture Only button.

To Do: Rotate and Wrap

▼ **To Do**

1. Begin in any pub containing both a picture and a column or more of text.
2. Drag the picture frame so that it intrudes upon the text. The text will wrap to the picture frame by default.
3. With the picture frame selected, click the Custom Rotate button; then adjust the Angle on the Custom Rotate dialog to 45 degrees. Close the dialog.
4. With the picture frame selected, choose Format | Picture Frame Properties and then click the Picture Only button on the dialog that appears. The text wraps to the contours of the rotated picture.

▲

Summary

Sometimes, it all seems like too much, doesn't it? There are so many things you can do to a frame—add borders or BorderArt, rotate, add a drop shadow, and more. But the thing to keep in mind is that all these techniques are additive—they add optional touches of style or visual interest, when needed.

So don't feel like you're obliged to apply any of these techniques. Just remember that they're available to you when a page appears to need just a little more *ooomph*.

Workshop

The following workshop helps solidify the skills you learned in this lesson.

Q&A

Q I wrapped text around a picture and it looks pretty cool, except my eye says there's not quite enough whitespace around the picture, between picture and text. What can I do?

A When you feel that the words are crowding the image—or, conversely, that there's too much whitespace around the picture—you can adjust the Margins measurements in the Picture Frame Properties dialog (the same one you used to make the text wrap).

If the Margins in the Picture Frame Properties dialog are already at 0, and you want to wrap even closer, select the text frame, open its Properties dialog (Format | Text Frame Properties), and decrease the margins there.

Quiz

Take the following quiz to see how much you've learned.

Questions

1. To add a heavy border line to just the cells in the top row of a table:

    a. Select the cells, click the Line/Border Style button, and choose a heavy line.

    b. Select the table, click the Line/Border Style button, click More Styles, and use the Select a Side box to apply lines only to those cells.

    c. Put box borders around each cell, one at a time.

    d. All the above.

2. If you see a perfect box made up of little apples, it must be

   a. BorderLine

   b. BorderLand

   c. BorderFruit

   d. BorderArt

3. When multiple frames are grouped, if you scale them down, they all scale down together, as a unit. (True/False)

Answers

1. (d) All would work, but (a) is probably easiest

2. (d)

3. True

Activities

Examine some of the less silly BorderArt options, and consider where they might play a role in your pubs.

HOUR 16

Controlling Color

You can do anything you want with color in a pub. Except that you can't. And that's the tricky part.

You see, Publisher's tools enable you to apply almost any imaginable color to text, borders, drawing objects, frame backgrounds, and more, in any combination. But your color choices must be limited to those colors that look good together, and to colors that can be produced effectively by the device on which the pub will ultimately be printed.

In this hour, you'll discover the considerations you must take into account before applying colors to objects. Then you'll learn how to apply those colors. At the end of the hour, you'll be able to answer the following questions:

- What do I have to know about color, and about where I will print my pub, before I can start using color in it?
- How can I avoid color problems by setting up my local printer properly?
- What's a color scheme and how do I choose one?

- How do I color objects in my pubs?
- How do I achieve dressy effects with color variants such as tints, patterns, and gradients?

What's the Big Deal About Color?

Of course, color matters because color matters. Using color in your pub draws attention to it and makes it more appealing to the reader. As when picking out an outfit of clothing, you must make sure that the colors you choose go well together, and that the colors (and amount of color) you use suit the occasion—or rather, the market or community the pub must appeal to.

But there's a lot more to consider about color than picking colors that look good. As you know, Publisher is a WYSIWYG (what you see is what you get) DTP program, which attempts to show onscreen an accurate representation of what you'll get when you print. It does a pretty good job at that, but where color is concerned, it can miss the mark to a greater or lesser degree, for a variety of reasons:

- Color matching between onscreen colors and colors of ink is never perfect, even with the best equipment. Colors that look great—and look great together— onscreen might not look so good on paper.
- Depending on how carefully you've configured the Print Setup dialog or outside printing options for your pub, Publisher might enable you to apply colors that can't be printed—or can't be printed well—on the device you'll use for printing.
- If you intend to save money on outside printing by applying spot color rather than full, or process, color, you must make this choice before applying colors so that Publisher can guide your color choices appropriately.

You deal with these color issues differently, depending on whether you'll print on a home or office color printer or use a professional "outside" printing service.

Color Considerations for Local Printing

If you will do your final color printing on your own color inkjet or thermal printer, the following steps will help ensure the best results. Note that the order of the steps matters.

1. Make sure that you have installed the proper printer driver for your color printer in Windows, and that you have used the Print Setup dialog (discussed in Hour 8, "Printing Proofs") to select your color printer for the pub.
2. Go to the General tab of Publisher's Options dialog (Tools|Options) and make sure that the check box for Improve Screens and Color Matching has been checked.

3. Begin to add a fill color to any frame, and then choose More Colors, just as an excuse to open the Color dialog. On the dialog, check the Mark Colors That Will Not Print Well On My Printer check box. All colors that are poor choices for your printer will remain available to you, but will have an X struck through them on all color dialogs to remind you to avoid them.

4. Choose a color scheme for the pub, as described later in this hour. After choosing a scheme, check the dialog's Custom tab to see if any colors in the scheme have Xs through them, and change any that do (or try another scheme).

5. Apply colors to the objects in your pub, as described in this hour. Apply only colors that are in the scheme.

6. Whenever you print, first click the Properties button on the Print dialog, and make sure the options for your printer have all been set to their highest quality color mode (see Figure 16.1).

FIGURE 16.1.

Clicking Properties on the Print dialog opens a dialog of options specific to your printer, which you can use to configure your printer to its highest quality color mode.

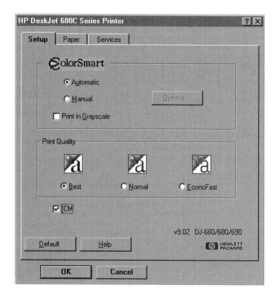

Color Considerations for Outside Printing

If you will hire a printing service to do your printing, you have the option to print all the color you want. But as you'll learn in Hour 17, "Setting Up for a Printing Service," the more colors you use, the more costly the job.

There's a reason why the only color you see in this book is on the cover. The cost of printing color on every page is so high that this book would have to cost $50 if printed in full color. Where this pub is concerned, the value added by color is not sufficient to justify the cost. That's the kind of choice you'll be making when planning the color in pubs that will be printed professionally.

I won't get into all the ins and outs of using a printing service now—that's coming up in less than an hour. All I want to tell you is that whenever possible, you should perform all the steps for setting up a pub to be printed by a service *before* you start choosing colors.

One step in that process requires choosing between simple spot color and full, or *process*, color. If you choose spot color, all the color dialogs from which you add colors will show only the colors your spot color choices allow. The dialogs prevent you from using a color you can't print.

If you choose the (usually) costlier Full Color option for a pub that will be printed by a service, Publisher enables you to apply virtually any color imaginable in your pub. But that's not a license to go nuts....

Choosing a Color Scheme

After you've configured for the final printing of a pub as described earlier, it's time to pick a color scheme. Color schemes are used in all pubs that will be printed locally or printed in full color (not spot color) by a printing service.

There's no need to choose a color scheme for a spot-color job (in fact, doing so is impossible); all the color dialogs are automatically limited to the spot colors you selected when setting up the pub for the printing service.

All pubs start out with a default color scheme, or one you selected in the wizard when creating the pub from a template.

Picking a Standard Scheme

To choose a color scheme for your pub, open the pub and choose Format | Color Scheme. The Color Scheme dialog opens (see Figure 16.2). Each of the Available Schemes has up to six different colors: a main color (usually black) and up to five accent colors.

FIGURE **16.2.**

*Choosing a color
scheme to keep all
your colors in order.*

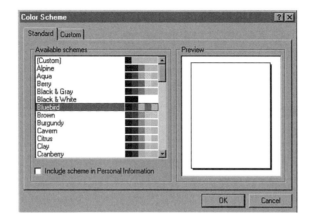

As you scroll through the list and single-click any schemes that look interesting, the
Preview pane shows how your pub would look if its current scheme were swapped for
the one you selected.

To Do: Choose a Color Scheme

1. From the Catalog, use the wizard to create a new newsletter (any type). When the
    wizard prompts you to choose a color scheme, choose one.

2. After clicking Finish and closing the wizard, choose Format I Color Scheme to
    open the Color Scheme dialog.

3. One by one, click through the Available Schemes shown in the Standard tab.
    Observe the way each new scheme changes the pub's appearance in the Preview
    pane.

4. When you come to a scheme you like, click OK to assign it to the pub.

> The colors in a pub are assigned, under the covers, to the color scheme cate-
> gories: main, accent 1, and so on. That's why Publisher automatically knows
> which color to use if you change schemes.
>
> However, all that matters when you're picking a scheme is which colors it
> includes, not where they're already applied. After picking a scheme, you can
> apply the accent 2 color where main used to be, for example. You can apply
> any color in the scheme to any object in the pub.
>
> So don't be put off if the preview doesn't show the colors where you want
> them applied. Just consider whether they're the right colors.

Creating a Custom Color Scheme

If none of the schemes listed in the Standard tab of the Color Schemes dialog floats your boat, pick the one that's closest to what you want, then click the dialog's Custom tab (see Figure 16.3).

FIGURE 16.3.

Use the Custom tab to make a new, customized color scheme.

The colors in the Custom tab at first show those in the scheme you clicked in the Standard tab. To change any color, click the arrow on the New box for that color to drop down a table of basic colors from which you can choose. Click a color to change that particular scheme color.

On the table of colors from which you can choose colors for custom schemes, you'll notice two buttons: More Colors and Fill Effects, each of which opens a dialog of the same name. These dialogs expand the range of colors you may choose and allow you to define patterns or textures as coloring for objects.

You'll learn more about these dialogs in the next section.

Coloring Objects

After all that preparation and consideration, actually adding color to objects is pretty easy.

When you choose colors, Publisher tries to help you keep to your chosen color scheme two ways:

The color menus that appear first always prominently display the scheme colors as your fastest, most obvious choices.

You can always choose the More Colors option (as you learn to do later) to choose any color, even those outside the scheme. But if you open the Color Scheme dialog in a pub that contains colors that are not in the scheme (either because you added those colors from outside the scheme or changed schemes), a dialog appears, asking whether you want colors outside the scheme changed to the nearest color in the scheme. Click Yes to make the change.

Coloring Text

To apply color to text, select the text and then click the Font Color button on the Formatting toolbar (or choose Format|Font, and drop down the Color list on the Font dialog). A menu appears, like the one in Figure 16.4. Choose one of the scheme colors from the top row.

FIGURE 16.4.

All menus for adding colors to objects appear very much like this one, for coloring text.

The other row of colored squares on the color dialog is a row of colors you've used recently, which might or might not be scheme colors.

If you want to step outside the scheme, click the More Colors button on the Font Color menu to open the Colors dialog. The Colors dialog can appear two different ways, depending on the option button you choose at its top:

- Click Basic Colors (see Figure 16.5) to see a table of 84 basic colors you can use, arranged in columns. Each column contains colors that work well together, so try to choose all colors from the same column.

- Click All Colors to display a palette from which you can choose from among thousands of colors. To use the palette, drag the big crosshairs around on it, watching the Color box in the lower-left corner. When the Color box shows the color you want, click OK.

In the All Colors view of the Colors dialog (see Figure 16.6), the Color box shows the closest approximation Windows can display onscreen of the color you selected, which might or might not be a perfect match. The Solid box shows the closest solid (Basic) color to the color in the Color box.

Onscreen in your pub, Publisher uses the color from the Solid box to represent the color you select. But when you print, Publisher will still attempt as close a match as possible to the actual color you selected.

FIGURE **16.5.**

*Use the Basic Colors
view of the Colors dia-
log to choose among
the 84 basic colors.*

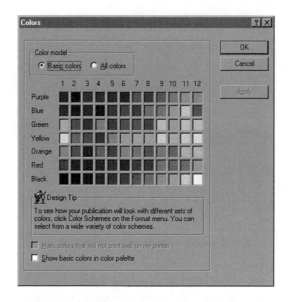

FIGURE **16.6.**

*Use the All Colors
view of the Colors dia-
log to choose any
color from an infinitely
variable palette.*

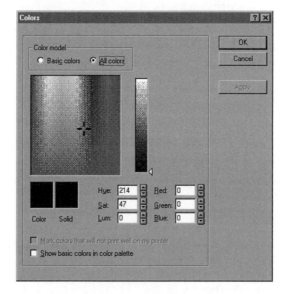

The All Colors tab enables you to easily select colors that might not display
accurately on your screen or print well. Using this tab of the Colors dialog
isn't recommended unless you will print in full (or *process*) color at a printing service (see Hour 17) and work closely with your printer to ensure that
colors are printed accurately.

Coloring Borders and Lines

To color any kind of line—frame borders, table borders and gridlines, shape outlines, and drawn lines—select the frame, table cells, or object to color, then click the Line/Border Style button on the Formatting toolbar (or choose Format|Line/Border Styles).

From the menu, choose More Styles to open the Border Style menu. Then choose a color from the list provided, which has the identical choices offered on the font color menu (refer to Figure 16.4).

16

Filling in a Frame or Shape with Color

NEW TERM A *fill* is a color that fills in the whole background of a frame (but doesn't cover the frame's contents) or fills in a drawn shape.

You can use a fill in a text frame to add a background color for the text, or fill in the background of a picture frame around the picture itself. You can even add colored fills to table cells. And of course, you can fill drawing objects to turn shape outlines into solid, colored shapes.

To fill, select the object you want to fill; then click the Fill Color button on the Formatting toolbar (or choose Format|Fill Color).

A color menu appears (it's almost identical to the font color menu), from which you choose the color. The menu for fill colors has an extra button on the top, No Fill, so you can easily remove the fill color.

To Do: Color Text and Fill Frames

1. Open (or create) a practice pub containing text.
2. Select a text frame.
3. Click the Font Color button on the formatting toolbar to open the color menu.
4. In the scheme colors shown, choose the lightest color. (Your text might become so light that it's hard to see, but don't worry about that now.)
5. With the text frame still selected, click the Fill Color button on the formatting toolbar.
6. In the scheme colors shown, choose the darkest color. A dark background fills the frame, and the light colored text stands out against it—this is known as *reverse text*.

Adding Fill Effects to Colors

Not every new color *is* a new color. What I mean is that existing colors can be given a new look through the use of three different kinds of patterns that change a color's appearance and sometimes also add textures or special effects to a color (see Figure 16.7):

- *Tints/Shades*: Variants of a color made lighter by adding white (tints) or made darker by adding black (shades).
- *Patterns*: Geometric patterns that subtly change the look of a solid color, adding texture and depth.
- *Gradients*: Like patterns, except that they change over the area they fill, getting lighter in some areas and darker or denser in others. Gradients add an irregular, attention-getting 3D effect to a color.

FIGURE 16.7.

Use fill effects to give plain colors more moxie.

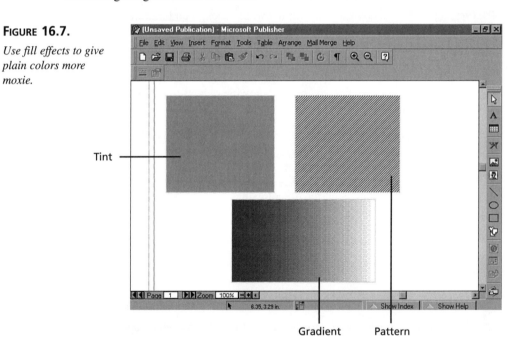

Anyplace you see the Fill Effects button, you have the option to add a fill effect to a color. That button appears on all the color menus, even those used to create custom color schemes.

Click the Fill Effects button to open the Fill Effects dialog (see Figure 16.8); then choose an option button along the top of the dialog to choose Tints/Shades, Patterns, or Gradients. Scroll through the options and click any that look interesting; the effect of your choice is displayed in the sample at the bottom of the dialog. When you see the desired effect, click OK.

To remove fill effects, return to the Fill Effects dialog and choose the tint, pattern, or gradient option farthest to the left.

FIGURE 16.8.

Choose fill effects from the Fill Effects dialog.

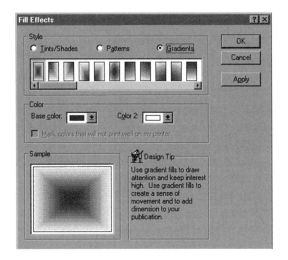

16

Patterns and gradients each are made up of two colors: A base color (the color already selected for the object before you clicked Fill Effects) and a contrasting second color. You can make a pattern or fill more subtle—or more bold—by varying the second color.

Recoloring a Picture

When a picture is made up of a single color—or you want it to be made up of just one color—you can change and choose the color and ensure that it's within the scheme.

Obviously, you don't want to knock a full-color photograph down to just a single color—unless you're doing so to use the photo in a more graphical way, deliberately dumping its realistic coloring. But you can change any picture to a single color of your choice, which can be very useful when you plan to print in spot color (see Hour 17).

To recolor a picture, select the picture and choose Format|Recolor Picture to open the Recolor Object dialog (see Figure 16.9). Choose a color from the Color menu, and observe the results in the Preview pane. When you see what you want, click OK.

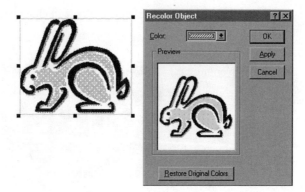

FIGURE 16.9.

Use Recolor Object to choose one—and only one—color for a picture.

To convert a color photograph to black-and-white, choose Black in the Recolor Object dialog.

To restore the original color or colors to a picture you've recolored, return to the Recolor Object dialog and click the Restore Original Colors button.

Summary

Just about any new car sold today can exceed 100 MPH, even though speed limits rarely exceed 60 or 70 MPH. Drive Publisher's color capabilities like a car: Choose colors not based on what Publisher *can* do, but on what's prudent, possible (through the device you'll print on), and tasteful. And always buckle up.

Workshop

The following workshop helps solidify the skills you learned in this lesson.

Q&A

Q A friend told me I need to learn about color models to do DTP. What's a color model? Is it like a supermodel?

A A *color model* is a way of standardizing how each color in the spectrum is described and represented by a device. Color models help printers and other graphics pros work with color more accurately, ensuring that the customer gets the colors he or she wants or expects.

There are several different standards for color models, and usually separate models for onscreen colors and ink colors. You'll learn a little bit more about color models in Hour 17, but the truth is that there's not much you can do in Publisher that demands any understanding of color models.

So when your friend starts showing off by blabbing about color models, just nod your head knowingly.

Quiz

Take the following quiz to see how much you've learned.

Questions

1. Which of the following usually should be done last?

    a. Configure the printer for a pub.

    b. Choose a color scheme.

    c. Choose colors for objects.

    d. Set up for outside printing.

2. The Fill Effects button you see on most color menus opens a dialog on which you can add

    a. Fill colors.

    b. A tint, shade, pattern, or gradient.

    c. Gravel, sand, or other clean fill (for drainage).

    d. All the above.

3. If you're careful about color, the colors you see onscreen will always be perfect matches for what you'll see on paper. (True/False)

Answers

1. (c) Set up printing and schemes before applying colors.

2. (b) Those are the "effects."

3. False. Being careful gets you closer, but a perfect match never happens. That's why careful proofing and working closely with your printer are essential.

Activities

Start a new pub, and choose or create a color scheme with nothing but black and one shade of gray. Now use all the color-free tools at your disposal—fonts, borders, drop shadows, gradients, and so on—to create a really snazzy page with nothing but black and gray. You might be surprised by how much you can do with little or no color.

PART V
Publishing on Paper

Hour

HOUR 17

Setting Up for a Printing Service

Publisher makes setting up for commercial printing easy—understanding your options is a little tricky. In this hour, I'll introduce you to the options and issues you must understand before you can select a printing service and set up for it. Then I'll show you how to set up and prepare your files for printing.

At the end of the hour, you'll be able to answer the following questions:

- What types of printing options do I need to discuss with a printing service, both to plan my pub and to choose the right service for me?
- How do I install a commercial printer driver in Windows to prepare for printing?
- How do I set up a pub for printing at a printing service?
- How do I print two documents that help me choose and communicate with a printing service?

Many DTP folks use the term *service bureau* to describe what I've been calling a *printing service*. Service bureau might be the more commonly used term, but I've favored printing service because that's the term you'll see in menu items and dialogs in Publisher, so I want to help you recognize it.

Service bureau recalls a time when there was a sharper distinction between services that prepared your pub for printing (*prepress* services) and those that actually printed it (printers). The line has blurred, and more companies do both jobs, especially for "short runs" (a small number of copies).

It's not a big deal either way. Just remember that a printing service and a service bureau are basically the same thing.

Planning for Printing

Before jumping into preparing your files for a printing service, you must know a little bit about the issues you will consider when dealing with a printing service. All these issues must be taken into account because each affects the other; for example, the paper or kind of color you choose might affect the choice of equipment required. And every choice you make—I mean every single one—can affect the cost of the job. After making your choices, you can solicit a quote from several different printing services to make an apples-to-apples comparison.

Of course, you probably won't choose a service by price alone. Available equipment, predicted turnaround time, and other factors should all play a role in your decision.

Frankly, because you're just starting out with printing services, the service that's most willing to take the time to explain your options to you and to provide helpful, patient service should rank high on your list.

I can't stress enough the importance of talking to printing services, both before choosing a service and after, to nail down the particulars of the job. In this hour I'm showing you the basics, but every service has its own approaches and method of doing things. To work productively with a service you must get to know the service, and the service needs to know you.

After setting up your pub for a printing service (as described later in this hour), you'll have the opportunity to print two important documents, one of which is the Printing Service Checklist.

The first part of that checklist is a questionnaire you can use with prospective printing services to evaluate the service and its capabilities. That's a valuable tool—but you don't get it until you finish setting up.

I therefore advise a four-stage approach to choosing a printing service:

1. Set up the pub for a printing service (even though you haven't chosen one yet), and supply your best guesses for the printing service particulars.

2. Print out the Printing Service Checklist.

3. Take the checklist and a printout of your pub to printing services, to help you choose one.

4. When you've chosen one, set up for a printing service again, this time plugging in the correct choices for the service you've selected.

Equipment

17

Most printing services have several different printers—or *output devices*—they use for different types of jobs. For example, the service might use a professional-quality laser, inkjet, or dye-sublimation printer for low-cost, medium resolution (300–600 dpi) prints when magazine-quality sharpness is not required.

Large print runs, true magazine-quality sharpness, and high-quality color photoreproduction typically demand a device called an *imagesetter*, which produces the best-looking output and runs at resolutions of 1,200 dpi, 2,000 dpi, and higher. Imagesetter services are more expensive than the alternatives and might not be available from smaller print services and copy shops.

Paper

The type of paper on which your pub is printed affects not only the way the pub looks and feels, but also its printing cost, turnaround time, and other factors. Pubs of certain sizes and configurations might require types or sizes of paper that the service can use only in a limited selection of devices, limiting your options.

A matte-finish, soft paper (like typical copier paper) absorbs ink in a way that slightly blurs the dots that make up the image, blending the dots together. This makes softer papers an excellent choice for medium-resolution budget printing on a laser or dye-sublimation printer—except when you've used very small text (6 points or less), which can get pretty blurry on soft paper.

However, shiny, glossy paper like magazines use tends to make the dots more apparent, which means the service will use an imagesetter to get satisfactory results on such paper.

If you've chosen to use any of the special papers supported by Publisher, you must make sure the print service carries that paper, or you must purchase the paper yourself and supply it to the printer.

The paper is sold by a company called Paper Direct. You may find a Paper Direct catalog and discount coupon in your Publisher box. You can also call Paper Direct toll-free at 800-A-PAPERS, or visit www.paperdirect.com.

Software

Any good service bureau can apply a range of software tools to improve your pub. In particular, the service can apply color management or *trapping* software (which prevents gaps between spot colors and adjacent text or other black objects) to ensure the best results.

Your print service need not use Publisher—as you learn later, you can easily prepare files for a print service that does not have Publisher. In fact, you can even use a print service that doesn't have PCs or Windows (some services use only Macs).

However, there are advantages to using a printing service that uses Publisher:

- The print service staff will know any quirks in the way Publisher files play on their equipment and can easily anticipate and correct any problems that might come up.
- If small, last-minute problems are discovered in your pub, such as copyfit troubles (discussed in Hour 18, "Working with Proofs"), the service can fix them for you in Publisher.
- The service might be able to apply its color management or other tools to greater effect when it can open and edit your pub.
- If there's a part of your pub you couldn't do yourself, the service can finish up for you. For example, if you want to add a photo but don't have a scanner, you can leave a hole in the layout and supply the service with your Publisher files and a snapshot. The service can take care of the rest.

My advice is this: Don't make having Publisher a requirement for your service, but all other things being equal, lean toward one that does.

Color: Grayscale, Spot, Full

There are three basic kinds of color printing, listed here from costliest to cheapest (generally). You and your printing service will work together to choose the best option for your pub.

- *Full color* (also called process color or CMYK color): If your pub includes color photographs, you need full-color printing to reproduce it effectively. Full-color printing not only costs the most, but depending on your service, it might require that you supply originals of any photos so that professional *color separations* (separate files for each of the four ink colors used in full-color printing) can be created.

- *Spot color*: In a pub without color photos, you can save on printing costs by foregoing full-color printing for one or more spot colors. A pub using only one spot color can actually have many "colors" in it, because it can show not only black, white, gray, and the spot color itself, but any tint or shade of that color (refer to Hour 16, "Controlling Color").

> Spot-color jobs using one or two spot colors are generally cheaper than full-color jobs (though some services might charge nearly as much for just two spot colors as for full color).
>
> A pub with three or more spot colors would almost certainly cost as much as a full-color job, in which case there's no point in not going to full color. For that reason, Publisher does not permit you to select more than two spot colors.

- *Black, white, and gray (or grayscale)*: The least costly option, good grayscale printing can even be done on a professional laser printer, which might be capable of imagesetter resolution (1,200 dpi).

Printing and Binding Options

Any pub printed on multiple sheets must be bound in some way to form the final pub. Printers bind pubs in two principal ways (although there are other, optional choices, such as spiral binding):

- *Saddle stitch*: The book is formed by printing four pages to a sheet (one spread on each side of a wide sheet or paper), and then folding the sheets together and stitching (or, more often, stapling) the fold. Saddle stitching is the cheaper option, but works only for shorter pubs (under 100 pages).

- *Perfect bound*: The book is formed by printing and binding several smaller booklets, called *signatures*, and then gluing the signatures into a flat spine. The book you're holding is perfect bound.

17

NEW TERM   A *signature* is a saddle-stitched, bound set of pages, often 16 or 24, that form
            one part of a book or magazine, which will be made by binding multiple signa-
tures together. If you look closely at the edge of the binding of this book, you'll see that
it's made up of a dozen or so signatures.

In a pub made of signatures, the total number of pages must be a multiple of the number
of pages in a signature. For example, in a pub printed on 24-page signatures, you cannot
have 230 pages. You must cut some pages to get down to 216 pages (nine 24-page signatures), or add pages (or allow some blank pages) to reach 240 pages (ten 24-page signatures).

Choosing a Commercial Print Driver

Ideally, after you've selected a printing service, that service will supply you with a disk
containing the Windows print driver for the device on which your pub will ultimately be
printed. Installing that driver and then selecting it when setting up for commercial printing (described next) will greatly improve the chances that what you see in print is a good
match for what you see onscreen.

If your print service supplies you with a driver, install it as follows:

1. Insert the disk in your PC and open your My Computer icon.
2. In My Computer, choose Printers. In the Printers folder, choose Add Printer to
   open the Add Printer Wizard; then follow the wizard's prompts.

If your printing service does not supply you with a driver disk, you might be able to use
one of the Microsoft commercial printing drivers, which were installed automatically
when you installed Publisher. The drivers support the commercial equipment listed in
Table 17.1.

If your pub uses spot color, you cannot use the Microsoft Publisher Color
Printer driver. You must use the Microsoft Publisher Imagesetter driver or a
driver from your printing service. Spot color generally requires an
imagesetter.

TABLE 17.1. COMMERCIAL PRINTERS SUPPORTED BY THE MICROSOFT PUBLISHER PRINTER DRIVERS.

Microsoft Publisher Imagesetter	Microsoft Publisher Color Printer
Agfa ProSet 9550	Canon CLC 500 with Efi Fiery RIP
Agfa SelectSet 5000	Compaq PageMarq 20
Linotronics 330	Hewlett-Packard Laserjet 4MV
Linotronics 530	Indigo E Print 1000
Linotronics Herkules 50	Tektronix Phaser 300l
Scitex Dolev 200 PS/M	Tektronix Phaser 340l
Varityper 4000	Tektronix Phaser llld
Varityper VT-800	Xerox Docutech
Xante PS 1200	

17

To use one of these drivers, select it when setting up your pub for commercial printing, as described next.

Setting Up a Pub for Commercial Printing

After you understand your options, actually setting up a pub for commercial printing takes only a minute or two, as you'll see in the following To Do. Note that you can repeat the procedure at any time to change your choices. That's important because you might want to do it once early in your pub's development to make a few basic choices and so you can get the Print Service Checklist (described next) to help you choose a service. After choosing a service, you can go back and firm up your settings.

To Do: Set Up for Commercial Printing

1. Open (or quickly create from a wizard) a pub containing at least some color. (Note that, depending on the specifics of the pub you choose, the dialogs that appear next might differ slightly from what I describe.)

2. Choose File | Prepare File for Printing Service | Set Up Publication. A dialog appears, asking you to choose your color printing options (see Figure 17.1). If you choose

   • Black, White, and Shades of Gray or Full Color, skip to step 4.

   • Spot Color, move ahead to step 3.

▼   . 3. From the list that appears after you choose Spot Color (see Figure 17.1), choose a color for Spot Color 1. If you will use two spot colors, choose a Spot Color 2 as well.

> After you've chosen spot colors, when you work in this pub Publisher will not show any other color except those that can print using your spot color selections: black, white, gray, and shades and tints of up to two spot colors. Any other color you add to the pub appears (and will print) in gray.

FIGURE 17.1.

When setting up for a printing service, begin by choosing your color options.

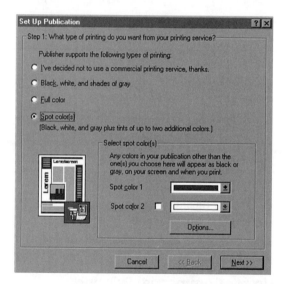

4. Click Next. A dialog prompts you to select a printer (see Figure 17.2). The choice you make here should be the device on which the pub will be printed at the service. (Your choice here has no effect on how the pub will print when you print proofs on your own local printer.)

If you have already installed a driver for the commercial printer you'll use, click the Select a Specific Printer button, then click the arrow button that appears on the dialog. A simplified Print Setup dialog appears, on which you can choose the

▼   printer from a list.

▼   If you know that the printer you will use is supported by one of Microsoft's commercial printer drivers (refer to Table 17.1), or if you have not yet chosen your service, choose Use Publisher's Commercial Printer Driver.

FIGURE 17.2.

Use this step to choose the printer driver for your service.

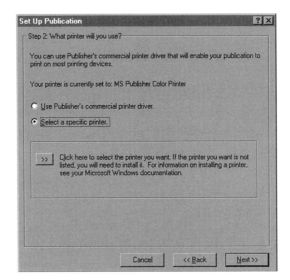

If you choose to use Publisher's commercial printer drivers just because you have not yet chosen a service and obtained a driver, do this after choosing a service:

Obtain and install the correct printer driver, and then open the pub and choose File | Prepare File for Printing Service | Change Printer Settings. The simplified Print Setup dialog appears, so you can select a printer from the list. As always, remember that the choice you make affects *only* how your pub will be prepared for the printer, not how it will print on your own local printer.

5. What happens next depends on whether you see a Done button on the dialog shown in Figure 17.2:

    • If you see a Done button, there are no more dialogs to complete. Click Done, and you're…done.

    • If you don't see a Done button, click Next to display a third and final dialog, and move to step 6.

▼

▼ 6. The third dialog (see Figure 17.3) is required for spot-color jobs and others going to an imagesetter. Choose your options (both check boxes are checked by default, which is usually best):

- *Automatically Choose "Extra" Paper Sizes*: Often, a pub must be printed on paper that's larger than the pub size, for a variety of different reasons. The larger paper is described as an "extra" paper size, one designed to allow the necessary extra space. Checking this check box instructs Publisher to auto matically allow for extra paper sizes when preparing files to print.

- *Show All Printer Marks*: In the extra space, Publisher can display standard printer's marks that tell the printing service where to trim the paper and how to align colors properly.

- After choosing your options, click Done.

FIGURE 17.3.

For some types of pubs, you can choose among options related to "extra" paper sizes.

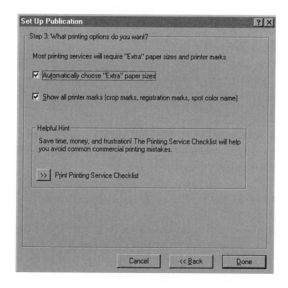

▲

After you prepare a pub for commercial printing, your printing options change slightly. The Print item on the File menu changes to Print Proof to indicate that when you choose it, you print a test printout on your own local printer, using your regular print driver (see Hour 8, "Printing Proofs").

Also, note that the Print button on the Standard toolbar also prints a proof on your local printer, using your regular driver as always.

Preparing a Pub for Printing

After setting up a pub for commercial printing, you can continue to work on it in Publisher until you feel it's ready for press. Then print your publication information and prepare your files.

> Before *really* preparing your pub for press, follow the steps in Hour 18 to make sure it's perfect. Then, after your printing service shows you a proof copy, check it again and make any little final fixes that are necessary.

Printing Publication Information

Setting up a pub for commercial printing makes two new menu items available, each of which prints an important document:

- *The Printing Service Checklist*: The Printing Service Checklist has two parts. Part A (see Figure 17.4) is a questionnaire you can take to a printing service (or use while talking to the service on the phone) to help you decide whether that service is equipped for you, and to help you decide which service is your best choice. Part B of the checklist is a rundown of all the choices you and your printing service must make together.

- *The Publication InfoSheet* lists all the particulars of your job—filename, paper size, colors, and so on. Give this to your printing service, and you will have supplied nearly all the information the service needs to do the job right.

To print these documents, choose File | Prepare File For Printing Service | Print Publication Information, and then choose Printing Services Checklist or Publication InfoSheet.

Preparing the Files

How you prepare files for your printing service depends on whether your service uses Publisher.

If Your Print Service Uses Publisher

Give your printer all of the following:

- The .pub file of the pub to print.

- A sample printout of the pub from your local printer, for reference.

- The Printing Service Checklist and Publication InfoSheet.
- Copies of all font files used in the pub. (You can see a list of the fonts used in your pub on the Publication InfoSheet.)

Your printing service might already have these fonts, but it's best to send them along. To copy a font file to a disk, click the Fonts icon in the Control Panel, click the icon for the font, and choose Edit | Copy. Then open your disk drive icon in My Computer, and choose Edit | Paste.

FIGURE 17.4.

Use the Printing Service Checklist to facilitate communication with printing services.

Printing Service Checklist

Following the steps below will help both you and your printing service get the results you want. This checklist assumes you've already read the Help topic "Decide which printing service options you will use" and know what kind of printing you need. To see that topic, in the Help Index, type **Printing services** and then click **options**.

Part A — Call several printing services to find one that meets your needs

If you need spot-color printing, or high-resolution printing (1200 dpi or higher):

- Tell them what kind of publication you're creating, how many pages it will have, and how many copies you'll need (for example, "I need 500 copies of a 2-page brochure").

Then ask the following questions:

• Can they create output with resolutions greater than 1200 dpi?	Required
• Do they do imagesetting, printing, or both? (Imagesetting creates a film version of a publication, which is then printed by a printing device.)	Service bureau ____ Printer ____ Both ____
• (If your publication uses spot color) Can they print spot color?	Required
• (If your publication uses two spot colors) Can they print two spot colors, or just one?	Required
• Are they familiar with printing from Microsoft Windows? (Recommended.)	____ Y ____ N
• Do they have Publisher 98? (Recommended.)	____ Y ____ N
• Roughly how much will it cost to print your publication? They won't be able to give you an exact figure until you've thoroughly discussed the details of your printing job, but they should be able to ask a few questions and give you a general idea.	Estimate

For full-color printing, or medium-resolution printing (usually between 400 to 600 dpi, and occasionally even higher):

- Tell them what kind of publication you're creating, how many pages it will have, and how many copies you'll need (for example, "I need 40 copies of a 2-page brochure").

Then ask the following questions:

• (If your publication is full color) Do they have a medium-resolution color printer (400 dpi or higher)?	Required
• Are they familiar with printing from Microsoft Windows? (Recommended.)	____ Y ____ N
• Do they have Publisher 98? (Recommended.)	____ Y ____ N
• Roughly how much will it cost to print your publication? They won't be able to give you an exact figure until you've thoroughly discussed the details of your printing job, but they should be able to ask a few questions and give you a general idea.	Estimate

If Your Printing Service Does Not Use Publisher

If your printing service does not use Publisher you must create a PostScript print file of your pub. A PostScript print file is a file that can be printed directly on a PostScript-compatible printer; the file uses the extension .prn.

To create a PostScript print file, choose File | Prepare File For Printing Service | Create File in PostScript. The Create PostScript File dialog opens (see Figure 17.5), which is virtually identical to the Print dialog you're already used to (see Hour 8).

Make sure all the options on the dialog are set as you want them to be when the printer prints, and click OK. A dialog opens from which you can choose a filename and folder for the file you're creating. Type a name, and choose your disk drive as the location.

FIGURE 17.5.

The Create PostScript File dialog.

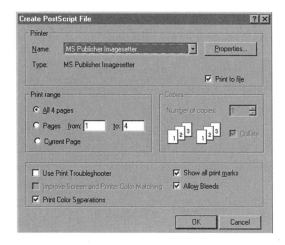

17

In addition to your PostScript file, be sure to supply the following to your printing service:

- A sample printout of the pub from your local printer for reference.
- The Printing Service Checklist and Publication InfoSheet.

Summary

Success with a printing service is all about preparation. Ask the right questions, choose the right settings, and you're set.

Workshop

The following workshop helps solidify the skills you learned in this lesson.

Q&A

Q My ready-for-the-printer file is too large to fit on a disk, and I don't have a writable CD-ROM drive or Zip drive. How can I get the files to the print service?

A Many printing services accept files by modem, either through the Internet or directly through the phone lines. You might also be able to fit the files on a disk (or make them travel through a modem faster) by using a file compression utility, such as WinZip, to compress the files. Talk to your printing service about what types of compressed files the service can accept.

You might also want to question why your pub file is so large; it's possible that you're using photos scanned at unnecessarily high resolutions (see Hour 13, "Getting Graphics").

Q You mentioned earlier that I can use online printing services on the Web. How would I do that?

A That depends on the service. Typically, you transmit your pub files (or PostScript print files) to the service through the Internet and supply a credit card number (for payment) and a mailing address (so the service knows where to send the job). In Appendix A, "Internet Resources for Publisher Users," you'll find addresses of a variety of online printing services; you can visit those pages to explore what they offer (no obligation!).

But for a beginner, it's important to have a helpful, local printing service you can deal with face to face. I don't recommend trying an online printing service until you've already had some experience dealing with a "live" one.

Quiz

Take the following quiz to see how much you've learned.

Questions

1. Which is the best printer driver to use for a pub that will be printed at a printing service:

    a. A driver supplied to you by your printing service

    b. One of Microsoft's commercial printing drivers

    c. Any old driver you happen to have

    d. A designated driver

2. A spot-color job may be no cheaper than a full-color job if it includes two or more spot colors. (True/False)

Answers

1. (a) Always use the driver your print service supplies.
2. True. The cost benefits of spot color erode as you add colors.

Activities

Find your local printing services. Look in the Yellow Pages under "Printers" and also "Copies." Drop by a few, pick up their brochures or price lists, and start to pick out shops you want to learn more about.

17

Hour **18**

Working with Proofs

There are two critical points at which to evaluate the final appearance of your publication: Right before you prepare it for a printer, and again when the printer shows you a proof before printing. Why check twice? Well, even though Publisher is WYSIWYG and all, there will inevitably be differences between what you see on your screen and printer and what you see in a proof from the printing service. Nothing's perfect.

For example, tiny, imperceptible differences in character spacing or line spacing might, multiplied over the course of a pub, change line breaks and hyphenation and add a line or two to a story (possibly pushing a line into the overflow area) or shorten the story by a line or two (creating unwanted whitespace). Also, picture and photo imperfections too small to notice on your equipment might become glaringly noticeable when printed by the printing service's equipment.

In this hour, you'll learn about finding and fixing some subtle, common flaws you'll likely find. At the end of the hour, you'll be able to answer the following questions:

- How can I solicit design cleanup advice from Publisher?
- What are widows and orphans, and how do I fix them?
- What other particular proof problems do I need to watch out for?
- What can I do if my photos look lousy in print?
- How do I mark corrections on a proof for a printer?

Asking Publisher to Critique Your Pub's Design

Always trust your eyes. If you like the way your pub looks, no arbitrary rules about how it's supposed to look should sway you. Then again, if you want a little professional advice about stuff in your pub, Publisher's Design Checker is there to help. The Design Checker scans your pub for potential problems and points these out to you. Like most critics, it doesn't really help you make changes, it just points out stuff you might consider fixing. Keep in mind that you're under no obligation to follow the Design Checker's advice.

To run the Design Checker, open the pub you want to check, choose Tools | Design Checker, and then follow the prompts. You can use the following To Do to get the hang of the Design Checker.

To Do: Check Your Design

1. Open a pub you've been working on, preferably one with a few obvious problems.
2. Choose Tools | Design Checker. A dialog opens to ask you which pages of the pub to check.
3. Click OK to use the default setting (check All Pages in the Pub).
4. The Design Checker locates the first object in the page that it considers a potential problem, and displays a dialog like the one in Figure 18.1.

FIGURE 18.1.

Choose Tools | Design Checker to locate design flaws.

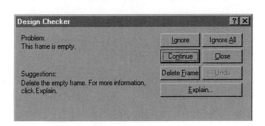

The dialog describes the problem and offers a suggestion for repairing it. While viewing the Design Checker's advice, you can do the following:

- Click in the pub and make whatever change the Checker recommends. Then click the Checker's Continue button to proceed to the next problem.
- Click Ignore to instruct the Checker to ignore this particular problem and move ahead to the next.
- Click Ignore All to instruct the Checker to ignore this type of problem, both here and anywhere else in the page or site.
- Click Explain to display Help Text about the problem at hand.
- Click Close to quit the Design Checker.

Watching for Widows and Orphans

Professional layout artists watch for two kinds of subtle flaws in text passages (see Figure 18.2):

- A single word standing alone as the final line of a paragraph, causing excess white-space.
- A single line of a paragraph alone at the top of a page or column, caused when a paragraph reaches the bottom of the preceding page or column just before its final line.

18

Some pros call both of these problems "orphans," some call both "widows," and still others like to call one problem an orphan and the other a widow, but there's disagreement on which is which. So pick what you like—you can't help but be both right and wrong.

When and whether these are really a problem is entirely subjective. For example, if a widow is a long word or it's within a narrow column it's really not worth fixing. You'll have to choose on a case-by-case basis when you want to fiddle with these.

The key to repairing these is to manipulate the length of text and where text lines break. You can fix windows and orphans in the following ways (in general order of preference):

- Change the wording of the paragraph leading up to the error. You can add words so that another word or two shares the last line, or cut words to "pick up" the widow into the preceding line.
- If the paragraph containing the widow (or the one following) is short, delete the paragraph mark after the widow to combine the widow's paragraph with the one that follows it.

- If the paragraph containing the widow is long, insert a paragraph break at an appropriate point in the middle of the paragraph to break it into two. (Watch that you don't create a new widow.)

- Adjust the hyphenation zone.

- Make a small adjustment to the font size, character spacing, or frame width for the entire story.

FIGURE 18.2.

Widows and orphans are among the text flow flaws to watch for.

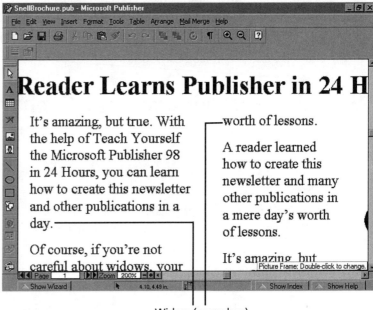

Widow (or orphan)

Note that any of the changes just described might inadvertently change other text in the story, causing new widows, orphans, or copyfitting problems. Often, getting the text just right means fixing one error, and then fixing other new errors that your first fix created.

Where Do Stories End?

Again, subtle differences in line and character spacing between your equipment and your print service's can produce dramatic changes in text flow over long text passages.

If your publication is a newsletter or other type of publication that allows stories in con-nected frames to flow through multiple pages, you must check the print service proof very carefully to see that the point at which a story "breaks" at the bottom of one column and starts at the top of another is a logical, clean place to break. If not, you can apply some of the same techniques offered earlier for fixing widows and orphans to fix story endings.

When the funky story endings show up not just in a proof, but also on your screen, Publisher's Copyfit feature (Format I Copyfit Text; see Hour 11, "Shaping Text in Its Frame") can offer a quick solution. I advised against using Copyfit as a replacement for careful font, size, and spacing selections. But when you just want a quick, subtle way to clean up story breaks, Copyfit might be your best option.

When the errors show up in the proof but not on your display, you can't fix them in Publisher. You must mark up the proof to tell the printing service to make corrections.

Nudging Frames

When frame alignment or positioning is a little off, you might be suffering from a clum-sy mouse hand (like mine) that has trouble with pinpoint positioning accuracy.

To make subtle, precise changes in frame positioning, try Publisher's Nudge facility. Select the frame you want to move, press and hold the Alt key, and press one of the arrow keys on your keyboard to gently nudge the frame in that direction.

To nudge even more precisely, choose Arrange I Nudge to open the Nudge dialog (see Figure 18.3). Check the Nudge By check box, and then enter the measurement by which you want the frame to move for each nudge. Then click the arrows in the dialog to nudge the frame into place.

FIGURE 18.3.

Use the nudge control to clean up object positioning if you can't quite get it right with your mouse.

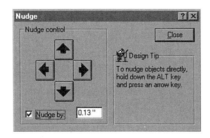

Checking Symbols

If you've used any symbols from the Symbol dialog (see Hour 10, "Dressing Up Your Words"), check the print service proof very carefully to ensure that they've been printed correctly—symbols very often get hinky at the printing service.

How you fix a hinky symbol depends on the following:

- If your printing service uses Publisher, mark the proof with the correct symbol.
- If your printing service doesn't use Publisher, consult with your printer about how you can change your symbol or font choices so that they will print correctly.

Symbol problems often result when you fail to supply all font files to your printer along with the pub, as I recommend in Hour 17, "Setting Up for a Printing Service."

Without your font files, the printer might use a slightly different version of the same font, or even a similar but different font. The differences between your fonts and the printer's can become most apparent in the printing of symbols, which can be very different in two otherwise nearly identical fonts.

Fixing Photos

Photographs are among the most troublesome parts of a pub, particularly when they're in color. Sometimes, photos that look great on your screen look crummy in print. I can't go over everything you can do to get better photo results, but here are a few ways to start:

- Rescan the photo with different color depth or resolution settings and see whether the results improve.
- Use a photo-editing program (see Hour 20, "Beyond Publisher: Exploring Other Desktop Publishing Tools") to scan, edit, and clean up photos before inserting them in Publisher.
- Ask your photo processor to supply photos to you on a Photo CD, and insert the files from there.
- Don't insert the photo at all. Leave a hole in the layout for it, and give the printed photo to your printing service along with your pub files (see Hour 17). The service can use its professional scanners, software, and expertise to get the best results with photos (at an added cost, of course).

Working with Printer Proofs

Print services provide two kinds of proofs:

- *Comp*, a full-color, accurate representation of the way your pub will appear when printed.
- *Blueline*, a pale blue proof used mainly to check that text will print correctly.

If you will mark corrections on proofs (for the print service to read and follow), you'll get the most reliable results if you apply the standard marks, often called proofreader's marks. There are many marks, but Figure 18.4 shows the most important ones.

 Always use red pen or red pencil to mark up a comp. Before marking a blueline, ask your service how they want it marked; some services require that bluelines be marked only with a special, nonreproducing blue pen or pencil.

FIGURE 18.4.

Proofreader's marks.

18

Mark	Action	Example
✗	Delete	Tayke my car ✗
◡	Close up space	Take m◡y car ◡
#	Insert space	Take#my#car #
‖	Align vertically	Item 1 Item 2 Item 3 ‖
tr. ∩	Transpose	T∩ke my ∩r. tr. ∩
•••• stet	Ignore marked correction	T∩ke my car stet ••••
╱ lc.	Lowercase	Take my ╱ar lc.
≡ Cap	Capitalize	take my car Cap ≡
wf	Wrong font	Take⟨my⟩car wf
∧	Insert comma	Take my car∧please ∧
⊙	Insert period	Take my car, please∧ ⊙
¶	Start new paragraph	Take my car, please. Let me tell you why I want you to take my car∧It all started when the timing belt went. ¶

Summary

Your pubs will most often come out of any printer 99% the way they appear onscreen—but that final 1% is a pain in the neck, especially when you fail to catch it. Your best defense is knowing what to look for and never, ever letting a pub go to print without checking the printing service proof carefully and fixing any errors you see.

Workshop

The following workshop helps solidify the skills you learned in this lesson.

Q&A

Q You used the word "hinky" in this chapter. Why did you do that? What does "hinky" mean, and will you promise not to do it ever again?

A I used it because we've now spent 18 hours together, and so I feel I know you well enough to reveal my true self. *Hinky* means weird, and I can't promise you anything.

Quiz

Take the following quiz to see how much you've learned.

Questions

1. To ask for design help from Publisher, choose

    a. Ebert | Critique Me

    b. Tools | Design Check

    c. Tools | Design Checker

    d. Tools | Siskel | Thumb

2. A word alone as the last line of a paragraph is called

    a. A widow

    b. An orphan

    c. An in-law

    d. It depends on who's talking

Answers

1. (c) Choose the Design Checker from your Tools menu.

2. (d) Some say widow, some say orphan, some say both. Hinky, ain't it?

Activities

Go back over pubs you've worked on and check for widows (or orphans). Consider whether any are worth fixing, and then practice fixing them. Pay special attention to how other text in the frame or story is affected by whatever you do to fix the widow (or orphan).

18

Hour 19

Creating and Printing Mass Mailings

Mail merge, as it has been called for many years in word processing programs, is the process of setting up a publication for a form letter, label form, or envelope and then automatically printing a separate copy (or label) for each entry in a list of names, addresses, or other information. Mail merge enables you, for example, to create a letter and then print dozens of copies, each personally addressed to a different recipient.

It's a great time saver and an easy way to produce direct-mail advertising, address newsletters or cards, and crank out labels or pre-addressed envelopes.

In Publisher, mail merge happens in four distinct steps or stages, so that's how I'll take you through the process in this hour. It's all pretty easy, actually, but a lot of people get hung up on some of the concepts, so I'll take it slow and steady so you can see exactly how everything comes together. At the end of the hour, you'll be able to answer the following questions:

- How do I create the list of addresses or other information to be used in a mail merge?
- Can I do a mail merge with an address list I already have from a different program?
- How do I attach a list to a pub and decide which information from the list to print?
- How do I choose where in the pub to print each piece of information from the list and format that text?
- Can I preview the results of a merge before printing?
- How do I print the results?

Step 1: Creating a Data Source

Before you can set up a pub for mail merge, you must have the data source ready from which Publisher will pull the information to be plugged into the pub.

NEW TERM   A *data source* is a list of names and addresses (or other information) to be used in a mail merge; it's the "source" for the "data" (information) that will be printed in the pub.

Creating a data source can be a bit of a chore the first time around—but don't let that hold you back. After you've created that source, you can use it again and again. The long-term time-savings of mail merge far exceed the time it takes to set up a list.

There are two ways to create a data source, each of which you discover next. You can

- Create a Publisher Address List
- Use a list already created in another program

Typing a Publisher Address List

To create a new address list in Publisher, begin with any pub open (even Unsaved Publication), and that pub doesn't need to be the one to which you'll attach the list later. In other words, the address list you create need not have anything to do with the pub that happens to be open when you create it.

To start, choose Mail Merge | Create Publisher Address List. The New Address List dialog opens (see Figure 19.1). For the first entry in the list, fill in all the fields you want to use (you can leave fields you don't need blank).

FIGURE 19.1.

To create a new address list, just fill in the fields for each entry.

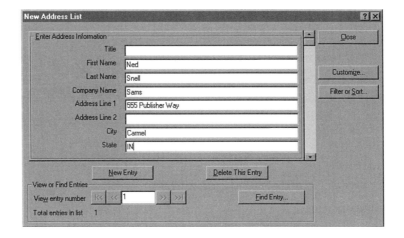

 Each discrete set of information in the list (one person's name, address, and so on) is an *entry*. Each piece of information within an entry—first name, last name, and so on—is a *field*. If your list were stored in a Rolodex file, each card would be an entry, and each line on the card would be a field.

After filling in any fields you want for the first entry, click the New Entry button. The fields clear, so you can type the information for Entry Number 2. To complete your list, just fill in one entry at a time and click New Entry after each.

Note the buttons and number shown at the bottom of the dialog, under View or Find Entries (see Figure 19.1). These controls work exactly like the Page controls you've used in Publisher to move among the pages of a multipage pub. The number shown is the number of the entry in the list; at the very bottom of the dialog, you'll see a report of the total number of entries in the list. Use these buttons to move back and forward to entries you've already typed, to check your work or make changes.

 Observe in Figure 19.1 that the New Address List dialog contains a scrollbar. That tells you that there are more fields available than those you see at first. You can scroll down to reveal such useful fields as ZIP Code, Home Phone, Work Phone, and E-mail Address.

When you finish typing new entries, click Close. A Save As dialog appears so you can give this list a name. Don't type a filename extension; Publisher automatically gives the list the extension .mdb.

To Do: Make a Short Mailing List

▼ To Do

1. Begin in any pub (it doesn't matter what pub is open when you create a list).

2. Choose Mail Merge | Create Publisher Address List. The New Address List dialog opens.

3. Fill in the fields for the first entry as shown below (leave any fields not mentioned blank). Remember that you might have to use the dialog's scrollbar to bring the last few fields into view.

   First Name: Ned

   Last Name: Snell

   Company Name: Sams

   Address Line 1: 555 Publisher Way

   City: Carmel

   State: IN

   ZIP Code: 55555

   Work Phone: 555-555-5555

4. Click New Entry. The fields in the dialog clear, and the blank fields for entry number 2 appear.

5. Add an entry for yourself (your name, your address), filling in only the same fields used in step 3. (After this entry, you can optionally fill in a few more entries for practice.)

6. Click Close. The Save As dialog opens.

7. Type TestList, and click the Save button. You have created and saved a short list called TestList.mdb, which you will use in a later To Do to merge data with a pub.

▲

A single address list can be used in as many different pubs as it's useful for; it's not married to a single pub.

Editing an Address List

You can easily add or change entries in a list at any time. Choose Mail Merge | Edit Publisher Address List to open the Open Address List dialog, which shows a list of the lists you've saved. Choose a list, click Open, and a dialog that looks just like the New Address List opens. On that dialog:

- Click New Entry to add a new entry to the list.
- Use the controls under View or Find Entry to move to an entry you want to change, and make any changes you like.
- Move to an entry you want to delete from the list, and click the Delete This Entry button to remove it.

Borrowing a List from Another Program

If you already have an address list entered in another program, you might be able to use it in Publisher as a mail merge data source, saving yourself the work of typing a new list and the work of keeping the list up-to-date separately in two programs (Publisher and the other).

Publisher can use lists from the following types of files (all except dBASE are from Microsoft programs for Windows):

- Word tables or mail merge data documents
- Access databases
- Excel spreadsheets
- FoxPro databases
- Microsoft Works databases (only if the database contains no formulas)
- dBASE versions III, IV, and V

To use a list in one of these file formats, you will select the file when attaching the data source to the pub, as you learn to do next.

19

Step 2: Attaching a Data Source to a Pub

Before you can begin inserting field data in a pub, you must attach a data source to that pub so that Publisher knows where the information is coming from.

To begin, prepare your data source as described earlier, and do most or all the layout and editing of the pub. You can do more layout and editing work after you add the merge fields, but it's easy when editing to inadvertently delete or otherwise scramble mail merge fields, so it's best to leave them for fairly late in the process of creating a pub.

When you're ready, open the pub to which you want to attach a list, and choose Mail Merge | Open Data Source. A dialog opens, asking whether you want to use a file you have or create a new list in Publisher. (Clicking the Create a New List option opens the New Address List dialog, shown earlier, so you can create a new address list.) Choose the top option, Merge Information from a File I Already Have, to display the Open Data Source dialog shown in Figure 19.2.

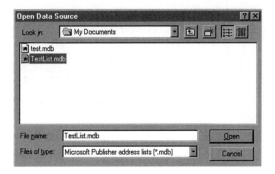

Choose your data source:

- To use a Publisher address list you've created, select it from the dialog and click the Open button.

- To use data from another data file supported in Publisher, drop down the Files of Type list at the bottom of the dialog and choose the type of file you'll use. Then use the Look In list at the top of the dialog to navigate to the folder where the data file is stored, choose the file, and click the Open button.

Step 3: Inserting Fields

Now the nitty gritty: choosing where in the pub each piece of information—first name, last name, and so on—will be printed. You do this by *inserting fields* in your pub.

To insert a field, create or select a text frame or table cell in which you want the field data to appear when the pub is printed. Then choose Mail Merge | Insert Field. The dialog shown in Figure 19.3 appears, listing all the fields in the data source that's attached to the current pub.

Choose a field name from the list, and its name appears in the selected frame or cell, surrounded by double carats (<< >>), as shown in Figure 19.3. The carats tell you that what you see in that spot is a field that will be replaced by data from a list when you print. Note that the carats will not appear when you print.

FIGURE 19.3.

Pick a field to insert it in your pub, where it appears surrounded by double carats (<< >>).

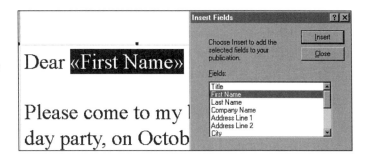

To control the look of the list text that will be printed in place of the field, just apply formatting to the field.

For example, suppose I want the First Name to appear in 12-point Arial, in bold. I simply click the field in my pub (<<First Name>>) to select it, and then apply the formatting from the Formatting toolbar.

After the field is in the pub, you can do anything to the field you can do to any text—move it, format it, delete it, and so on.

To Do: Make Simple Address Labels

1. In Publisher, open the Catalog by choosing File | New.

2. In the list of wizards on the Publications by Wizard tab, choose Labels.

3. Choose the first Labels template, euro7159, and click Start Wizard.

4. Click the wizard's Finish button, and click Yes when asked if you want to skip the wizard's questions. A single label appears on your screen, with placeholder text in a single text frame.

5. Click the placeholder text to select it, and press your Delete key. The placeholder text is deleted, but the empty frame remains.

6. Choose Mail Merge | Open Data Source, and on the dialog that appears choose Merge Information from a File I Already Have. The Open Data Source dialog opens.

7. Choose TestList (the simple list you created in this hour's first To Do), and click Open. TestList has been attached to the new label pub.

8. Make sure the text frame in the pub is still selected, and choose Mail Merge | Insert Field to open the Insert Field dialog.

▼ To Do

19

▼   9. Click First Name and then click the Insert button. The field <<First Name>> appears in the pub.

     10. Press Enter to start a new line.

     11. Repeat steps 8, 9, and 10 for the remaining fields of the name and address. Note that in practice, you need not insert all fields in the list; you can select only the ones you want for the pub at hand.

▲   12. Save your new labels pub. When you print this pub (as described next) on label stock, a label will be printed for each entry in the list.

> You can put a field anywhere—on a line by itself, or run in with other text. For example, you could create the sentence
>
> `Dear <<First Name>>, my old friend:`
>
> and the printout of the first entry (using our TestList) would read
>
> `Dear Ned, my old friend:`
>
> If you string fields together, don't forget to insert any necessary spaces between them. The phrase
>
> `<<First Name>><<Last Name>>`
>
> produces
>
> `NedSnell`
>
> Putting a space between the fields would get you the necessary space between the words.

Step 4: The Big Merge

Now comes the fun part, the reward for all your efforts—*merging*, plugging the actual list data into multiple copies of the pub. You can merge data two ways, both of which you discover next:

- Preview the merge results onscreen
- Print the multiple copies of the pub, each containing an entry from the list

Previewing the Merge

To preview your merge results onscreen (to test them before printing), open the pub and choose Mail Merge | Merge. The onscreen view of the pub shows the first entry in the list as it will appear in print, and the Preview Data dialog opens (see Figure 19.4).

Use the controls on the Preview Data dialog to display the other entries, to see how each copy of the printed pub (or each label in a sheet of labels) will appear.

FIGURE 19.4.

You can preview the merge to check results before printing.

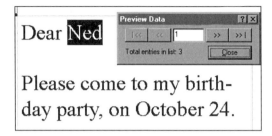

Printing the Merge

To print a mail merge pub, you don't need to preview it. Just open it as always and choose File | Print Merge to open the Print Merge dialog (see Figure 19.5).

Use the Print Merge dialog just as you would the regular Print dialog—just press Enter (or click Print) and a copy or label prints for each entry in the list.

FIGURE 19.5.

Choose File | Print Merge to produce a copy (or label) for each entry in the list.

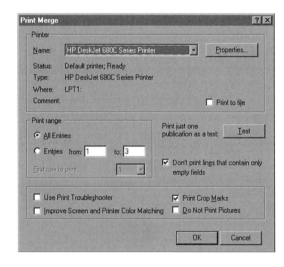

19

When you need to, though, take advantage of the Print Merge dialog's special features:

- Under Print Range, you can choose to print a copy for all entries (the default setting), or print only selected entries or a range of entries.
- Click the Test button to print a single copy for a single entry (or a few rows of labels) as a test, to judge the appearance of the results without printing the whole list.

Summary

As you can see, setting up for mail merge takes some work. But if you often address multiple copies of letters, envelopes, and such, the rewards of creating lists and inserting fields are well worth the effort.

Workshop

The following workshop helps solidify the skills you learned in this lesson.

Q&A

Q What if I need different fields than the ones I see in the New Address List dialog?

A There's no need to change the standard list of fields in a Publisher Address List—Title, First Name, and so on—as long as the list includes all the fields you need. If the list contains fields you don't need, you can just leave those blank, or not insert those fields in the pubs where you don't need them.

However, you can optionally customize the names of the fields for a particular list, adding new fields, deleting fields, or changing the names of existing fields. To customize the list, click Customize on the New Address List dialog to open the Customize Address List dialog where you may add, delete, or rename fields. After customizing the list, return to the New Address List dialog and fill in entries as usual.

Quiz

Take the following quiz to see how much you've learned.

Questions

1. Which of the following steps of a mail merge comes first?

    a. Creating the data source

    b. Inserting fields in a pub

    c. Attaching a data source to a pub

    d. Licking the stamps

2. An _____ is a set of _____ about one person or organization.

    a. autobiography, lies

    b. autopsy, tissue samples

    c. entry, fields

    d. estimate, unreliable guesses

3. You can create one address list and then use fields from it in many different pubs, as needed. (True/False)

Answers

1. (a) The data source always comes first.

2. (c) One set of fields makes an entry.

3. True. After you've got the list, use it wherever, whenever you need it.

Activities

That's almost it for printing pubs—after a quick Hour 20, "Beyond Publisher: Exploring Other Desktop Publishing Tools," you'll move ahead to the wonderful world of Web pages. If you want to create and publish Web pages, but don't yet have an Internet account, now would be a good time to go get one.

19

Hour 20

Beyond Publisher: Exploring Other Desktop Publishing Tools

At the beginning of this book, I told you that Publisher was designed for two types of users: Those who want to create professional-looking publications without having to acquire the complete skills of a desktop publishing pro, and those who are on their way to becoming DTP pros but want an easy program to start with.

If you're in the latter group—or you're toying with joining it—you must know about other DTP tools available to you. When you've mastered Publisher, you're fully prepared to step up to the more difficult, more powerful professional page layout programs. And whether you'll do layout in Publisher or in another program, you'll need to learn about other tools DTP pros use, such as draw, paint, and photo-manipulation programs.

In this hour, I'll introduce you to the most popular options. Within each category, I've listed the programs by level of difficulty (in my opinion—others might differ), from the easiest choice to more difficult ones. At the end of the hour you'll be able to answer the following questions:

- What other page layout programs might I move up to when I've outgrown Publisher?
- What tools can I use to draw and paint my own images for pubs?
- How can I do more with photographs?

> All programs described in this hour are available for Windows 95, but most are also available for other systems, particularly Macintosh. When buying one or asking for more information, be sure to select the version for your system.

Page Layout Programs

PageMaker and Quark are used by the overwhelming majority of professional desktop publishers, and also by most printing services. Both are more difficult to learn and use than Publisher, but both also offer a far greater degree of precision in layout control, graphics manipulation, text formatting, and color.

Perhaps more important, both of these programs each support multiple *color-matching* systems that are also widely supported by printing services.

NEW TERM A *color-matching* system is a way of assigning codes or names to particular colors for two purposes: To help you and your printing service ensure that you're talking about the same color, and to enable systems that improve the color matching between onscreen colors and ink colors (also called *pigment* colors).

Publisher includes a rudimentary color-matching system (see Hour 16, "Controlling Color"), but PageMaker and Quark support the systems used and understood by most printing services, such as Pantone and Duotone. These matching systems can dramatically improve the accuracy of the color you'll get in print.

In fact, most printing services actually use one or the other of these programs (or both) for their own DTP work. That expands your options for asking your printing service to help you fine-tune your pub for press. You can give your PageMaker or Quark files to the service, and the service can apply its expertise to fixing any little last-minute glitches that might come up.

Adobe PageMaker

It's billed by Adobe as "the world's leading professional publishing software," and it just might be. Easier to learn and use than Quark, and a little more in tune with a Windows way of working (even in its Windows version, Quark feels a little Mac-like), PageMaker makes an excellent next step up from Publisher.

PageMaker's interface, redesigned for version 6.5, makes PageMaker look and feel just like other Adobe products such as Illustrator or Photoshop (both described later in this hour). That, plus a level of enhanced integration between PageMaker and those products, makes PageMaker a strong choice if you also use Adobe's other tools.

PageMaker includes a selection of multimedia tutorials and tips to help you learn the program quickly. Other strengths include comprehensive color management and matching tools, supporting advanced techniques such as trapping, imposition, and separation.

Quark

DTP veterans often swear by Quark, claiming that it's more powerful and versatile than PageMaker. That's a matter of opinion, but it's safe to say that the longer someone's been doing DTP, the more likely that person is to be a Quark user. Quark proficiency is a badge of honor among DTP folks; a Quark user sniffs at a PageMaker user the way a farmer might at a gardener.

Does that mean Quark's better? Maybe yes, maybe no, depending on what you need. There are a few things Quark does better than PageMaker, but it's also harder to learn.

One neat thing about Quark is that it has a distinct view and file format for books (see Figure 20.1). In that view, it helps you easily deal with the unique demands of book publishing, such as maintaining a consistent layout and page numbering across multiple chapters.

Other Quark features of particular value to Publisher converts include the following:

- Customizable tool palettes in which you can rearrange and hide tools. (Quark has a zillion tools, so the ability to limit the visible tools to those you use often is important.)
- Zoom levels from 10% to 800%.
- The ability to view multiple spreads simultaneously.
- A tool for calibrating your monitor's resolution for more accurate display of a pub.
- The ability to open up to 25 documents or templates at once.

20

FIGURE 20.1.

Quark is a more advanced, and more difficult, page layout program than Publisher or PageMaker.

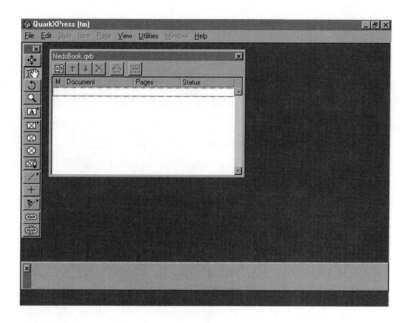

Draw and Paint Programs

Use these programs to create and edit your own artwork, from simple shapes to freehand drawings. At their most basic level, using any of these is much like using Publisher's drawing tools, although these programs are far more powerful and sophisticated.

CorelDRAW!

One of the most popular drawing tools for both professionals and amateurs, CorelDRAW! (see Figure 20.2) is really a suite of graphics creation tools that includes a great draw program (for vector images), a paint program (for creating and editing bitmaps), a library of clip art you can edit, and other handy utilities.

The most recent release (version 8) of CorelDRAW! includes the following features, of special value to a Publisher user:

- Transparent drop shadows.
- Intuitive, interactive filters for creating effects in a drawing, such as Push and Pull, Zipper and Twister, Extrude, Envelope, and Blend.
- Special tools for creating pictures to be used in Web pages.
- Text wrapping to a curve or shape.
- Onscreen kerning and line spacing.

- A Digger function for easy location of hidden objects.
- Rotate, nudge, and multiselect guidelines for pinpoint positioning.

FIGURE 20.2.

CorelDRAW! is a valuable suite of draw and paint tools.

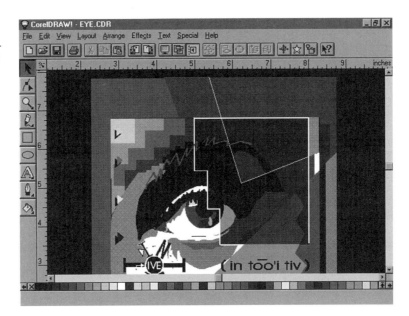

NEW TERM Used in draw, paint, and photo manipulation programs, *filters* let you apply formatting to an image in one click. For example, most photo-manipulation programs have one or more fish-eye lens filters which, when applied to a photograph, distort the image to make it appear as though it's being viewed through a fish-eye lens or the bottom of a bottle. Another common filter *posterizes* an image, giving it a sort of Andy Warhol, pop art quality.

Adobe Illustrator

A more elaborate drawing tool than CorelDRAW!, Adobe Illustrator has been the dominant illustration program among computer graphics professionals for several years. It's probably the most powerful one you can get, and also the most demanding of you. Illustrator not only edits artwork, but also enables you to do powerful type design—like WordArt, only far more versatile.

Illustrator is essentially a paint program in that its principal job is producing beautiful bitmapped images. But it can optionally turn its bitmaps to vector graphics when vector-style manipulation is required.

20

Like so many other graphics programs, recent versions of Illustrator have added Web-page creation tools. These tools might be handy, but there are easier, cheaper ways to get Web pages—one of which is Publisher.

Like its Adobe cousins, Illustrator includes sophisticated color management capabilities and support for color-matching systems. Other features include

- Multiple layers to overlay graphics and text.
- Grids and Transform and Align palettes that help you manipulate objects precisely.
- Nearly 50 different filters for distortions or fine art effects.

Photo-Manipulation Software

Photo-manipulation—or photo-editing—programs are graphics editors specifically designed to help you capture (from a scanner or digital camera), clean up, and customize photographs.

When your photos need a lot of cropping, sizing, or cleaning up before printing, you'll get better results if you perform all such tasks in a photo-editing program before you insert the photo in your pub.

Microsoft Picture It!

Picture It! is to photo manipulation as Publisher is to DTP: It's the easy program for people who don't really want to learn this stuff at a professional level. Picture It! makes common tasks—such as removing scratches from a scanned photo or fixing "red eye" reflections in people's eyes—fast and simple, often achievable with just one click.

In addition to helping you fix up photos, Picture It! includes several templates that enable you to produce—right from within Picture It!—a variety of home and business publications, such as greeting cards, calendars, and flyers.

To a Publisher user, the advantage of Picture It! is that, as a Microsoft program, it looks and feels very much like Publisher, and is therefore very easy to learn and use. Features include

- Automatic fixes for red eye, scratches, and dust on photos.
- Publisher-style wizards and design templates to speed up tasks.
- Over 500 photo-quality backgrounds, templates, and clip art images.
- The ability to crop, zoom, rotate, and flip photos.
- Paint-program tools and filters for painting, distorting, adding fancy text, or turning photos into impressionist paintings and watercolors.

Adobe PhotoDeluxe

An easier, scaled-down cousin to Adobe's Photoshop (call it Photoshop Lite), PhotoDeluxe (see Figure 20.3) is very much like Picture It! and plays the same role. Its major difference is that it's a little more powerful than Picture It!, and probably a little tougher to learn for a Publisher user. Features include

- Fifty step-by-step guided activities.
- Dozens of templates for creating calendars, cards, flyers, and so on.
- Thirty effects filters.
- Powerful editing tools, including a clone tool and one-step red-eye removal.
- An EasyPhoto organizer for creating albums or galleries of photos.

FIGURE 20.3.

Beginner's photo editing programs like Picture It! and PhotoDeluxe (shown here) are mainly for cleaning up snapshots.

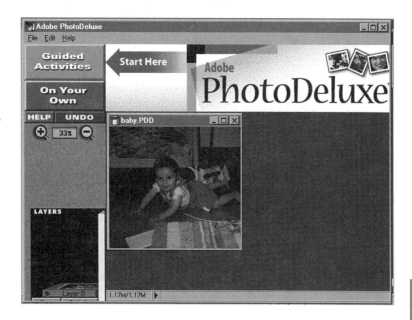

Adobe Photoshop

A few years ago, a whole new artistic medium was born. There are now thousands of professional artists whose medium is, in effect, Adobe Photoshop (see Figure 20.4). They shoot photos, and then pull them into Photoshop and manipulate them in a thousand different ways to make unique, wonderful images. When you see a cool-looking picture in an ad that appears to be some slicked-up variant of a real photo, odds are pretty good that you're looking at a Photoshop project.

20

FIGURE 20.4.

Photoshop has spawned a whole new medium: art by computer photo manipulation.

You could use Photoshop to do everything that PhotoDeluxe and Picture It! do—but doing so would be more difficult. Photoshop isn't built for cleaning up snapshots in a snap; it's for making photos into art.

Using Photoshop, you can retouch photos, combine multiple photos into one, or add any kind of effect—there's pretty much nothing you can't do to a photo in Photoshop.

For the Publisher user, Photoshop provides not only photo manipulation, but also professional-quality color management and matching and color separations. Other features include

- Continuous zoom levels from 0.2% to 1600%.
- More than 95 filters, including filters for image sharpening, softening, stylizing, natural media, distortion, removal of dust and scratches, and lighting.
- Layers that you can merge, flatten, flip, copy, and clip together.
- A custom gradient tool that supports named, multicolor designs with varying opacity.
- Professional photography tools, including Dodge and Burn (to correct exposure) and Sponge (to correct color saturation).
- A full assortment of drawing and painting tools, including Pencil, Brush, Airbrush, Clone, Text, and Line.

- User-definable soft-edged brushes, with preview of brush size.
- Retouching tools, including Smudge, Sharpen, Blur, and Rubber Stamp for cloning.
- Feather-edge selections for blending backgrounds and combining foreground and background images.

Summary

Publisher is an excellent introduction to the world of DTP, but there's much more to that world than Publisher shows you. When you feel you have Publisher well under your belt, start "Teaching Yourself" the next level of DTP and graphics tools.

Workshop

The following workshop helps solidify the skills you learned in this lesson.

Q&A

Q Doesn't Publisher have any better built-in drawing tools than the ones I learned to use in Hour 14?

A Well…sort of. Bundled with Publisher, Microsoft Draw occupies a slot somewhere between Publisher's simple drawing tools and a full-scale drawing program like CorelDRAW!. It gives you the ability to draw more sophisticated shapes than the drawing tools, but for all intents and purposes it's just a slightly more advanced set of drawing tools. But at least it's handy.

- To create and insert a Microsoft Draw picture in a pub, choose Insert | Picture | New Drawing from within Publisher.
- To edit that picture later, double-click it.

Quiz

Take the following quiz to see how much you've learned.

Questions

1. Why might you find Microsoft's Picture It! photo-manipulation program especially easy to learn?

   a. It has no moving parts.

   b. It looks and acts a lot like Publisher.

20

      c. It looks and acts a lot like CorelDRAW!.

      d. All the above.

2. What's a color-matching system?

      a. A system of names or numbers for standardizing colors across print and display devices.

      b. The opposite of a black-and-white matching system.

      c. The opposite of a color unmatching system.

Answers

1. (b) As a Publisher user, you'll find Picture It! pretty familiar territory.

2. (a) Color matching helps ensure you get exactly the color you expect.

Activities

Got an Internet account? In Appendix A, "Internet Resources for Publisher Users," you'll find the addresses of the Web pages from which you can learn more about all the products mentioned in this hour. In a few cases, you can even purchase the software online or download a free trial version straight from the Web.

PART VI

Publishing Online

Hour

Hour **21**

Understanding Online Publishing

Publisher without paper? It's possible, and no more difficult than the Publisher you already know. In this hour, you'll learn about using Publisher to produce pubs for online consumption, and also discover how to set up the software you'll need to make online publishing happen.

At the end of the hour, you'll be able to answer the following questions:

- What exactly is a "Web page" and how is it different from a regular print pub?

- What do you need—besides Publisher—to create and publish a Web page?

- How do you prepare for Web page authoring by installing Internet Explorer 4 from your Publisher CD-ROM?

Understanding Web Pages

Before you can dive into creating a Web page (as you will in the next hour), you must pick up a more intimate understanding of how a Web page works than you get simply by surfing the Web.

To effectively create Web pages, you needn't be any sort of Internet guru, but you really do need to have surfed the Web enough to have a general sense of what Web pages are like and how a visitor operates one.

In particular, you must understand what Web page addresses—often called *URLs*—are, and you'll need to know about hyperlinks, the text or pictures a visitor can click to jump to another page or download a file. To publish your finished Web pages, you'll need access to the Internet and some space on a Web server (see Hour 24, "Putting Your Page on the Web").

If you're completely new to the Web or the Internet, get your bearings first before moving ahead with this tutorial.

What's in a Web Page?

If you've been online, you know what a Web page is from a Web surfer's point of view. But before you can begin creating—or *authoring*—Web pages, you must learn what a Web page is from an author's perspective.

A Web page is actually just a file in a format called HTML, using the file extension `.htm` (or `.html`). When you create a Web page in Publisher or convert a pub to a Web page, you end up with an HTML file instead of a `.pub` file.

An HTML file contains nothing but text (see Figure 21.1): the actual text readers see online and instructions for how that text is to be formatted onscreen. The text in an HTML file also includes the URLs to which the links in the page lead, and the filenames, locations, and page positions of any pictures or other multimedia files, which are stored in their own separate files.

FIGURE 21.1.

The actual contents of an HTML Web page file, created in Publisher.

```
index.html - Notepad
File  Edit  Search  Help
<td width=549 height=58 valign=top align=left>

<p align=center><center><font face="Impact" color=#000000 size=6>NED'S BIG PAG
</td>
<td></td>
</tr>
<tr>
<td height=4></td>
<td colspan=2><img src="blnk.gif" width=553 height=1></td>
</tr>
</table>



</td>
</tr>
<tr>
<td height=22></td>
<td colspan=8><img src="blnk.gif" width=556 height=1></td>
</tr>
<tr>
<td height=1></td>
<td width=152 height=46 colspan=1 rowspan=3 valign=top align=left>
<map name="map350">
<area shape="rect" coords="0,0,152,46" href="index.html">
<area shape="rect" coords="0,34,152,46">
<area shape="rect" coords="0,0,152,35">
</map>
```

It's important to understand that in a Web page, the pictures and any other multimedia files (such as sound or animation) are stored in their own individual files separate from the HTML file. So except when a Web page contains only text, it is made up of a collection of files: the HTML file plus any media files. If you convert a pub containing pictures to a Web page, the pictures are automatically separated out to their own files.

Keeping the files of a Web page organized is an important aspect of creating and publishing a Web page.

When an HTML file is viewed through a browser such as Internet Explorer or Netscape Navigator, the browser interprets the instructions in the file, formatting the text onscreen as ordered, and adding the picture files in their specified positions. The browser also reads and remembers the URLs the links point to, so it knows where to take a visitor who clicks one. Figure 21.2 shows the very same file as Figure 21.1, but now interpreted by a Web browser.

21

FIGURE 21.2.

The same file as Figure 21.1, now interpreted by a browser.

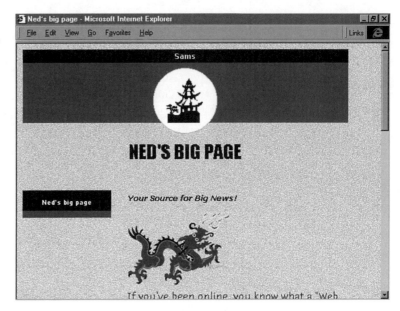

A Web page can be made up of many different parts, but most Web pages contain most or all of the following core elements. When you create a Web page, these are the parts you insert and format. And when you convert a pub to a Web page, the objects in the pub are converted into their nearest equivalents in this list.

The standard Web page parts include

- A *title*, which browsers typically display in the title bar of the window in which the page appears. Note that the actual title does not appear within the layout of the page, although many authors repeat the title in a big heading near the top of the page layout.

- *Headings*, which browsers typically display in large, bold, or otherwise emphasized type. A Web page can have many headings, and headings can be *nested* up to six levels deep; that is, there can be subheadings, and sub-subheadings, and so on.

> In HTML, there are six levels of headings, beginning with Heading 1 (the biggest and boldest, usually reserved for creating a title) and going down to Heading 6 (a very small, minor heading, indistinguishable from Normal text in many browsers).

- *Normal text*, which makes up the basic, general-purpose text of the page.

- *Horizontal lines* (sometimes called *rules*), which dress up the page and separate it into logical sections.

- *Hyperlinks* (or simply *links*) to many different things: other Web pages, multimedia files (external images, animation, sound, video), document files, email addresses, and more. Links might also lead to specific spots within the current page.

- *Lists*, bulleted (like this one) or numbered, just as in a pub.

- *Inline images*, pictures that are incorporated into the layout of the page to jazz it up or make it more informative.

- *Inline multimedia*, sound, animation, or video clips that play automatically when the page appears (see Hour 23, "Adding Links, Motion, and Other Web Goodies").

- A *background*, an inline image that, unlike a regular image, covers the entire background of the page so that text and other images can be seen on top of it. Instead of an image, you can use a solid background color.

- *Tables*, text and inline images organized in neat rows and columns.

How's a Web Page Different Than a Pub?

Obviously, a Web page is not a pub in many ways. Its dimensions conform to the width of a computer screen, and that screen can be scrolled down a long way. So all the considerations related to paper size, folding, spreads, and so on become moot on the Web—one size fits all.

But there are other, subtler differences. In general, the formatting instructions contained in an HTML file do not precisely control how the page will appear. Instead, the file provides a general idea of how the page is to appear, and each browser realizes those instructions slightly differently. That's why the very same Web page often looks different in two different browsers.

For example, the HTML file might specify that a particular line of text is to be displayed as a heading. One browser follows that instruction by making the text big and bold, whereas another might follow it by underlining the text. This idea is often difficult to get used to after you have had complete control of every aspect of a pub, down to the smallest fraction of an inch. Web page formatting is looser and more general than DTP formatting.

Figure 21.3 shows a pub in Publisher, and Figure 21.4 shows the exact same pub immediately after conversion to a Web page, with no other changes made. Note how different the two displays are.

21

A regular print-ready pub in Publisher.

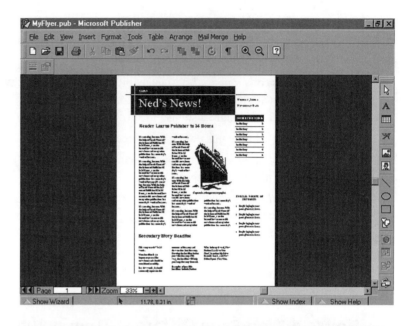

FIGURE 21.4.

The same file as Figure 21.3, converted to a Web page.

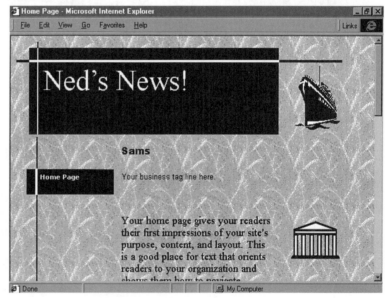

There are new, advanced Web authoring techniques that give you greater control over Web page formatting, but for most authors today (and certainly all beginners), formatting a Web page is not about controlling exactly how the page will look, but rather about designating the role each element plays in the page: a heading, a normal paragraph, and so on. You will need to keep this principle in mind when creating and editing your own Web pages.

Installing Internet Explorer 4 and the Web Publishing Wizard

Your Publisher 98 CD-ROM includes Internet Explorer 4 (IE4), along with IE4's Web Publishing Wizard. These programs are not simply favors from Microsoft—you need them if you'll author Web pages.

- While working on a Web page in Publisher, you can click a Web Site Preview button on the Standard toolbar to automatically view the page in Internet Explorer (see Hour 22, "Creating a Web Page in Publisher").

- When your page is finished, you can use the Web Publishing Wizard to publish it online (see Hour 24) through your Internet account.

The following To Do shows you how to install IE4 and the Web Publishing Wizard from your Publisher CD-ROM, to prepare for using these tools in the final three hours of this tutorial.

If you've already installed IE4, either from the Publisher CD or from any other source, make sure that you've included the Web Publishing Wizard.

Open your Windows Start menu and choose Programs | Internet Explorer. If you see Web Publishing Wizard on the menu that appears, you're all set.

If not, you need to add the Web Publishing Wizard. You can do that without having to re-install IE4 simply by double-clicking the Setup for Microsoft Web Publishing Wizard icon that appeared on your desktop after you installed Publisher.

21

To Do: Install Internet Explorer 4

Before starting the To Do, prepare your PC by closing all programs (except Windows 95). If you've opened and closed several programs since last starting Windows, it's a good idea to restart your PC just before beginning the installation, to clear out the odds and ends that a few nasty programs can leave in your PC's memory.

1. Insert your Publisher 98 CD-ROM.

2. On your Windows desktop, double-click the icon labeled Setup for Microsoft Internet Explorer 4. (The icon was deposited there when you installed Publisher.) A Welcome dialog appears.

3. Click Next to open the license agreement. Read through the license agreement, select I Accept the Agreement, and click OK. The Installation Option dialog box appears (see Figure 21.5).

FIGURE 21.5.

Choose Full Installation to be sure to include the Web Publishing Wizard in your installation.

4. Drop down the list and choose Full Installation. (The default choice, Standard Installation, does not include the Web Publishing Wizard.)

5. In the Windows Desktop Update dialog, select Yes to install the Active Desktop or No to avoid it.

▼ 6. On the next dialog, choose the country in which you'll use Publisher.

▼

In step 5, you'll be asked whether you want to install the Web Desktop Update. Choosing Yes installs IE4's Active Desktop, which dramatically affects the way you work in Windows, even off the Internet. For example, you'll open icons by single-clicking rather than double-clicking.

If you install the Active Desktop and decide you don't like it, you can easily restore your original Windows desktop by opening your Start menu, choosing Settings | Folder Options, and then choosing Classic Style on the Folder Options dialog.

To learn how to use the Active Desktop, see *Sams' Teach Yourself Internet Explorer 4 in 24 Hours* by Noel Estabrook.

7. In the next dialog, the setup routine asks whether it's okay to store your Internet Explorer 4 files in the directory C:\Program Files\Microsoft Internet. Unless you can think of a good reason why it's not okay, just click Next to accept that location.

After you choose the storage location, the setup routine begins setting up files on your PC. As it does, it displays a progress report to let you know how things are going. When the process is complete, a dialog appears to tell you setup is complete.

▲ 8. Click OK to close the dialog.

Your PC restarts automatically; if after a minute or so it has not restarted, restart it yourself. Windows might take a few minutes longer than usual to stir back to life, but that's just because Setup is still finishing up. The next time you start Windows, it will come up about as quickly as it ever did.

After installing the IE4 software, you have done all you need to do to set up IE4 for previewing Web pages you create in Publisher; in Hour 24, you'll learn about the remaining steps required to set up the Web Publishing Wizard.

However, to use IE4 for actual Web browsing, you still must tell it how to communicate with your Internet provider. You do this by running the Internet Connection Wizard, which prompts you step-by-step for each piece of required communications information.

To start the Connection Wizard, open IE4 by double-clicking the icon labeled The Internet on your desktop, or open your Start menu and choose Programs | Internet Explorer | Connection Wizard.

21

Summary

Web pages are the hot new publishing medium, and for good reason. Put your pub in a Web page, and virtually anyone with an Internet account and Web browser anywhere in the world can see it, no matter whether they use a PC, Mac, or other computer type.

Workshop

The following workshop helps solidify the skills you learned in this lesson.

Q&A

Q My company has an intranet. Can I publish stuff there, like the company newsletter I'm developing?

A Sure, you leading-edge-type techno-worker, you. A growing number of internal company networks are designed as *intranets*—private company networks designed to operate like the Internet. All users of an intranet have a Web browser for accessing company information, which is stored in regular Web page files on a company server computer and is accessible only within the company (not to others out on the Internet).

If your company uses an intranet, you have the option of creating Web pages in Publisher, then publishing those files on the company intranet rather than the Internet.

Create the files using the same steps you're about to learn in Hours 22 and 23. Then talk to the administrator of your intranet to learn how to publish those files on the company's intranet server. To create the HTML files for publication, you won't need the Web Publishing Wizard. Just create the site in Publisher, and then choose File | Save As HTML to save the Web site files on your own hard disk. Your administrator will tell you where to copy those files to put them on the intranet.

Quiz

Take the following quiz to see how much you've learned.

Questions

1. After you install Internet Explorer, what role does it play in Publisher?

    a. It lets you preview Web pages in a real browser.

    b. It converts pubs into pages.

    c. It converts pages into pubs.

    d. It gets Microsoft in hot water with the Justice Department.

2. The Web Publishing Wizard helps you

    a. Create Web pages

    b. Format Web pages

    c. Publish Web pages on an intranet

    d. Publish Web pages on the Internet

Answers

1. (a) IE4 is for testing your work.

2. (d) In Hour 24 you'll learn how to use the Wizard to copy Web page files onto the Internet.

Activities

Review any pubs you've been working on, and think about who those pubs are intended for. Do any of those pubs match an audience that might be better reached online than in print?

21

Hour **22**

Creating a Web Page in Publisher

I feel a little guilty—I've been leading you on. I've promised since the Introduction that in this part of the book you'd learn how to create Web pages in Publisher. But you know what? You already know how to create Web pages. Surprise!

For all intents and purposes, creating, editing, and formatting a Web page in Publisher is not really any different from what you do with a printed pub. You create and arrange frames and put text and pictures in 'em. Easy.

All you need to know now is the few simple steps you must take to tell Publisher that the pub is for the Web, not for paper. Doing so instructs Publisher to limit the kinds of formatting choices available in that pub to those that work on the Web (and to add a few Web-specific tools, too). In this hour, you'll discover those steps. At the end of the hour, you'll be able to answer the following questions:

- In what special ways does Publisher manage the fundamental difference between a Web page file and a regular pub?

- How can I create a fully formatted Web site in a flash, with a wizard?
- How do I give my page a title and choose other optional properties for it?
- How can I preview my page in Internet Explorer to see what my visitors will see?
- What special helping tools can I call upon to assist me when editing a Web page?
- Can I convert an existing print pub file into a Web page file?
- How can I design a Web page specifically for display on an 800×600 display?

Understanding the Weird, Wonderful Way Publisher Webs

In Hour 21, "Understanding Online Publishing," you learned that a Web page file is in a special format—called HTML and using the extension .htm or .html—that's different from a regular .pub file.

But Publisher isn't built for editing HTML files, so it cheats a little. When you work on a Web site in Publisher, the whole time you're working on it it's still a pub file (see Figure 22.1), using the extension .pub. (It's a special kind of pub file, though, that Publisher knows is intended as a Web page.) When you open or save a Web page in Publisher, you open or save a .pub file, as always.

FIGURE 22.1.

Publisher's view of a Web site, as you edit it, is not exactly WYSIWYG; you must preview the file in Internet Explorer to get a real WYSIWYG view.

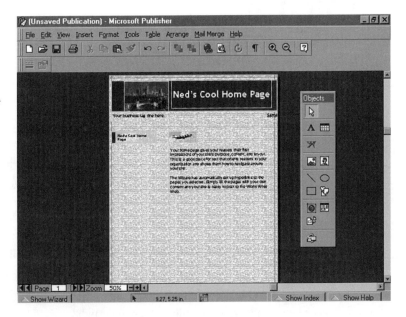

22

But when you finally publish the file (copy it to a Web server, as you learn to do in Hour 24, "Putting Your Page on the Web"), Publisher then converts the pub file into HTML format, giving it a new filename and extension online. Publisher calls this process of converting the pub file to HTML at publishing time *generating the Web site*.

NEW TERM A *Web site* is a set of separate Web pages, each in its own file, that are linked together to function as a single, multipart document. Most Web sites have a beginning home or top page containing links that the visitor clicks to jump to the site's other pages. In Publisher, you create, open, or edit whole Web sites at once (as a single pub), and move from page to page just as you'd move among the pages of a print pub. The pages are automatically separated into individual files when published.

There's an advantage to this weird approach. After a pub has been designated as a Web site (either because you created it as such or because you converted it from a print pub), you edit and format it exactly as you would any other pub, adding and positioning frames and formatting their contents. Publisher's cheating enables you to apply your familiar Publisher skills to the new job of Web authoring.

As you know from Hour 21, a Web page does not support all the formatting possible in a print pub, and a Web page does support a few things—such as multimedia—that a print pub doesn't.

But you needn't think too much about those differences because when you're working in a pub file that you've designated as a Web page, Publisher changes the toolbar buttons, menu items, and other options to those required for Web page work. It limits your work to the stuff that can go in a Web page, so you don't have to think about what you can and cannot do.

Although Publisher helps you avoid formatting that's not supported in a Web page (especially if you run the Design Checker, as described later in this hour), there are a few big differences you should consider when creating and formatting text and pictures. (These subtle, sneaky differences are one reason it's important to regularly preview your Web page in Internet Explorer, as you learn to do later in this hour.)

Text Tips

You create and edit text frames and text in a Web site exactly as you do in any other pub. But because the options for text formatting are much more limited on the Web than in print, a few things will happen a little differently in order to best preserve the formatting choices you make while also maintaining Web compatibility.

Fancy formatted text is converted to a picture, so that it still looks the way you want it to online. The types of text that turn into pictures include

- WordArt (which is pretty much a picture anyway)
- Text in table cells
- Text in a frame with a fill color or shading in it
- Rotated text
- Text that overlaps another object
- Text in a frame that is very close to another object

It's important to know when text is turned into a picture for two reasons:

- The more pictures in a Web page, the larger its files and the slower it will materialize on the visitor's screen. When performance is important to you, you must be careful that your pages do not include too many pictures.
- Some people use text-only Web browsers or switch off picture display in their browsers, and thus see only the text in Web pages. If important text in your page has turned to pictures, it's invisible to these visitors. To make your page work for them, you'll need to simplify the text formatting so that Publisher does not turn text into pictures, or you'll need to repeat any text turned to pictures in simple text elsewhere on the page.

Text not formatted in one of these ways will remain text in the Web page. However, it might not show up in the size or font you selected. The Web supports a limited selection of text sizes, so all text is converted to the closest supported size, which might not match what you intended.

More importantly, the fonts you choose will show up on the visitor's browser only if the visitor also has those same fonts installed on his or her computer. If you set text in, say, the Garamond font, any visitor who does not also have Garamond on his PC will instead see that text in a standard default font selected in his browser. That's not a big deal—your words still get through. But as always with Web pages, you cannot assume that what you create is *exactly* what the visitor sees.

A few standard fonts are widely supported, so using these most often in your Web pages improves the chances that your visitors will see text as you intend (although there's still no guarantee). In Publisher, you apply the standard Web fonts by using the TrueType fonts shown in Figure 22.2.

FIGURE 22.2.

Use these fonts to improve the chances that text will be formatted in the visitor's browser as you intend—or at least pretty close to it.

Arial (and **Arial Black**)
Comic Sans MS
Courier New
Georgia
Impact
Σψμβολ
Times New Roman
Trebuchet MS
Verdana
♦)(■ ℔Ω)(■ ℔♦   (Wingdings)

22

Pic Tips

Although you can use many different types of graphics files in a print pub (see Hour 13, "Getting Graphics"), only two types are technically supported in Web pages: GIF (.gif) and JPEG (.jpg). However, that rule has no effect on what files you can use in a Publisher Web page. You can insert pictures in any of the file formats Publisher supports (including any object from the Clip Gallery or Design Gallery). When it generates the Web site from your pub, Publisher automatically converts all graphics to .gif format.

Wizarding Up a Web Page

The best way to create a Web site in Publisher is to start with a wizard; doing this gives you a great-looking Web layout quickly, and helps you avoid adding elements or formatting that won't play well online.

You start a Web Site Wizard from the Catalog, like any other wizard. The Web site templates are easy to spot in the Catalog, because they all have the words "Web Site" in their names:

- To see all the Web site template previews at once, open the Catalog's Publications by Wizard tab and choose Web Sites from the Wizards list (see Figure 22.3).

- To see Web site templates matched with stylistically similar print templates, open the Catalog's Publications by Design tab, choose the Design Set you want, and scroll to the templates that include Web Site in their names.

FIGURE 22.3.

To start a new Web site, choose a template with the words Web Site in its name.

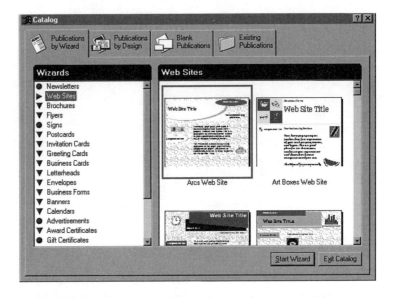

After choosing a template, click Start Wizard to run through a series of questions as you would for any other wizard. The following To Do shows what each of the questions means.

To Do: Run a Wizard to Make a New Web Site

1. Open the Catalog's Publications by Wizard tab, and click Web Sites in the column of Wizards.

2. In the panel of Web Site template previews to the right, click any one you like (your choice!).

3. Click the Start Wizard button. The Web Site Wizard opens. Click Next to move past the Welcome. (As you perform the remaining steps, click Next after each step.)

4. Choose a color scheme just as you would for a print pub.

5. Check the check box for any pages you'd like in your site. If you check no check boxes, the Wizard will produce a single home page. Check check boxes to add pages with a particular layout: Story is formatted as a general-purpose, text-oriented page; Calendar provides a calendar of events, and so on.

6. The next part of the wizard offers you a chance to add a *form*, a page containing boxes in which visitors can enter information, as in an order form. You'll learn a little more about forms—including reasons you'll probably not use them just yet—in Hour 23, "Adding Links, Motion, and Other Web Goodies." For now, choose None.

22

▼ 7. When a site contains multiple pages, the wizard can automatically add a navigation bar to every page that provides links for jumping among the pages of the site. You can choose to make those links out of text labels alone (which improves your page's performance by not including a graphical navigation bar), graphics alone (which adds a spiffy graphical navigation bar), or graphics and text (so that text-only browser users still get links they can use).

8. Next, the wizard lets you add a background sound that plays automatically when the visitor arrives (if the visitor's computer and browser support sound). Click Yes to add the sound. (You'll learn more about adding sounds in Hour 23.)

9. Next, the wizard lets you add a texture covering the background of all pages, which can look pretty neat. (In Hour 23, you'll learn how to choose your background color or texture manually.)

▲ 10. Finally, the wizard lets you add a good old personal information set. After choosing one, click Finish to finish up. Save your new Web site.

When looking at your new Web site, keep in mind that some aspects of it won't function properly in Publisher:

- The navigation bar doesn't work; use the regular Publisher page controls to move among pages in the site.

- Animations and background sounds do not play. (You can, however, test a link to a sound clip from within Publisher, as described in Hour 23.)

To see how these objects work, you must preview the site as described later in this hour.

Choosing Properties for Your Page

You learned in Hour 17, "Setting Up for a Printing Service," about optionally setting up properties for a pub file to identify the file and stamp your name on it for a printing service. But when you create a Web site, there's one property that's never optional.

It's very important that you take a few moments after creating a new Web site to give its top page a title. While on the top page, choose File | Web Properties to open the Web Properties dialog (see Figure 22.4), where you can enter a title on the Page tab (required) and change other properties on either of the two tabs (optional). When working with properties, remember that

- Items on the Site tab of the Web Properties dialog affect all pages in the current Web site open in Publisher.

- Items on the Page tab of the Web Properties dialog affect only the page you were viewing when you opened the dialog. You can choose these items separately for each page.

FIGURE 22.4.

Identify your page to the Web by giving it a title on the Page tab of the Web Properties dialog.

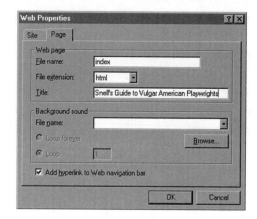

Giving Your Page a Descriptive Title

The most important item on the Web Properties dialog—and the only one you absolutely *must* change—is the title that appears on the Page tab. Publisher fills this in automatically with a generic, default title, but you should replace that with a short title that concisely but accurately describes the contents of your page.

"Ned's Home Page," for example, is too generic—it doesn't tell a visitor enough about what the page contains. Better titles might be "Ned Snell's MS Publisher Home Page," or "Ned's Movie Reviews Page," or "The Snell Guide to Vulgar American Playwrights."

It's important that the title you enter is descriptive and engaging because it identifies your page to the Web in all the following ways:

- When a visitor displays the page, the page's title appears in the title bar of the visitor's Web browser.
- If a visitor uses his browser to create a Bookmark or Favorite for your page (to revisit it easily), the title is what appears in the visitor's bookmarks or favorites list.
- When a search engine that automatically catalogs the contents of the Web—such as Excite or AltaVista (see Hour 24)—creates a listing for your page, it will use information from the title to decide under what categories to list your page.
- When a visitor finds your page in a list of pages generated by a search, what the visitor sees in the list is the title.

Besides the title, the other properties a search engine looks for are the key-words and description, both of which you can supply on the Site tab of the Web Properties dialog.

In Keywords, type one or more keywords that describe the contents of your site. In a search engine, whenever anyone searches for pages that match one of those words, your page will appear among the search results.

For The Snell Guide to Vulgar American Playwrights, my keywords might be *play*, *playwright*, *theatre*, *drama*. (Note that you separate multiple keywords with commas.)

In Description, type a brief, general description of your site. Some search engines display the description along with the title.

Choosing Other Optional Properties

When you're just starting out, it's best to leave everything else on the two tabs of the Web Properties dialog—besides Title and maybe the Keywords and Description—alone. But in case you run into problems or get an attack of technical ambition, it's valuable to know what a couple of these other options are about.

Target Audience

Every few years, a new standard is approved for HTML file formats, and the new stan-dard always includes support for new, fancier formatting options. To display those options, however, a visitor must have a newer browser that's compatible with the new standard.

By default, Web pages created in Publisher conform to an older, well-established stan-dard called HTML 2.0, which is supported by virtually every browser around. If you leave this choice in place, Publisher helps ensure that you don't apply formatting that isn't supported by HTML 2.0 browsers *and* all browsers that support more recent stan-dards, too.

If you will publish to a corporate intranet (see Hour 24) or other environment where you can be certain that all visitors use state-of-the-art browsers that support HTML 4.0, switching to that option allows Publisher to apply some kinds of advanced formatting, such as better font control, that aren't supported in HTML 2.0.

File Name and File Extension

When you publish, new HTML files are generated and copied to the Internet. Publisher automatically assigns filenames to the HTML files it generates: the top page is named `Index.htm` and any other pages are named `page1.htm`, `page2.htm`, and so on.

If you have your own private directory on the Web server where you publish your files (see Hour 24), these filenames will work fine. However, if you share that directory with someone else, that person might already have published a file named Index.htm. In such cases, you can use the File Name and File Extension options on the Page tab to choose new filenames.

Evaluating Your Page

A Web page is not meant to be viewed through Publisher—it's supposed to be viewed through a browser, such as Internet Explorer or Netscape Navigator. And as you've seen, the process of generating a Web page from the pub you see in Publisher brings about several important changes, such as converting fancy text into pictures. More importantly, multimedia in the page—sound and animation—will not play in Publisher.

So you can do broad, general work on your page within Publisher's view of it, but to get a fully accurate view of the way it will appear to others online, you must preview the page through Internet Explorer. In addition to previewing, you have a few other tools at your disposal—the Design Checker and the Troubleshooter—to help you smooth out any problems you might find.

You must have Microsoft's Internet Explorer installed on your PC to use the preview. See Hour 21 for more details.

Previewing the Page

To preview your page, open the page in Publisher and click the Web Site Preview button on the Standard toolbar. Internet Explorer opens (see Figure 22.5) and shows your page as it will appear to visitors on the Web—or at least to visitors using Internet Explorer or Netscape Navigator, who together make up the overwhelming majority of Web users.

In the Preview, the page behaves exactly as it will online: Navigation buttons work (so you can jump from page to page) and animated graphics and sounds play.

To return to Publisher after previewing the page, close Internet Explorer or click Publisher's button on the Windows taskbar.

FIGURE 22.5.

Click the Web Site Preview button to get a WYSIWYG view of your Web site in Internet Explorer.

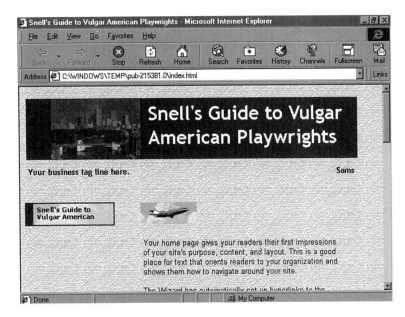

You can leave Internet Explorer open after previewing and return to Publisher by clicking its button on the Windows taskbar. However, after you make more changes to the page in Publisher, you can't preview the page again simply by switching back to Internet Explorer.

Every time you preview—even if Internet Explorer is already open—you must click the Web Site Preview button so that Publisher can generate a new preview file containing all the changes you've made since the last time you previewed the site.

Displaying the Preview Troubleshooter

Publisher offers a Preview Troubleshooter that's akin to the Print Troubleshooter you met in Hour 8, "Printing Proofs"—only not as useful. Publisher can't show its own help contents atop Internet Explorer, so to read the troubleshooter's advice you must switch back and forth between the preview and Publisher (you can use the button on the Windows taskbar to do this).

Setting Up the Troubleshooter

To set up the Preview Troubleshooter, first open or create any Web page in Publisher (the option you need in order to enable the troubleshooter is available only when a Web site is the current pub). Then open Publisher's Options dialog (Tools | Options).

On the General tab, check the Preview Web Site with Preview Troubleshooter check box. As long as you do not later remove that check mark, the troubleshooter will appear automatically any time you preview a Web page.

Using the Troubleshooter

To use the Preview Troubleshooter, preview a Web page and evaluate its appearance. When you notice any problem you don't already know how to fix, click the Publisher button on the Windows taskbar to return to Publisher, where you'll see the Preview Troubleshooter displayed in the Help Contents (see Figure 22.6).

FIGURE 22.6.

Use the Preview Troubleshooter to figure out and fix flaws you see in your Web pages.

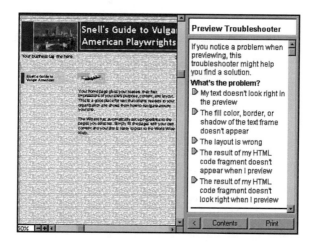

In the Contents, choose the item that most closely describes the problem you observed in your Web page. You'll see another set of more specific problem descriptions. Continue choosing the items that best match your problem until you arrive at help text that tells you how to fix it.

Checking a Web Page's Design

Publisher offers a special Design Checker, different from the regular Design Checker for Print pubs (see Hour 17). This Design Checker checks for design problems in a Web site and offers suggestions for improvement.

The Design Checker is especially helpful when you're starting out because it alerts you to many of the ways a Web page is different from a print pub. For example, it tells you where and when fancy text will be converted into a picture. Knowing such information can help you find and fix problems later.

You can run the Design Checker from time to time when developing a page to help guide its evolution, and you should always run the Design Checker before publishing the page to help perform any final cleanup steps.

To run the Design Checker, choose Tools | Design Checker. The Design Checker at first displays a simple dialog on which you can choose to check the design of the whole Web site or only selected pages. After you click OK on that dialog, the Design Checker locates the first object in the page it considers a potential problem, and displays a dialog like the one shown in Figure 22.7.

FIGURE 22.7.

The special Web site Design Checker alerts you to objects and formatting that won't work well online.

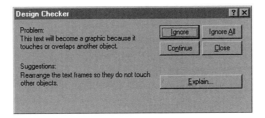

The Design Checker dialog describes the problem it has found and offers a suggestion for repairing it. While viewing the Design Checker's advice, you can do the following:

- Click in the pub and make whatever change the Checker recommends. Then click the Checker's Continue button to proceed to the next problem.
- Click Ignore to instruct the Checker to ignore this particular problem and move ahead to the next.
- Click Ignore All to instruct the Checker to ignore this type of problem, both here and anywhere else in the page or site.
- Click Explain to display Help text about the problem at hand.
- Click Close to quit the Design Checker.

Wizardless Ways to Start Web Pages

Again, the best way to start a Web page in Publisher is to choose an appropriate Web site template from the Catalog—and when you want a Web site, I *highly* recommend you start that way.

But you do have two other options: You can create a blank Web site into which you can pour whatever contents you like, or you can convert an existing print pub file into a Web site.

Creating a Blank Web Site

When starting from scratch, even when you don't want to use a wizard, it's important to determine from the outset that the pub you're creating is a Web page, so that Publisher can present you with the proper tools and options for Web work.

To create a new, blank Web page, open the Catalog's Blank Publications tab, choose Web Page from the list, and click the Create button. A new, completely blank Web page appears, ready for your objects.

Converting a Print Pub to a Page

When you convert an existing pub to a Web page, the results are never perfect; you typically must do a substantial amount of editing and formatting in the resulting Web page to make it look the way you want it.

For that reason, the only time it makes sense to convert an existing print pub to a Web page is when the original pub contains so much content—text and pictures—that also belongs in the Web page that cleaning up the Web page is less work than starting over from scratch. Keep in mind that there is a happy medium: You can start a new Web page and selectively copy to it any text or pictures you want from the print pub.

The following To Do shows how to convert an existing print pub to a Web site.

When you convert a print pub to a Web site, you really create a copy of the print pub to use as a Web site—the original pub file is unaffected. When you save the Web site, give it a filename different from the pub from which it was created, so the Web page file doesn't replace the original.

To Do: Convert a Print Pub to a Web Site

22

1. Open the pub you want to convert to a Web site.

2. Choose File | Create Web Site from Current Publication. What happens next depends on the complexity of the original pub:

   For most simple, one-page pubs, Publisher simply designates it a Web site, makes no other changes, and displays a dialog asking whether you want to run the Design Checker (to look for objects and formatting that won't work well on the Web). It's a good idea to run the Checker, and then preview the page to assess the situation before moving ahead to editing.

   For more complex pubs (especially multipage ones), Publisher displays the Convert To Web Site dialog (see Figure 22.8). On the dialog, choose Use the Web Site Wizard… to run the wizard (as described earlier in this hour) and let it rework your pub for the Web, creating a home page with a navigation bar leading to other pages. Choose Add My Own Hyperlinks… to simply designate the file a Web page, and edit it from there.

FIGURE 22.8.

When converting a complex pub to a Web site, Publisher offers the option to call upon the wizard's design assistance.

Designing for Different Resolutions

By default, Publisher's Web pages are designed to look their best when the visitor's display is running in 640×480 resolution (the standard screen resolution for both Windows 95 and the Macintosh). This resolution is often called *standard VGA* resolution.

However, a growing number of computer users routinely use a higher screen resolution of 800×600 (called *SVGA* resolution) or even higher resolutions. Higher resolutions make graphics and some text appear smaller, altering the overall look of a Web page.

A page designed for VGA screens still looks pretty good when displayed on an SVGA screen, but the reverse is sometimes not true. A Web page designed for SVGA might be too wide for a VGA display, forcing the visitor to do a lot of annoying horizontal scrolling to see both sides.

On the Web, you'll get visitors using both VGA and SVGA resolutions. For that reason, I recommend sticking with the default VGA setup in your Publisher Web pages so they look good to everybody. But if you intend to publish on a company intranet (see Hour 24) where you might know that all your visitors will use SVGA resolution, you may choose to design your Web pages specifically for that resolution.

To design a page for SVGA, open the page in Publisher, and choose File | Page Setup. On the Web Page Setup dialog (see Figure 22.9), change the Page Width from Standard (VGA) to Wide (SVGA).

FIGURE 22.9.

Use the Web Page Setup dialog to create wide pages for 800×600 display.

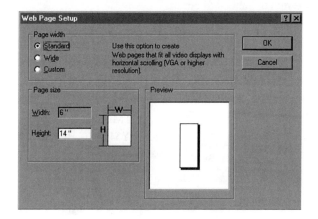

If you design pages for SVGA, you'll get an accurate preview on your PC only if your PC is configured for 800×600 resolution, too.

To configure Windows 95 for SVGA display, right-click an empty area of the desktop to open the pop-up menu, choose Properties, and then click the Settings tab on the Display Properties dialog. In the Desktop Area part of the dialog, drag the slider control to the right until it reads 800 By 600 Pixels.

Summary

At its heart, a Web page is a pub. But you can't control it quite as finely as you can a print pub. In a way, that sets you free. Use all your Publisher skills (plus the new ones you'll pick up in the next hour) to make your pages shine, then trust Publisher to keep your work within the boundaries of Web formatting.

Workshop

The following workshop helps solidify the skills you learned in this lesson.

22

Q&A

Q I'm comfortable with Publisher and all that, but are there better programs for creating Web pages? Somebody told me I can actually use Internet Explorer or Netscape to write pages.

A When installed with their Full installation options, both Internet Explorer 4 and Netscape Communicator include Web authoring programs. Internet Explorer's is called FrontPage Express (and is included with Internet Explorer on your Publisher 98 CD-ROM), and Communicator's is called Composer. In addition to these easy-to-use, beginner's Web authoring programs, there are many other, more sophisticated programs, such as Microsoft's FrontPage 98.

Are they better than Publisher for creating Web pages? That depends. These programs let you work directly on the HTML file, and what you see while you work comes much closer to an accurate, WYSIWYG representation of the way the page will look online. On the other hand, switching to a new program forces you to learn a whole new way of working—and you're already comfortable with Publisher.

So if you create many print pubs and only an occasional Web site, it's probably best to stick to Publisher. If you'll do a lot of Web authoring, it might be worth your while to learn one of these other Web-specific programs.

Quiz

Take the following quiz to see how much you've learned.

Questions

1. While you edit a Web site in Publisher, you're actually editing

   a. An HTML (Web site) file.

   b. An ordinary Publisher `.pub` file.

   c. A pub file specially designed to generate a Web page file when you preview or publish.

   d. A pub file specially designed to generate applause.

2. Which of the following places will your Web site's title appear?

    a. In visitors' bookmarks or favorites menus.

    b. In the title bar of a visitor's browser.

    c. As an item—leading to your page—in a list generated by a search tool.

    d. All the above.

3. A great way to develop a new Web site is to fully develop it first as a print pub, then convert it to a Web site. (True/False)

Answers

1. (c) What you see in Publisher is a special pub file; the real Web site files are created only when you preview or publish, and are never seen in Publisher.

2. (d) The title shows up in all these places to identify your page or site.

3. False. If it's a Web page you want, make that choice from the outset.

Activities

Open up any of the regular print pubs you've created so far (or make new ones with wizards), quickly convert them into Web sites (using the wizard, if Publisher offers it), and then preview the results. How much more work would you need to do to make these converted pubs into good-looking Web sites?

HOUR 23

Adding Links, Motion, and Other Web Goodies

Now you know how to create Web pages—but the stuff you know how to put in those pages is pretty much the same stuff you've been putting in print pubs for about the last 14 hours. So your question is fair: "Ned, what have I taught myself *lately*?"

In this penultimate hour, you'll learn how to add to your Web pages all the cool, online-only stuff like music, animation, and the ever-popular hyperlinks.

At the end of the hour, you'll be able to answer the following questions:

- What does *penultimate* mean? (Next to last.)
- How can I add new hyperlinks to my Web pages to give my visitors new places to go?
- Can I put different links on different parts of a picture?
- How do I add music, sound effects, and animated pictures to a page?

- How do I add a background sound to a page and control how it plays?
- How can I add a background color or texture?
- What are online forms all about?

Adding Links

You know from your own surfing excursions that *links*—more fully and properly described as *hyperlinks*—are the text or pictures in a Web page that make something happen when you click them. A link can

- Jump the visitor from your Web site to anywhere else on the Web—another Web page, a link in a Web page that opens or downloads a file, and so on. All you need to know is the address, or *URL,* you would enter to go there yourself.

- Jump the visitor to another page within your Web site. The links in the navigation bar added by the Web Site Wizard are these kinds of links.

- Open or download a file of yours (such as a text or word-processing file) that's not a Web page. When you add the link, the file is on your hard disk. But Publisher automatically copies that file to the Internet when you publish, so that visitors can download or open the file but don't have any access to your PC or hard disk.

- Open the visitor's email program and preaddress a new message to a particular email address, so the visitor can conveniently send a message to that address. You might use this type of link to supply a button or text visitors can click to send email to you, to tell you how they like your Web site.

> Some folks on the Web use browsers that don't open their email programs when they click an email link. So when you create a link to an email address, include that address in the onscreen text to which you attach the link; for example, you might attach an email link to the phrase:
>
> `Send me email at neddy@sample.com.`
>
> That way, visitors whose browsers don't support email links can simply read the address to which the link leads and enter that address manually in their email programs.

You create all these links in roughly the same way: By first adding to the page the text or picture you want the visitor to click, and then attaching the link to it. The following To Do shows how to add a new hyperlink.

Before publishing a Web page containing a link to someone else's Web site, email the *Webmaster* of that site—the person who manages it—and request permission to use the link in your page. You can often find the Webmaster's email address in an email link near the bottom of the site's home page.

To Do: Add Hyperlinks

1. Open or create any Web page pub in Publisher.
2. Locate the text or a picture you want to make into a link.
3. Select the object:
   - If text, you can actually highlight only a portion of the text in the frame to make that text alone the link. Whatever text you select will be underlined and displayed in a unique color when the visitor views it, to show that it's a link.
   - If a picture, just click the picture to select it.
4. Click the Insert Hyperlink button in the Standard toolbar, or choose Insert | Hyperlink. The Hyperlink dialog opens (see Figure 23.1).

23

FIGURE 23.1.

Select an object and click the Insert Hyperlink button to add any kind of link.

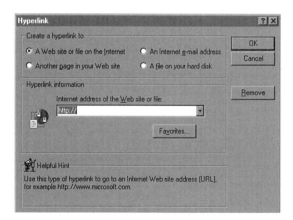

5. In the Create a Hyperlink To section at the top of the dialog, select the type of hyperlink you want to create. (The options available in the next box, Hyperlink Information, change depending on your selection.)

▼ 6. Fill in the Hyperlink Information box, supplying the information requested. For a
    link to

  • A Web site or file on the Web, fill in the complete URL of the site. Note that
    the `http://` part is already supplied for you.

> When filling in a Web site link, you can fill in the URL easily by clicking the
> Favorites button, then choosing one of the favorite pages you've selected
> while browsing the Web with Internet Explorer.

  • Another page in your Web site, choose the page from the list presented.

  • An email address, fill in the complete email address (for example,
    `fredo@server.com`).

  • A file on your hard disk, enter the complete path and filename (for example,
    `C:\readme.txt`), or click Browse to navigate to the file and select it from a
    dialog.

  7. Click OK. The link has been attached to the selected object. To edit the link later,
▲   select the object and choose Insert | Hyperlink again.

> When you attach a link to a picture, it's customary to create elsewhere on
> the page (usually near the bottom) a second link that leads to the same
> place, but is attached to text instead of a picture. That gives users of text-
> only browsers a link that works for them, too.

Putting a Bunch of Links in One Object

If you're an experienced Web surfer, you might have noticed that some pictures contain
more than one link. For example, clicking on different heads in a group photo can acti-
vate different links, each leading to information about the person whose head you
clicked. Such multilink pictures are called *image maps*, and you can create them very
easily in Publisher through a tool called Hot Spots.

Using the Hot Spots tool, you draw Hot Spots areas—just the way you'd draw a frame—
over the part of a picture you want assigned to a particular link; then you define the link
for the spot. You'll get the picture in the next To Do.

Some browsers don't support the kind of image maps created by Publisher's Hot Spots, and some browsers don't support pictures at all. Always create a second set of text links elsewhere on the page to repeat any Hot Spot links for those whose browsers don't support them.

To Do: Make Hot Spots

23

1. Start in any Web site pub, and locate or insert a picture you want to attach multiple links to. (If you need an example for practice, open the Clip Gallery's Clip Art tab, choose People from the list of Categories, and insert a clip art picture showing two or more people. That way, you can assign a different hot spot to each person.)

2. Click the Hot Spot tool in the Objects toolbar.

3. Point to the picture, and click and drag to draw a box around the portion of the picture to which you want to attach a link. (For example, drag to draw a box around one person in a multiperson picture.) When you release the button, the Hyperlink dialog opens automatically.

4. Define the link in the Hyperlink box, as usual.

5. Repeat steps 2, 3, and 4 for other areas of the picture to which you want to attach links.

Adding Mondo Multimedia

Multimedia—sound and motion—are the fun part of the Web, and they're pretty easy to add in Publisher, as you're about to see. Just keep in mind that the more pizzazz you add to a page—pictures, sounds, and motion—the larger that page's files, and the slower it will materialize on the visitor's screen.

You want to use enough cool stuff to make the page fun, but not so much that the visitor visibly ages while waiting for your page to show up. You probably know from your own Web travels how frustrating it is to wait for a Web page. So do unto others…

Adding Sound and Motion Clips from the Clip Gallery

The easiest and best way to add the zip of multimedia to your Web pages is to pull it from the Clip Gallery.

You insert sounds (sound effects or music) or "motion clips" from the Clip Gallery exactly as you would a clip art image: Click the Clip Art Gallery tool on the Objects toolbar and draw a frame (or click in your Web page and choose Insert | Picture | Clip

Art). Then choose a file from the Sounds or Motion Clips tab of the Gallery (see Figure 23.2).

FIGURE 23.2.

Add multimedia from the Sounds and Motion Clips tabs of the Clip Gallery.

Note that most of the multimedia files are on the Publisher CD, not on your hard disk, so it's smart to insert your Publisher CD before opening the Clip Gallery to get multimedia files. However, if you select from the Gallery a sound or animation that's only on the CD, and you have not inserted the CD, Publisher reminds you to insert it.

On the Sounds and Motion Clips tabs of the Clip Gallery, you'll notice a new button: Play. Click the Play button so you can hear the sound or watch the animation to evaluate it before inserting it in your Web page.

In your Web page:

- The sound clips show up as little sound clip icons (see Figure 23.3), which you can size and position like any picture. When your visitors click that icon, the sound plays. (To add a sound that plays automatically and without showing an icon, see "Adding a Background Sound," later in this hour.)

FIGURE 23.3.

When you add a sound from the Clip Gallery, this icon appears in your page.

23

- The motion clips appear in your pub as pictures, which you can position and size like any other picture. When your visitors display the page, the motion will play automatically, and will *loop*, or play over and over, as long as the visitor views the page.

To test your animations, preview the Web page in Internet Explorer. To test a sound clip, preview the Web page and click the sound clip icon, or double-click the sound icon in Publisher. (Sound clips are the one kind of multimedia that can be tested from within Publisher.)

When sizing and positioning a motion clip, be careful not to overlap any other frame. If you do, Publisher converts the motion clip to an ordinary picture when you publish. (It warns you about this when you preview the page, so you can easily go back and fix any overlapping before you publish.)

The motion clips you insert from the Clip Gallery are actually a special kind of GIF graphic file called an *animated GIF*. You can find new animated GIFs in clip art collections and all over the Web; in Appendix A, "Internet Resources for Publisher Users," you can learn the addresses of Web pages where you can pick up new animated GIFs.

When you get a new animated GIF file, you insert it in your pub exactly as you would a regular GIF file: Insert | Picture | From File. You can size and position the file any way you want (but don't overlap another frame!) and preview the Web page to see the animation play. You can also use drag and drop to copy an animated GIF from another publication or document into a Web page.

However, you cannot use copy and paste (or cut and paste) to insert an animated GIF from another document; doing so inserts it as an ordinary, still picture, losing the animation. Also, note that when you publish the page, the animated GIF gets a new filename (`img1.gif`, `img2.gif`, and so on).

Adding a Background Sound

When a Web page has a background sound effect or music clip, no icon appears on it. Instead, the sound simply plays, automatically and invisibly, when a visitor arrives at the page (or when you preview the page).

The easiest way to add a background sound is to let the Web Site Wizard do it for you, as shown in Hour 22, "Creating a Web Page in Publisher." But you can optionally add a sound to any page of a site, and you can also control the way the sound plays (even if you used the wizard to add it).

To add a background sound, open the page on which you want the sound to play, choose File | Web Properties, and then choose the Page tab of the Web Properties dialog (see Figure 23.4). Click Browse to browse for a sound clip file; when you select one, its path and filename appear in the Page tab.

FIGURE 23.4.

Use the Page tab of the Web Properties dialog to add a background sound and control how it plays.

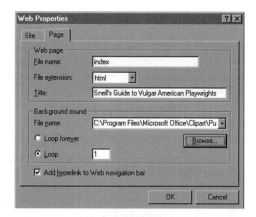

Also on the Page tab, observe that you have two choices for how the sound plays:

- *Loop Forever*: The sound will repeat continuously as long as the visitor views the page. This is often a good choice for a music clip, but use it carefully. If the page is a type that the visitor might stay on for awhile (one with a lot to read), the sound can become annoying after three or four loops.

- *Loop*: Choosing this option makes the sound play only the number of times indicated in the number following Loop. This option, used with a number of 1 (the sound plays just once, to welcome the visitor, then stops), is usually best for sound effects.

Choosing Background Colors and Textures

Web page backgrounds and textures are a very popular way to quickly and easily dress up a page. In Publisher, you choose a Web page's background texture or color on the same dialog you use to choose a color scheme.

Why? Well, it's important to select text colors and background colors that contrast, to make sure the text is legible. So it makes sense to choose all your colors from the same dialog—although you can still use the regular Font Color button to choose the color of selected text.

To choose a background color, open the page where you want the color to appear, and select Format | Color and Background Scheme. The Color and Background Scheme dialog opens (see Figure 23.5).

FIGURE 23.5.

Choose a Web page's color scheme, background color, or texture all from one dialog.

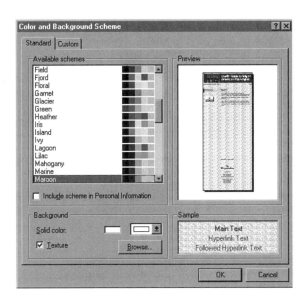

Choose an overall color scheme from the list provided, and move to the Background part of the dialog. Drop down the list next to Solid Color to choose a color that contrasts with (and also complements) your color scheme; the Preview and the Sample along the right side of the dialog show the effects of your choices.

Instead of choosing a background color, you can choose a *texture*, which is really a GIF image repeated over and over across the whole page background. Some such images are designed to create the effect of an even texture—marble or a geometric pattern—across the background, but you can choose any GIF image to create fun, tiled effects (see Figure 23.6).

FIGURE 23.6.

You can choose any GIF file as your background texture to achieve fun effects.

To choose a GIF image for the background, check the Texture check box; then click the Browse button and select the file.

You can't use both a background color and a background texture. Choose one or the other.

Understanding Forms

You can create online forms (see Figure 23.7) on your Web pages in two ways:

- The Web Site Wizard offers to create one for you (see Hour 22).
- While editing a Web page, you can click the Form Control tool on the Objects toolbar (see Figure 23.8) to open a menu of form objects, choose an object, and then draw a frame in your pub to add that object.

FIGURE 23.7.

The Web Site Wizard can create a form like this, but can't configure the processing of the information it collects.

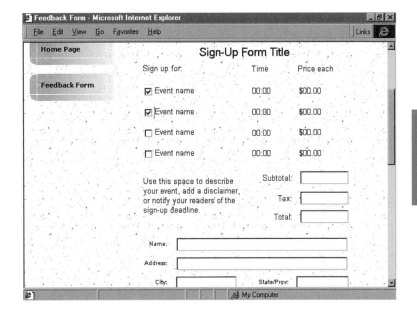

23

FIGURE 23.8.

You can use the Form Control tool on the Objects toolbar to add new form objects.

That sounds pretty simple, but there's a problem: The only reason to add a form of this type to a Web page is because you want your visitors to be able to fill in the form, and then have the information they supply delivered to you or processed in some way. And that part of creating forms—controlling how information is collected and processed—is a little tricky.

For information to be collected from your forms and delivered to you, the Web server on which your Web page is published must have certain special Microsoft software running on it (called *FrontPage extensions*), or a programmer must write a program (using a language such as JavaScript or CGI) to process your form data. On top of all that, any time you use a form you run up against a variety of security issues that must be resolved with the administrator of the Web server. And finally, if you publish your page on your Internet provider's Web server, you will probably be required to pay an extra monthly fee for any forms processing.

So the bottom line is this: Fully functional forms require expertise and instruction beyond the scope of this book. Feel free to play around with the Form Control tool—you can't hurt anything. But if you want your forms to function, you're going to have to sit down with the administrator of the Web server—and probably a programmer, too—to discuss how you want the information to be processed, after which they will take care of all that for you.

You and I haven't the time for a programming tutorial—there's only one hour left, and I still need to show you how to get your Web pages onto the Internet!

Summary

Multimedia and links are easy to add—maybe too easy. Add a touch here and there—a sound, an animated GIF—but don't go nuts. It isn't just the activity in your pages that makes them valuable, but the quality of their content.

Workshop

The following workshop helps solidify the skills you learned in this lesson.

Q&A

Q What about adding my own movie clips and such?

A When you're on the Web, with rare exceptions, really heavy-duty files such as movie clips are offered as files you download by clicking links. When you click a link that downloads a file, most browsers detect whether it's a file the browser can play (such as a movie clip), and offer the visitor a choice between simply downloading and saving the file or playing it right away.

So to offer multimedia files—or any files—other than animated GIFs and sounds, all you need to do is create or acquire the file (trying the best you can to ensure that the file uses a format common on the Web, such as the `.avi` or `.mov` types used most often for video clips); then create a link of the "A file on your hard disk" variety.

When you publish as described in the next hour, that file is automatically copied to the Web server along with the rest of your Web page files. When a visitor clicks the link, the file is downloaded from the Web server where you published it to the visitor's computer.

Quiz

Take the following quiz to see how much you've learned.

23

Questions

1. To what can a link point?
    a. A file on your PC.
    b. An email address.
    c. A Web page.
    d. All the above.

2. Hot Spots enable you to
    a. Boogie the night away.
    b. Scratch off a patch of fur.
    c. Put several different pictures into one link.
    d. Put different links into different parts of a picture.

3. You can change the size and position of a motion clip or other animated GIF. (True/False)

Answers

1. (d) You can link to all this stuff.
2. (d) Hot Spots allow you to attach different links to different parts of a picture.
3. True. You can size, scale, and move an animated GIF as you would any picture.

Activities

In the next hour, you'll learn how to publish your pages on the Web. To do that, you'll need space on a Web server, probably one at your Internet provider. If you haven't already done so, now is a good time to talk to your provider about Web server space.

HOUR 24

Putting Your Page on the Web

What's a Web page off the Web? It's a song sung in a vacuum. It's a painting in the dark. It's watching the Dustin Hoffman sci-fi movie *Sphere*—lots of time and effort for no discernible payoff. (I *still* don't understand what's in that silly sphere…do you?)

In this final hour, I'll show you how to set up and run the Web Publishing Wizard to copy your Publisher Web creations onto the Internet, and also offer a few tips for what to do after that. At the end of the hour, you'll be able to answer the following questions:

- How do I prepare to publish?
- How do I copy my page files onto a Web server to publish them online?
- After my files are published, how do I get the word out so people will visit them?

Getting a Home for Your Page: Server Space

After your Web page is finished, you must *upload* it to a Web server so that others on the Internet can see it.

NEW TERM Copying files from your PC to a server computer (through a network, such as the Internet) is called *uploading* them. (Copying files from a server to your PC is *downloading*.) To publish a Web page, you upload its files to a computer called a Web server.

First, you need space on somebody's Web server—enough to hold all the files that make up your page (the HTML file plus any pictures or multimedia files). A typical Web page with a picture or two usually requires less than 100KB (kilobytes) of space on a server. The larger and more picture-laden your page, the more server space you'll need.

- If your page is related to your job, you might be able to get permission to publish it on your company's Web server; talk to your company's network administrator or Webmaster. Most colleges and universities also have Web servers and often allow students and faculty to publish pages on them.

- If you don't have permission to publish your Web page on your company's or school's server and don't plan to create your own server (which is prohibitively expensive and technical for beginners), you must acquire space on somebody else's Web server, usually one operated by your Internet provider.

After you know whose server will hold your Web page files, you must upload the files from your PC to the server. You can use the Web Publishing Wizard to upload, as described next.

Before you start the wizard, though, you must contact the administrator of the Web server you will use and jot down some information you'll need during the uploading procedure. In particular, you need to know the following:

- The server's address—for example, `http://www.server.com`

- The *uploading protocol* used by the server; for example, HTTP or FTP

- Any username and password that you are required to use to gain access to the server

- The particular directory in which your files will be stored; for example, `http://www.server.com/ned/`

Running the Web Publishing Wizard

The first time you publish a page using the Web Publishing Wizard, you'll need to supply it with information about how to publish your files, such as the server address and
uploading protocol.

Supplying this information to the Web Publishing Wizard takes only a few minutes, but
after you've done it, later uploads will be even easier. The Web Publishing Wizard
remembers all your server information so that after you enter the information once, you
don't need to fiddle with the wizard again unless your server information changes.

> If you've been advised by your Web space provider to use a different pub-
> lishing technique than the Web Publishing Wizard, you still need to get the
> finished HTML files from Publisher so you have the files ready for publishing.
>
> To get those files, open the Web site file in Publisher, and choose File I Save
> As HTML to generate the Web site and save it in HTML format. You can then
> publish the resulting HTML files in whatever way your Web space provider
> has advised.

24

To Do: Upload a Web Page Using the Web Publishing Wizard

1. Finish your page in Publisher, and preview it in Internet Explorer to make sure it's
   finished and ready for public consumption. (If you discover flaws after uploading,
   however, you can fix them as described later.)

2. When the page is ready to be published, open the page in Publisher, and then choose File I Publish to Web. A dialog appears briefly, reporting that Publisher is generating the Web page files. Then the Web Publishing Wizard's Welcome dialog
   appears.

3. Click Next to clear the Welcome dialog, after which you'll see the Select a Web
   Server dialog shown in Figure 24.1. Click the New button to configure a new
   server.

> The next time you publish, you'll be able to simply select the preconfigured
> server from the Select a Web Server dialog, bypassing all the setup you're
> about to do in steps 4 through 7.

▼   4. On the Name the Web Server dialog, type a descriptive name for the server. Use
         anything you like; this is not the technical name of the server.

FIGURE 24.1.

Begin configuring the Web Publishing Wizard by setting up a server to which you'll publish.

5. Still on the Name the Web Server dialog, click the Advanced button. The Select
   Your Service Provider dialog opens. Drop down the list, choose the uploading protocol your server provider uses, and then click Next.

6. On the next dialog (shown in Figure 24.2), you must type the server address and
   directory in which you will store your page files. The URL is made up of the server address, your directory on that server, and the filename of the HTML file.

FIGURE 24.2.

Enter the server address and directory where your pages will be stored.

▼

▼   For example, suppose that my Internet provider's server is called
        `http://www.server.com`. On that server, my ISP has given me a directory called
        ned, and the filename of my page is `WhatWasInTheSphere.htm`. Put those together
        (separating the parts with forward slashes), and the URL is
        `http://www.server.com/ned/WhatWasInTheSphere.htm`.

> When typing a URL or server address in the Web Publishing Wizard, you
> must include the `http://` part, even though you can leave off that part
> when performing most other Web tasks in Internet Explorer or Netscape
> Navigator.

        When finished, click Next.

24

7. What the next dialog shows depends on the protocol you selected in step 6; this
    dialog collects the specific information required for uploading with the selected
    protocol.

    Complete the Provide Posting Information dialog, using the information your serv-
    er provider gave you for uploading, and then click Next.

    A final dialog appears, announcing that the wizard is ready to publish the files.

8. Click Finish. The wizard connects to the Internet (if necessary) and uploads your
▲   files.

> In the future, if you decide to make changes to the page you just published,
> simply edit the original copy of the file on your PC in Publisher, then publish
> again to the same server directory. The new, edited files will replace the last
> ones you published as long as you use the same filenames.

Announcing Your Page

After your page is on the server, it doesn't do you much good if nobody knows it's there.
(Just as a *Sphere* doesn't matter when nobody knows what's inside…oh, never mind.)
Here are a few final ideas for letting the world know your pub is online.

Listing Your Page in Web Directories

To start off, you must get your pages into the proper category listings of the major Web
directories and search tools, such as Yahoo! and Excite. Each has its own form and rules
for entering and describing your page.

When adding the URL of a business page to directories, do searches to find out how your competitors are listed. Then be sure your document is associated with the same categories or keywords. If anyone finds your competitors, they find you, too.

For example, to enter your page in the category listings for Yahoo!, perhaps the most popular directory, choose How to Suggest a Site from the bottom of the main Yahoo! page (www.yahoo.com). A list of instructions appears.

Following the instructions, you select a category in which you want your page listed and then scroll down to the form shown in Figure 24.3. In this form, you can enter your document's title and its URL and any additional categories in which you want it listed.

FIGURE 24.3.

Adding your page to the Yahoo! directory.

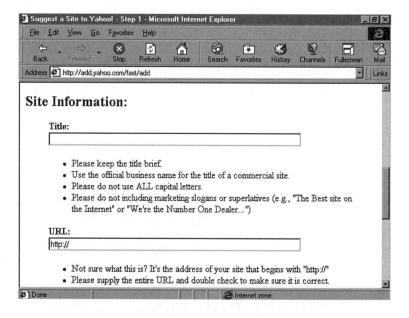

Like other search tools based on spiders or crawlers (including WebCrawler and AltaVista), Excite crawls around the Web cataloging its contents, and would eventually catalog your page. But you can speed up the process by suggesting your page. Choose Add URL from the bottom of the main Excite page (www.excite.com), and complete the form (see Figure 24.4).

FIGURE 24.4.

Suggesting your page to Excite.

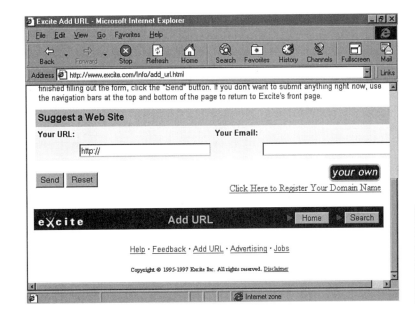

To make sure your page is located and properly cataloged by Web spiders, be sure to carefully and thoughtfully phrase the page's title, description, and keywords in the Web Properties dialog (see Hour 22, "Creating a Web Page in Publisher").

Commercial services have emerged that offer (for a fee) to list your page with many of the most popular directories and spiders, all in one quick step. If you care more about saving time than saving money, check out the following:

- The PostMaster (see Figure 24.5) at www.netcreations.com/postmaster/.
- Submit It! at www.submit-it.com.

There are also a few free site submission services that register your site with search engines, although these are not as powerful as those you pay for. Try Martin's Search Engine Submission Site at www.coollinks.com/submit/.

FIGURE 24.5.

The PostMaster.

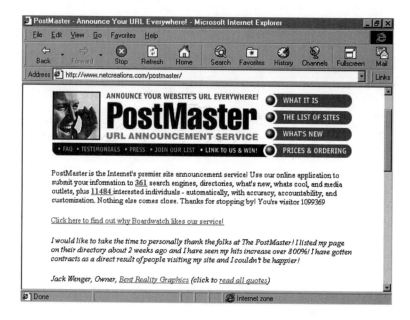

Publicizing Your Page off the Web

Don't forget that not all ways to publicize your Web page are on the Web (or even online). Be sure to list your Web page on all print publications you create, and also in all your communications and correspondence. (In fact, adding the URL to all your pubs is a great update project!)

Get that URL onto your

- Email signature
- Business cards
- Company or personal stationery
- Advertising and marketing collateral

Summary

Setting up to publish on the Web can be a little tricky, but Publishing itself is a snap. When you get it right once, repeating it is easy. That opens the door to more and better Web pages. Have fun!

Workshop

The following workshop helps solidify the skills you learned in this lesson.

Q&A

Q I want one of those cool little counters on my page that tells me how many visitors I've had. How do I get one?

A Counters require a special script as well as access to server logs. Typically, your Web server provider will add one for you for free if you have a business Internet account, or for a small fee if you have a personal Internet account.

Quiz

Take the following quiz to see how much you've learned.

24

Questions

1. Which of the following might be a source for server space for your Web page?

    a. Your Internet provider

    b. Your company

    c. Your school

    d. All the above

2. A typical Web page holding a picture or two usually takes up roughly how much disk space?

    a. Less than 100KB

    b. More than 2MB

    c. About an acre

    d. A couple of bytes

3. To update pages on the Web, you upload new files to replace the old ones. (True/False)

Answers

1. (d) All are space sources.

2. (a)

3. True

Activities

Enjoy Publisher. See you around!

PART VII

Appendix

Hour

APPENDIX **A**

Internet Resources for Publisher Users

This appendix is a directory of resources you can access on the Internet to support your work in Publisher, and to grow beyond it. To access these resources, you must have an Internet account.

If you're new to the Internet, consult the following:

- *Sams' Teach Yourself the Internet in 24 Hours*, 2nd Edition, by Ned Snell
- *Sams' Teach Yourself Internet Explorer 4 in 24 Hours*, by Noel Estabrook
- *Sams' Teach Yourself Netscape Communicator 4 in 24 Hours*, by Galen Grimes

Microsoft's Publisher Page

You can access Microsoft's Publisher page at

`http://www.microsoft.com/publisher`

You can jump to this page from within Publisher by choosing Help |
Microsoft Publisher Web Site.

Printing Services/Service Bureaus

Advanced Web Offset

`http://207.67.226.117/awo/content.htm`

GlobalPrint Directory

`http://www.globalprint.com/`

PrintBuyer.com

`http://www.printbuyer.com/`

PrintersLink Directory

`http://www.abcdprint.com/p-link/`

PrintersMart

`http://printersmart.com/`

Printovation

`http://www.printovation.com/`

VBS Services

`http://www.vbsnet.com/vbs.services1.htm`

General DTP Pages

Adobe Systems Incorporated

`http://www.adobe.com/`

Corel Corporation

`http://www.corel.com`

Desktop Publishers Journal

`http://www.dtpjournal.com/`

Desktop Publishing.com

`http://www.desktoppublishing.com/open.html`

First Guide to PostScript

`http://www.cs.indiana.edu/docproject/programming/postscript/postscript.html`

Freedom System Integrators, Inc.

`http://southwind.net/fsi/`

Global Prepress Center (The DTP Jumplist)

`http://www.ledet.com/prepress/`

Macromedia Software

`http://www.macromedia.com/Tools/`

Quark, Inc.

`http://www.quark.com/`

Yahoo!'s DTP Resources

`http://www.yahoo.com/Computers_and_Internet/Desktop_Publishing/`

Clip Art

A

Barry's Clip Art

`http://www.barrysclipart.com/`

Clip Art Connection

`http://www.clipart.com/`

Clip Art Directory

`http://www.clipart.com/`

Clip Art Now

`http://clipartnow.com`

Clip Art Review (Directory)

`http://www.webplaces.com/html/clipart.htm`

Clip Art Universe

`http://www.nzwwa.com/mirror/clipart/`

WebSpice

`http://www.webspice.com`

Yahoo!'s Clip Art Directory

`http://www.yahoo.com/Computers_and_Internet/Multimedia/Pictures/Clip_Art/`

Fonts

AdobeStudios

`http://www.adobestudios.com/`

Attention Earthling Type Foundry

`http://www.attention-earthling.com/`

Bitstream, Inc.

`http://www.bitstream.com/`

Cosmonaut Fonts

`http://www.hypenet.com/cosmonaut/`

Fonts Online

`http://www.fontsonline.com/html/enter.html`

Fontz (freeware)

`http://indigo.simplenet.com/fontz/`

Internet Type Foundry

`http://www.typeindex.com/`

Omega Font Labs

`http://members.tripod.com/~DrNimbus/`

Serif, Inc.

`http://www.serif.com/`

World Wide Fonts

`http://wwfonts.com/`

Yamada Language Center Non-English Fonts

`http://babel.uoregon.edu/yamada/fonts.html`

Web Authoring

The following sites will help you do your own Web authoring.

Browsers

Microsoft Internet Explorer

`http://www.microsoft.com/ie/`

Netscape Communicator (Navigator)

`http://home.netscape.com/`

General Web Development

Yahoo!'s WWW Listings

`http://www.yahoo.com/Computers/World_Wide_Web/`

The Virtual Library

`http://WWW.Stars.com/`

The Web Toolbox

`http://www.rtis.com/nat/user/toolbox/`

The Developer's JumpStation

`http://oneworld.wa.com/htmldev/devpage/dev-page.html`

Multimedia Files (GIF and JPEG Clip Art, Animations, Sound, and Video)

Index to Multimedia Information Sources

`http://viswiz.gmd.de/MultimediaInfo/`

MPEG Archive

`http://www.powerweb.de/mpeg`

Multimedia Directory

`http://www.clipart.com/`

A

GLOSSARY

alignment The way text conforms to the boundaries confining it (column, frame, or page margins). Horizontal alignment (left, right, center, justified) describes how the lines of text align to the sides, and vertical alignment (top, center, bottom) describes how a line or block of text aligns to the top and bottom.

background Every pub has a background, which holds the grid guides that control page layout and any text, pictures, or other objects that must appear on every page of a multipage pub. See also *foreground*.

bleed Describes when objects print all the way to the edge of the paper with no margins.

body text General-purpose paragraphs in a publication that contain most of the pub's text content.

border A printable box added to a frame or table to enclose it, visually separating it from surrounding objects.

browser An Internet software program that enables one to explore the World Wide Web. Internet Explorer and Netscape Navigator are the two most well-known browsers.

bulleted list   A list in which each item is preceded by a graphical symbol. See also *numbered list*.

catalog   Opened automatically each time you start Publisher, the Catalog is a dialog on which you start a new publication or open an existing one. It's divided into four parts, or *tabs*. You use the first three tabs to create new publications, and the fourth tab (Existing Publications) to locate and open pubs you've already created.

cell   The box in a table formed by the intersection of a row and column.

clip art   Artwork made available (free or for a fee) for use by those other than the original artist. Publisher includes a library of clip art you access through the Clip Gallery.

Clip Gallery   A large collection of clip art and multimedia objects included with Publisher.

color depth   Describes the number of colors that can be displayed or printed simultaneously by a device. Usually expressed as a number of colors (16 million colors) or a number of bits (24-bit color).

compression   The process of making a computer file smaller so that it can be copied more quickly between computers. Compressed files, sometimes called Zip files, must be decompressed on the receiving computer before they can be used.

copy   A word used casually to describe the text in a publication.

copyfit   The use of various techniques to make a story fit within its space in the layout. Copyfitting techniques include shortening or lengthening the story or reworking the layout to make the frame larger or smaller.

cyberspace   A broad expression used to describe the activity, communication, and culture happening on the Internet and other computer networks.

data source   A list of names and addresses (or other information) to be used in a mail merge; it's the "source" for the "data" (information) that will be printed in the pub.

dialog box   Any of many different boxes displayed by Windows or Publisher in which you can perform an action by typing something, choosing among options, or clicking a button.

domain   The address of a computer on the Internet. A user's Internet address is made up of a username and a domain name.

drop cap   An oversized, decorative first letter of a paragraph, often used to mark the very beginning of a chapter or article. Also called a "fancy first letter."

drop shadow   A gray shadow applied to the right side and bottom of a frame (or text characters in WordArt) to add a 3-D effect.

edit cursor   A bold, vertical bar a little taller than the letters that surround it. It typically flashes on and off so it's easy to see. The edit cursor marks the place where anything you do on the keyboard happens within text.

email   Short for *electronic mail*. A system that enables a person to compose a message on a computer and transmit that message through a computer network, such as the Internet, to another computer user.

Explorer   See *Internet Explorer*.

fancy first letter   See *drop cap*.

FAQ   Acronym for *Frequently Asked Questions*. A list containing the answers to frequently asked questions on just about any topic.

flush   On a side of a paragraph where the lines of text align evenly, they are said to be flush on that side. See also *ragged*.

font   A particular style of text, or typeface, that can be used in a variety of sizes.

footer   Objects that are repeated across the very bottom of all pages of a pub or major section. See also *header*.

foreground   Everything in the pub that's not part of the background, including all objects on a page.

frame   In Publisher, a container used to hold objects in the layout. In a Web page, each discrete part of a page that has been divided into sections.

freeware   Software available to anyone, free of charge (unlike shareware, which requires payment).

GIF   A form of image file using the file extension `.GIF`, commonly used for pictures in Web pages.

grid guides   Vertical and horizontal lines you add to all pages in a pub to guide the layout. See also *ruler guides*.

handle   Little black squares that appear along the frame outline when a frame is selected, used to change the size or shape of the frame.

header   Objects that are repeated across the very top of all pages of a pub or major section. See also *footer*.

Hot Spots   A Publisher tool used to create image maps in Web pages.

HTML (Hypertext Markup Language)   The document formatting language used to create pages on the World Wide Web.

hyphenation zone   A measurement for the width of the area between the right margin and the point at which an automatic hyphen will be applied. For example, if the hyphenation zone for a story is 0.25 inches, any word that comes within a quarter-inch of the right margin but can't fit completely will be broken and hyphenated.

image map   In a Web page, a single picture that contains several links, each activated when a visitor clicks on a different area of the picture. In Publisher, image maps are created with the Hot Spots tool.

import file   The action of converting a document from another program into a pub.

import text   The action of copying all the text from a file created in another program into a frame in a pub.

inline image   An image that appears within the layout of a Web page.

Internet   A large, loosely organized internetwork connecting individuals, universities, research institutions, governments, businesses, and other organizations so that they can exchange messages and share information.

Internet Explorer   A browser for the World Wide Web; included with Publisher.

intranet   An internal company network, usually a local area network, that is based on Internet technologies.

justify   To line up a column of text so that both sides are flush.

kerning   A technique in which the spacing between specified characters in some fonts is adjusted to make those characters look better when used together.

landscape orientation   See *orientation*.

layout   The general term for the size, shape, and arrangement of objects on a page.

margin   Areas around the top, bottom, and sides of a page outside the print area, where nothing is to be printed.

menu   A list of choices on a computer screen.

Microsoft Word   A popular word processing program that can work together with Publisher for some functions.

multimedia A description for the combination and presentation of various types of media—text, pictures, sound, video, animation—in a Web page or other online document.

netiquette The code of proper conduct (etiquette) on the Internet (the Net).

Netscape Short for *Netscape Communications Corporation*, a software company that developed and markets a popular World Wide Web browser called Netscape Navigator.

nonprinting character A character you type—such as a paragraph break or tab—that affects the text but does not itself appear in print.

numbered list A list in which each item is preceded by a number or letter, and the numbers and letters increase as the list proceeds. See also *bulleted list*.

object Everything that appears in a pub—a block of text, a picture, and so on. You add new elements to a pub by creating new objects, and you design a page by arranging, sizing, and shaping the objects on it, in frames.

orientation A way to describe the shape of a page or pub when held upright. When the page is taller than it is wide (like the pages of this book), it's in *portrait* orientation. When the page is wider than tall (like a dollar bill), it's in *landscape* orientation.

overflow When more text is inserted in a frame than the frame has space for, the excess stays in the overflow area (unseen) to return when you successfully copyfit the frame.

password A secret code, known only to the user, that allows the user to access a computer system that is protected by password security.

personal information set Contains information about you or your company, such as your name, company name, and address. When you insert a personal information set in a pub, the text it contains appears in the pub automatically, saving you the time of typing it.

point A unit of measurement for characters in typography. One point equals 1/72 of an inch and describes the height of the capital letters. In 12-point type, a capital I is 1/6 of an inch high.

pointer The onscreen icon that moves when you move your mouse. In Publisher, different pointers are used for different jobs.

portrait orientation See *orientation*.

preview   A small, rough image of a page or pub, used in many dialogs in Publisher to show you a pub or the results of a change you may make in a dialog.

print area   The part of the paper within which your pub will appear, not counting any margins or parts of the paper to be trimmed away.

printing service   A company that takes your desktop publishing files and prints them on professional-quality equipment. Sometimes also called a *service bureau*.

pub   Short for publication, the general term for what you produce in Microsoft Publisher.

ragged   On a side of a paragraph where the lines of text are allowed to end at natural break points between words (creating an uneven pattern), the text is said to be ragged on that side. See also *flush*.

resolution   A description for the number of lines or dots that make up the grid from which an image is produced, onscreen or on paper.

reversed text   Light-colored text on a dark background.

rotate   The process of turning or tilting an object in a pub to make it print sideways, upside-down, or at any other angle.

ruler   Inch-marked scales along the left side and top of Publisher's workspace that provide visual reference for the size and spacing of objects, tab positions, and ruler guides.

ruler guides   Vertical and horizontal lines you add to particular pages to guide the layout. See also *grid guides*.

scratch area   The gray area of the workspace, used for temporary storage of objects.

search page (or search engine)   A Web page that provides a way to search for other Web pages that contain specified information.

server   A networked computer that serves a particular type of information to users or performs a particular function.

service bureau   See *printing service*.

shade   A variation on a particular color, darkened by adding black.

shareware   Software programs that users are permitted to acquire and evaluate for free. Shareware is different from freeware in that, if a person likes the shareware program and plans to use it on a regular basis, he or she is expected to send a fee to the programmer.

signature   A saddle-stitched, bound set of pages, often 16 or 24, that form one part of a book or magazine that will be made by binding multiple signatures together.

snake   When a single story or article is set in multiple columns, the text "snakes" its way through the columns, beginning in the leftmost column and continuing at the top of each column to the right.

story   A particular article or other discrete chunk of text. All the text in one frame is one story, but a single story can continue across multiple frames when those frames are connected.

symbol   A character that does not appear on the keyboard, such as a trademark or copyright symbol. In Publisher, you type symbols by choosing them from the Symbol dialog, or in a few cases letting the AutoCorrect facility add them for you.

tab   A non-printing character that aligns the text following it to a preset position, a tab stop.

template   A pub that's already been completely designed, provided as a head start you can edit to create a new pub.

tint   A variation on a particular color, lightened by adding white.

upload   Copying files from your PC to a server computer (through a network, such as the Internet).

URL   Short for *Universal* (or *Uniform*) *Resource Locator*. A method of standardizing the addresses of different types of Internet resources so that they can all be accessed easily from within a Web browser.

username   Used with a password to gain access to a computer. A dial-up IP user typically has a username and password for dialing the access provider's Internet server.

Web   See *World Wide Web*.

Web page   A single document on the World Wide Web.

Web site   A set of separate Web pages, each in its own file, that are linked together to function as a single, multipart document. Most Web sites have a beginning "home" or "top" page containing links that the visitor clicks to jump to the site's other pages.

whitespace   Any area on a page not covered by words, pictures, or other objects. Whitespace can appear in lots of places: around the page margins, around text as the frame margin, between columns, around pictures, and even where a line of text stops short before reaching the right margin.

wizard   Automated routines, used throughout Windows 95, for conveniently performing a step-by-step procedure, such as setting up Windows 95 or configuring it for the Internet. Used in Publisher for installation and for creating new pubs from templates in the Catalog.

Word   See *Microsoft Word*.

WordArt   Included with Publisher, a program you use to create highly graphical objects, such as logos, out of words.

workspace   The large area in the Publisher window in which the pub appears, flanked by the scratch area.

World Wide Web   (WWW or Web) A set of Internet computers and services that provides an easy-to-use system for finding information and moving among resources. WWW services feature hypertext, hypermedia, and multimedia information, which can be explored through Web browsers.

wrap   To make a column of text conform to the contours of an object.

zoom factor (or zoom)   Describes the extent to which a pub's appearance is magnified or reduced onscreen. A zoom of 100% means that the pub appears onscreen at roughly its printed size.

INDEX

Sams' Teach Yourself the Internet in 24 Hours, Second Edition

—Ned Snell

Sams' Teach Yourself the Internet in 24 Hours, Second Edition is a guide book and quick step-by-step tutorial broken up into 24 short, one-hour chapters that are easy for the busy beginner to read and digest. Updated with the latest technological and software developments such as Internet Explorer 4.0, Netscape Communicator, channels and Netcasting, HTML mail, and Web integration. Internet technology focus will appeal to users of all versions of Windows, Mac, and UNIX. Covers all aspects of the Internet such as establishing a connection, using the World Wide Web, searching for information, sending and receiving email, using newsgroups, security issues, and more.

Price: $19.99 US/$28.95 CAN   *User Level: Beginning–Intermediate*
ISBN: 1-57521-393-1   *408 pages*

Sams' Teach Yourself Microsoft Internet Explorer 4 in 24 Hours

—Noel Estabrook and Maxine London

This beginner-level book shows readers how to browse the Web with Microsoft Internet Explorer, send email, and find newsgroups. Everything from configuration to creating a Web page is covered. Each of its 24 lessons can be completed in one hour or less, making this book the best way to learn everything about Internet Explorer! Readers learn how to install, configure, and use Microsoft Internet Explorer and how to create an easy and reliable method of navigating the Web. Details all the new features of the latest version of Microsoft Internet Explorer.

Price: $19.99 US/$28.95 CAN   *User Level: New–Casual*
ISBN: 1-57521-233-1   *300 pages*

Sams' Teach Yourself Netscape Communicator 4 in 24 Hours

—Galen Grimes

This beginner-level book shows readers how to browse the Web with Netscape Communicator, send email, and find newsgroups. Everything from configuration to creating a Web page is covered. Readers learn how to install, configure, and use Netscape Communicator and how to create an easy and reliable method of navigating the Web. Details all the new features of the latest version of Netscape.

Price: $19.99 US/$28.95 CAN   *User Level: New–Casual*
ISBN: 1-57521-227-7   *350 pages*

Sams' Teach Yourself HTML 4 in 24 Hours, Second Edition

—Dick Oliver

Sams' Teach Yourself HTML 4 in 24 Hours, Second Edition provides a quick step-by-step tutorial that is broken up into 24 short, one-hour chapters that are easy for the busy beginner to read and digest. Updated to cover all the latest developments in HTML 4, Microsoft Internet Explorer 4, and Netscape Communicator 4, including Dynamic HTML and Cascading Style Sheets. The HTML Cafe support site is set up on the Sams Web site, providing online examples from the book, easy access to Web publishing shareware products, and updated material.

Price: $19.99 US/$28.95 CAN   *User Level: New–Casual*
ISBN: 1-57521-366-4   *440 pages*

Sams' Teach Yourself Microsoft Office 97 in 24 Hours

—Greg Perry

Sams' Teach Yourself Microsoft Office 97 in 24 Hours shows readers how to use the most widely requested features of Office. This entry-level title includes many illustrations, screen shots, and a step-by-step plan to learning Office 97. You learn how to use each Office product and how to use them together. You also learn how to create documents in Word that include hypertext links to files created with one of the other Office products.

Price: $19.99 US/$28.95 CAN   *User Level: New–Casual–Accomplished*
ISBN: 0-672-31009-0   *450 pages*

Sams' Teach Yourself Windows 95 in 24 Hours, Second Edition

—Greg Perry

With learning broken down into 24 one-hour lessons, this easy-to-follow tutorial can be used by individuals, in seminars, training sessions, and classrooms. Whether users are just starting out or are migrating from previous versions of Windows, this is a must-have resource to get them up and running quickly and easily. Loaded with "quick-start" chapters, "Do and Don't" tips, Question and Answer sections, quizzes, and exercises to help users master the concepts with ease.

Price: $19.99 US/$28.95 CAN   *User Level: New–Casual*
ISBN: 0-672-31006-6   *550 pages*

Sams' Teach Yourself Microsoft FrontPage 98 in 24 Hours

—Andy Shafran

Sams' Teach Yourself Microsoft FrontPage 98 in 24 Hours provides a quick step-by-step tutorial that is broken up into 24 short, one-hour chapters. This book is the quickest, easiest way to learn to create great-looking Web pages with Microsoft FrontPage 98. FrontPage 98 follows on the tremendous success of FrontPage 97, bringing even more power tools to the user. Covers everything from the basics of Web publishing to wizards, WebBots, forms, and style sheets and embedding Java, ActiveX, VBScript, and JavaScript.

Price: $19.99 US/$28.95 CAN
ISBN: 1-57521-367-2

User Level: New–Casual
350 pages

Sams' Teach Yourself Microsoft Excel 97 in 24 Hours

—Lois Patterson

Sams' Teach Yourself Microsoft Excel 97 in 24 Hours uses a task-oriented format to help you become productive in this spreadsheet application with just 24 one-hour lessons. Many new features of Excel 97, including increased connectivity and the enhanced Chart Wizard, are covered in this book so that it is also a tutorial for those who are upgrading from previous versions of Excel. Accomplished users will find tips to help increase their productivity. Includes numerous illustrations and figures that demonstrate how to operate Excel's key features as well as more mathematical and scientific examples than many texts.

Price: $19.99 US/$28.95 CAN
ISBN: 0-672-31116-x

User Level: New–Casual
400 pages

Sams' Teach Yourself Microsoft Word 97 in 24 Hours

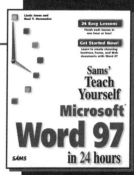

—Linda Jones

Written in a straightforward, easy-to-read manner, *Sams' Teach Yourself Microsoft Word 97 in 24 Hours* enables you to become productive quickly with Word 97. From very basic concepts such as opening new and existing documents to more complex features like using styles and macros, beginning users will learn how to quickly utilize the new features of the most popular word processing application. This book includes coverage of concepts relating to the Office 97 suite—how applications relate to each other as well as how to interface with online resources.

Price: $19.99 US/$28.95 CAN
ISBN: 0-672-31115-1

User Level: New–Casual
400 pages

Sams' Teach Yourself Microsoft PowerPoint 97 in 24 Hours

—Alexandria Haddad and Christopher Haddad

Sams' Teach Yourself Microsoft PowerPoint 97 in 24 Hours is an introductory tutorial enabling the reader to quickly create dynamic, captivating presentations. Beginning users will quickly learn how to utilize the new features of PowerPoint 97 with the easy, task-oriented format. The material is presented in manageable one-hour lessons. Practical easy-to-follow exercises walk you through the concepts. Sections on free informational resources (templates, graphics, and so on) are included.

Price: $19.99 US/$28.95 CAN   *User Level: New–Casual*
ISBN: 0-672-31117-8   *400 pages*

Sams' Teach Yourself Illustrator 7 in 24 Hours

—Mordy Golding

Adobe Illustrator 7 is the first major release of this application for Windows users since 1994. This book discusses raster objects, input issues, filters, backgrounds, navigating, and more. Readers can explore type, graphics, layers, and Web graphics.

Price: $19.99 US/$28.95 CAN   *User Level: Beginning–Intermediate*
ISBN: 1-56830-410-2   *284 pages*

Sams' Teach Yourself to Create a Home Page in 24 Hours

—Rogers Cadenhead

This book is a carefully organized tutorial that is divided into 24 short, one-hour chapters that teach the beginning Web page author what he needs to know to make a Web page operational in the shortest time possible. No HTML is required. The book steps the reader through the process using Claris Home Page, a leading entry Web page editor for novices. Truly a "Starter Kit," the Windows and Macintosh CD-ROM includes a full working copy of Claris Home Page Lite and a collection of examples from the author.

Price: $24.99 US/$35.95 CAN   *User Level: New–Casual*
ISBN: 1-57521-325-7   *336 pages*

Add to Your Sams Library Today with the Best Books for Programming, Operating Systems, and New Technologies

The easiest way to order is to pick up the phone and call

1-800-428-5331

between 9:00 a.m. and 5:00 p.m. EST.

For faster service please have your credit card available.

ISBN	Quantity	Description of Item	Unit Cost	Total Cost
1-57521-393-1		Sams' Teach Yourself the Internet in 24 Hours	$19.99	
1-57521-233-1		Sams' Teach Yourself Microsoft Internet Explorer 4 in 24 Hours	$19.99	
1-57521-227-7		Sams' Teach Yourself Netscape Communicator 4 in 24 Hours	$19.99	
1-57521-366-4		Sams' Teach Yourself HTML 4 in 24 Hours, 2E	$19.99	
0-672-31009-0		Sams' Teach Yourself Microsoft Office 97 in 24 Hours	$19.99	
0-672-31006-6		Sams' Teach Yourself Windows 95 in 24 Hours, 2E	$19.99	
1-57521-367-2		Sams' Teach Yourself Microsoft FrontPage 98 in 24 Hours	$19.99	
0-672-31116-X	·	Sams' Teach Yourself Microsoft Excel 97 in 24 Hours	$19.99	
0-672-31115-1		Sams' Teach Yourself Microsoft Word 97 in 24 Hours	$19.99	
0-672-31117-8		Sams' Teach Yourself Microsoft PowerPoint 97 in 24 Hours	$19.99	
1-56830-410-2		Sams' Teach Yourself Illustrator 7 in 24 Hours	$19.99	
1-57521-325-7		Sams' Teach Yourself to Create a Home Page in 24 Hours	$24.99	
❏ 3 ½" Disk		Shipping and Handling: See information below.		
❏ 5 ¼" Disk		TOTAL		

Shipping and Handling: $4.00 for the first book, and $1.75 for each additional book. Floppy disk: add $1.75 for shipping and handling. If you need to have it NOW, we can ship product to you in 24 hours for an additional charge of approximately $18.00, and you will receive your item overnight or in two days. Overseas shipping and handling adds $2.00 per book and $8.00 for up to three disks. Prices subject to change. Call for availability and pricing information on latest editions.

201 W. 103rd Street, Indianapolis, Indiana 46290

1-800-428-5331 — Orders   1-800-835-3202 — FAX   1-800-858-7674 — Customer Service

Body Text Fonts

Arial
The quick brown fox jumps over the lazy dog 1234567890

Arial Narrow
The quick brown fox jumps over the lazy dog 1234567890

Arial Rounded MT Bold
The quick brown fox jumps over the lazy dog 1234567890

Baskerville Old Face
The quick brown fox jumps over the lazy dog 1234567890

Bell MT
The quick brown fox jumps over the lazy dog 1234567890

Book Antiqua
The quick brown fox jumps over the lazy dog 1234567890

Bookman Old Style
The quick brown fox jumps over the lazy dog 1234567890

Calisto MT
The quick brown fox jumps over the lazy dog 1234567890

Centaur
The quick brown fox jumps over the lazy dog 1234567890

Century Schoolbook
The quick brown fox jumps over the lazy dog 1234567890

Comic Sans MS
The quick brown fox jumps over the lazy dog 1234567890

Courier New
The quick brown fox jumps over the lazy dog 1234567890

Eras Medium ITC
The quick brown fox jumps over the lazy dog 1234567890

Footlight MT Light
The quick brown fox jumps over the lazy dog 1234567890

Franklin Gothic Book
The quick brown fox jumps over the lazy dog 1234567890

Garamond
The quick brown fox jumps over the lazy dog 1234567890

Georgia
The quick brown fox jumps over the lazy dog 1234567890

Gill Sans MT
The quick brown fox jumps over the lazy dog 1234567890

Goudy Old Style
The quick brown fox jumps over the lazy dog 1234567890

Lucida Bright
The quick brown fox jumps over the lazy dog 1234567890

Lucida Sans
The quick brown fox jumps over the lazy dog 1234567890

Lucida Sans Typewriter
The quick brown fox jumps over the lazy dog 1234567890

Maiandra GD
The quick brown fox jumps over the lazy dog 1234567890

Modern No. 20
The quick brown fox jumps over the lazy dog 1234567890

Perpetua
The quick brown fox jumps over the lazy dog 1234567890

Tahoma
The quick brown fox jumps over the lazy dog 1234567890

Times New Roman
The quick brown fox jumps over the lazy dog 1234567890

Trebuchet MS
The quick brown fox jumps over the lazy dog 1234567890

Tw Cen MT
The quick brown fox jumps over the lazy dog 1234567890

Verdana
The quick brown fox jumps over the lazy dog 1234567890

Impact Fonts

Arial Black
The quick brown fox jumps over the lazy dog 1234567890

Bernard MT Condensed
The quick brown fox jumps over the lazy dog 1234567890

Bauhaus 93
The quick brown fox jumps over the lazy dog 1234567890

Brittanic Bold
The quick brown fox jumps over the lazy dog 1234567890

Broadway
The quick brown fox jumps over the lazy dog 1234567890

Cooper Black
The quick brown fox jumps over the lazy dog 1234567890

COPPERPLATE GOTHIC
THE QUICK BROWN FOX JUMPS OVER THE LAZY DOG 1234567890

Elephant
The quick brown fox jumps over the lazy dog 1234567890

Eras Bold ITC
The quick brown fox jumps over the lazy dog 1234567890

Franklin Gothic Heavy
The quick brown fox jumps over the lazy dog 1234567890

Gill Sans Ultra Bold
The quick brown fox jumps over the lazy dog 1234567890

Haettenschweiler
The quick brown fox jumps over the lazy dog 1234567890

Impact
The quick brown fox jumps over the lazy dog 1234567890

Matura MT Script Capitals
The quick brown fox jumps over the lazy dog 1234567890

Playbill
The quick brown fox jumps over the lazy dog 1234567890

Rockwell Extra Bold
The quick brown fox jumps over the lazy dog 1234567890

Wide Latin
The quick brown fox jumps over the lazy dog 1234567890

Display Fonts

ALGERIAN
THE QUICK BROWN FOX JUMPS OVER THE LAZY DOG 1234567890

Blackadder ITC
The quick brown fox jumps over the lazy dog 1234567890

Bradley Hand ITC
The quick brown fox jumps over the lazy dog 1234567890

Brush Script MT
The quick brown fox jumps over the lazy dog 1234567890

CASTELLAR
THE QUICK BROWN FOX JUMPS OVER THE LAZY DOG 1234567890

Chiller
The quick brown fox jumps over the lazy dog 1234567890

Colanna MT
The quick brown fox jumps over the lazy dog 1234567890

Curlz MT
The quick brown fox jumps over the lazy dog 1234567890

Edwardian Script ITC
The quick brown fox jumps over the lazy dog 1234567890